JOURNEYS OF DISCOVERY IN VOLUNTEER TOURISM

International Case Study Perspectives

JOURNEYS OF DISCOVERY IN VOLUNTEER TOURISM
International Case Study Perspectives

Edited by

Kevin D. Lyons

School of Economics, Politics and Tourism
University of Newcastle
Callaghan, NSW 2308
Australia

and

Stephen Wearing

School of Leisure Sport and Tourism
University of Technology Sydney
PO Box 222
Lindfield, NSW 2070
Australia

www.cabi.org

CABI is a trading name of CAB International

CABI Head Office	CABI North American Office
Nosworthy Way	875 Massachusetts Avenue
Wallingford	7th Floor
Oxfordshire OX10 8DE	Cambridge, MA 02139
UK	USA
Tel: +44 (0)1491 832111	Tel: +1 617 395 4056
Fax: +44 (0)1491 833508	Fax: +1 617 354 6875
E-mail: cabi@cabi.org	E-mail: cabi-nao@cabi.org
Website: www.cabi.org	

A catalogue record for this book is available from the British Library, London, UK.

Library of Congress Cataloging-in-Publication Data

Journeys of discovery in volunteer tourism : international case study perspectives/editors, Kevin D. Lyons, Stephen Wearing.
      p. cm.
    ISBN 978-1-84593-380-7 (alk. paper)
    1. Volunteer tourism–Case studies. I. Lyons, Kevin D. II. Wearing, Stephen. III. Title.

G156.5.V64J68 2008
361.3 ' 7--dc22

                                                      2007038282

ISBN-13: 978 1 84593 380 7

Typeset by SPi, Pondicherry, India.
Printed and bound in the UK by Biddles Ltd., King's Lynn.

Contents

Contributors

Dr Kathleen Andereck is a Professor in the Department of Recreation and Tourism Management at Arizona State University. Her research is focused on the tourism experience from the perspectives of both residents and tourists. She has conducted recreation and tourism-related research projects for many US state and federal agencies including the Arizona Office of Tourism, Arizona Department of Transportation, USDA Forest Service and Bureau of Land Management. She is an associate editor for five academic journals and is the author of many refereed journal articles and numerous conference papers and professional reports.

Dr Sue Broad completed her PhD from the University of Newcastle, Australia, in 2001. Her research interests capture the intersection between wildlife tourism and volunteer tourism. She has presented her research at international conferences and has published her work in a number of tourism journals and edited books. After completing her postgraduate studies she worked as a research associate at Monash University, Melbourne. She now runs her own business in personal development and life coaching.

Dr Alexandra Coghlan has a PhD in tourism from James Cook University in Townsville and 6 years of industry experience in marine environments, as a dive master, whale-watching guide and researcher. Her areas of interest focus on tourism in natural environments. She is currently researching reef tourism through the Marine and Tropical Sciences Research Facility/Reef and Rainforest Research Centre, examining the sustainability of reef tourism experiences over time, in the context of increasing anthropogenic pressure on the Great Barrier Reef (GBR). Other areas of work include ongoing research into the volunteer tourism experience which was the focus of her PhD thesis.

Professor Chris Cooper is Foundation Professor of Tourism at the School of Tourism, The University of Queensland. He has an honours degree and PhD from University College London and before beginning an academic career worked in market planning for the tourism and retail sectors in the UK. Chris has authored a number of leading textbooks in tourism and worked closely with the United Nations World Tourism Organization in developing the status of tourism education on the international stage and is currently the Chair of the Education Council.

Adrian DeVille is undertaking a PhD at University of Technology, Sydney, Australia, on the phenomenon of travelling volunteers known as WWOOFers (Willing Workers on Organic Farms). His research focuses upon what WWOOFers seek and gain and the contributions made to the lives and livelihoods of various 'hosts' engaging with sustainable agriculture and earth care through the exchange of labour for food and accommodation.

Dr Deborah Edwards is the STCRC Senior Research Fellow in Urban Tourism in the School of Leisure, Sport and Tourism at the University of Technology, Sydney. Her interests are in sustainable tourism management, urban attractions, tourism planning, community volunteers in tourism attractions and the social impacts of events. She is on the steering committee of the Best Education Network (BESTen).

Dr Eduardo Fayos-Solá is the Director of the Education and Knowledge Management Department of the United Nations World Tourism Organization. He is also the President of the UNWTO Themis Foundation for Quality in Tourism Education and Training. From 1991 to 1994 he was the Director General of Tourism for Spain, in the Ministry of Industry, Commerce and Tourism. He has been Professor of Applied Economics and Economics of Tourism at the University of Valencia (Spain) since 1977 and previously was Assistant Professor of Economics of Development at the University of Stockholm (Sweden).

Dr Freya Higgins-Desbiolles is a Lecturer in Tourism with the School of International Business of the University of South Australia. She received her PhD from Flinders University of South Australia. She was a Peace Corps volunteer between 1987 and 1989 to the Kingdom of Tonga. She then moved to the UK in order to obtain a Master's degree in International Relations. Moving to Australia in 1995, she worked as the coordinator of an NGO called the Global Education Centre in Adelaide for 3 years. She has an interest in the topic of tourism as a force for peace through the life experiences she has accumulated.

Dr Kirsten Holmes is a Research Fellow at Curtin University of Technology, Perth, Australia, investigating the contribution of volunteers to tourism. Previously she was a Lecturer in Tourism at the University of Surrey and also a Lecturer in Leisure Management at the University of Sheffield in the UK. Her research focuses on various aspects of volunteering within tourism but she also researches more widely within cultural tourism, particularly the role of culture within urban regeneration, and has recently completed work for the UK government on notions of sustainable leisure.

Professor John Jenkins is Head of the School of Tourism and Hospitality Management at Southern Cross University in Australia. His research has a strong interdisciplinary base. Key research foci include the interrelated themes of environmental management, outdoor recreation management, tourism, politics and public policy and business–government relations. His research has appeared in a variety of leading international journals, including *Journal of Sustainable Tourism*, *Pacific Tourism Review*, *Tourism Geographies*, *Current Issues in Tourism* and *Annals of Leisure Research*, and in books with international publishers.

Dr Andrew Lepp is a Professor in the Recreation, Park and Tourism Management programme at Kent State University (USA). He has an MS degree from Oregon State University and a PhD from the University of Florida. As a researcher, one area of interest has been tourism and sustainable development in East Africa and he has published several papers on the subject. His interest in the subject grew from the 2 years he spent working as a Warden of Tourism in Uganda's national parks and wildlife reserves. He has also worked for the US National Park Service and the US Forest Service.

Dr Kevin Lyons is a Senior Lecturer in Leisure and Tourism Studies at the University of Newcastle, Australia. He received his Master's and Doctoral degrees from the University of Georgia, USA, in 1998. Prior to his career as an academic, he worked for 15 years in community-based leisure and tourism services in New York where he was responsible for recruiting and managing large teams of paid staff, international volunteers and cultural exchange participants. This experience led him to develop his research interests in volunteering and travel. He has also conducted research into the relationships between leisure and communities, and has examined the impacts of volunteering upon life trajectories. He has published his research in a number of international refereed leisure studies and tourism studies journals. He is on the Board of Directors of the Australian and New Zealand Association for Leisure Studies (ANZALS), and is an associate editor for a number of international refereed journals.

Amie Matthews is a PhD candidate at the University of Newcastle, Australia. Her research focuses on the experiential significance of travel in the lives of young Australians and the impacts extended international journeys have on identity formation. Having spent a number of years working in the tourism industry and having been privileged enough to travel to a number of Australian and international destinations with backpack in tow, she has both a professional and personal interest in the backpacking culture, tourism and volunteer travel. Her broader research interests include youth culture, alternative spiritualities, contemporary secular ritual and social change movements.

Dr Nancy McGehee is an Associate Professor in the Hospitality and Tourism Management Program at Virginia Tech. She is a sociologist. She has spent over a decade studying and writing about volunteer tourism both in the USA and abroad. Her current interests centre on resident perceptions of volunteer tourism, as well as the exploration of how better to match volunteers with community needs.

Dr Alison McIntosh is an Associate Professor at the Department of Tourism and Hospitality Management, University of Waikato, New Zealand. Her main research interests are in tourists' experiences of heritage, spirituality and culture, and the sustainable development of cultural tourism, particularly with reference to issues of interpretation and hosting. This also involves other aspects of her career as she has been a director of, and associated with, different heritage organizations. She is predominantly a qualitative researcher with an interest in critical perspectives. She has published in leading journals such as *Annals of Tourism Research, Journal of Travel Research, Tourism Management* and *Journal of Sustainable Tourism*.

Professor Philip Pearce is the Foundation Professor of Tourism at James Cook University. He undertook his doctoral studies at the University of Oxford and has always been interested in tourist behaviour and analysis. He has held a Fulbright scholarship to Harvard University and has published widely in tourism journals and books. His most recent book with Channel View (2005) is *Tourist Behaviour: Themes and Conceptual Schemes*. He is a foundation member of the International Academy for the Study of Tourism, an Honorary Professor at Xi'an International Studies University in China and teaches in graduate-level courses in Italy. He maintains active publishing interests in tourists' motivation, experiences, satisfaction and impact.

Eliza Raymond migrated from England to New Zealand in 2001 where she studied Geography and Spanish at the University of Otago. Following her experience as a volunteer in Guatemala and Chile, she returned to Otago to research good practice in volunteer tourism. She is now working as the International Programs Coordinator for Maximo Nivel in Cusco, Peru. Maximo Nivel's volunteer programmes cater for international volunteers seeking to contribute to the social, cultural, economic and/or natural environment of Cusco and the surrounding region.

Dr Lisa Ruhanen is a Lecturer at the School of Tourism, the University of Queensland. She has an honours degree from James Cook University and a PhD from the University of Queensland. She has been involved in a number of research projects in both Australia and overseas. She is a visiting scholar with the United Nations World Tourism Organization's Education and Knowledge Management department and is involved in the Education Council as part of the University of Queensland's current role as Council Chair.

Dr Gabrielle Russell-Mundine obtained her PhD from Southern Cross University where she investigated the experiences of an Aboriginal Corporation as they undertook the process of investigating and developing sustainable community enterprise options including tourism, forestry, education and social enterprises. Gabrielle started out her working life in the small business sector learning about business in industries as diverse as office products to baby products. Her real interest, however, was in the volunteer work she was doing in youth programmes and later in politics. Eventually she moved full time into the not-for-profit sector and has since worked for NGOs such as Amnesty International, The Futures Foundation and the Minerals Policy Institute. She has also worked as a political adviser to an NSW Senator, researching and advising on corporate social responsibility, human rights and foreign affairs issues.

Dr Suzanne Snead holds a BSc in Psychology and MSc in Therapeutic Recreation from the University of Southern Mississippi, USA. She spent several years as a practitioner in the disability and recreation fields before returning to academia to complete a PhD in Social Sciences at the University of Newcastle, Australia, and a research fellowship with the University of Sydney, Australia. She has presented at numerous conferences in the USA, Canada and Australia on topics such as inclusive community recreation, client autonomy, leisure education and staff–client interactions in allied health settings. She has recently returned from a year-long 'working holiday', teaching English in Russia.

Nadia Söderman has a Master's degree in German, French and Marketing from Åbo Akademi University in Finland and is currently completing her MPhil at the Centre for Tourism Policy Research at the University of Brighton, England. She is interested in languages and speaks English, Swedish, German, Spanish, French and Italian, some Finnish and a little Russian, Japanese and Maori. Her research interests lie in the fields of youth tourism, educational tourism, volunteer tourism, rural tourism, ecotourism, indigenous cultures and Latin America as a destination.

Dr Rochelle Spencer is a Postdoctoral Research Fellow in the Centre for Research on Social Inclusion at Macquarie University, Australia. Her doctorate explores alternative touristic models of 'doing' rights-based community development in Cuba, notions of transformative learning and new social movement participation. She is keenly interested in the social development of socialist Cuba in the current age of globalization and neoliberalism as a site of educational and humanitarian tourism. Drawing on her tourism and NGO sector experience, Rochelle's current research is situated within the local government context. She is exploring the diverse possibilities of harnessing social capital, local networks and partnerships, including volunteering, for building sustainable communities and social transformation from 'within'.

Dr Tamara Young is a lecturer in the School of Economics, Politics and Tourism at the University of Newcastle, and a research associate in the School of Social Sciences at the University of Western Sydney. She completed her PhD at the University of Newcastle in 2005. Her doctoral thesis examined guidebook constructions of traveller and travelled cultures, and the interplay between text and audience in the context of independent backpacker travel in Aboriginal Australia. Her research interests include representation and interpretation in tourism, guidebooks and travel media, travel experiences and identity, cultural tourism and Aboriginal Australia.

Dr Stephen Wearing is an Associate Professor at the University of Technology, Sydney (UTS). He has been responsible for a variety of projects in the area of Leisure and Tourism Studies at an international and local level. Stephen received his PhD from Charles Sturt University, Australia. He has served as chair and on the Board of Youth Challenge Australia for over 12 years. He has directed a number of leisure and tourism community-based projects in Costa Rica, Solomon Islands, Guyana and Australia receiving a special citation from the Costa Rican Government for services to community, conservation and youth and an outstanding contribution award from Youth Challenge International in Canada. His published research in refereed journals and books on volunteer tourism and ecotourism is internationally recognized and highly cited. He is managing editor of a new refereed international journal entitled *Journal of Volunteer Tourism and Social Development*.

Dr Anne Zahra is Senior Lecturer at the Department of Tourism and Hospitality Management, University of Waikato, New Zealand. Her current research areas include tourism policy, tourism organizations, destination management, volunteer tourism, multi-paradigmatic research methodologies and the ontological and epistemological foundations of tourism and hospitality research. She has had a 25-year involvement in volunteering both as a volunteer working with rural and urban poor in less-developed countries such as the Philippines, and as an organizer of education development projects for volunteers in Fiji, Tonga, India and the Philippines. She has also coordinated AusAid projects in South America through her long-term involvement with Reldev Australia Limited, an NGO registered with AusAid.

Preface

A central question that led us to develop this volume of international case studies asks whether volunteer tourism is an example of a niche product in the broader arena of tourism or whether it is an alternative social phenomenon that challenges the commodity-intensive underpinnings of tourism. In seeking answers to this question we realized that volunteer tourism manifests in diverse ways and a rigorous understanding of it requires casting the analytical net widely. To this end, we have sought out a collection of theoretically and empirically grounded case studies that we feel provide a rigorous and critical vehicle for understanding the relationship between volunteering and tourism broadly. This book explores the experiences of the volunteer tourist and the ensuing narrative between host and volunteer as it manifests in diverse and increasingly contested political international contexts. As such, this volume includes case studies conducted in 12 countries across six continents.

In order to understand the extent and nature of volunteer tourism and to ask critical questions of it, we have invited scholars from around the globe who are actively involved in knowledge generation and research activism related to volunteer tourism to contribute chapters to this book. These contributors include established leaders in tourism research and emerging researchers who represent a 'new wave' of scholarship that is developing in response to this fast-growing area of tourism.

This book is organized into three parts that explore key approaches to, and dimensions of, volunteer tourism. In the opening chapter for each part we provide an in-depth discussion of relevant approaches and issues that link and frame the ensuing cases.

Part I considers the perspectives of host communities and the organizations that provide them with volunteers as part of a process of social and community development. Part II presents case studies that focus upon the experiences of the volunteer tourist and considers issues of the self, motivation, identity and the impact of volunteer tourism upon the volunteer. The case studies presented in Part III consider new and emerging trends that challenge traditional conceptualizations of volunteer tourism and open the door for further investigation that explores their implications in the future. In this concluding part, we ask questions about the future of volunteer tourism and the dialogue that arises if we examine how a commodified or decommodified frame is used to examine it.

This book was developed as a resource for scholars, commercial and non-commercial service providers and students alike who seek a deeper understanding of how volunteer tourism is growing and developing, the potential power of this form of alternative tourism and the potential challenges it presents. We hope it opens the door for critically informed practice in the future.

Kevin Lyons and Stephen Wearing
Editors

Acknowledgements

There are several people who have been instrumental in enabling us to complete this collection of international case studies. We thank the contributors to this book who represent the full spectrum of scholarly experience from the well-published through to those whose chapter in this volume is their first foray into published scholarly work. We also thank a number of the contributors who agreed to blind peer review other chapters in this book. This extra layer of work has strengthened this volume considerably. We would also like to thank Suzanne Snead, PhD and Research Associate at-large for her work on the final drafts of the chapters in this book. Her 'ninth-hour' assistance was invaluable. We thank those volunteer tourists who agreed to participate in the empirical research that features in a number of the cases presented. Finally, we thank those host communities who opened their doors to scrutiny and analysis. Through your participation we believe this volume provides rich insights into the phenomenona of volunteer tourism.

Kevin Lyons and Stephen Wearing

I Journeys Beyond Otherness: Communities, Culture and Power

1 Volunteer Tourism as Alternative Tourism: Journeys Beyond Otherness

K.D. Lyons[1] AND S. Wearing[2]

[1]School of Economics, Politics and Tourism, University of Newcastle, Callaghan, Australia; [2]School of Leisure Sport and Tourism, University of Technology Sydney, Lindfield, Australia

Seismic changes in leisure time, disposable income, mobility and communication technologies have created a context in which tourism has thrived, grown and diversified to encompass a wide array of leisure travel behaviours that were not imagined even as recently as a couple of decades ago. Leading the way in this process of diversification is alternative tourism, which describes a form of tourism that rebukes mass tourism and the consumptive mindset it engenders and instead offers alternative, more discriminating, socially and environmentally sustaining tourist experiences (Wearing, 2001). The demand for alternative tourism has led to a diverse array of niche products and services, each the subject of critical scholarly analysis including educational tourism, farm tourism, cultural exchange tourism, scientific tourism and volunteer tourism, which is the subject and focus of this book.

Definitions of volunteer tourism have begun to emerge in the academic and popular literature and are cited in a number of the case studies presented in this volume. Some of these definitions are relatively narrow in their focus. For example, Wearing (2002) defines volunteer tourists as those who 'volunteer in an organized way to undertake holidays that may involve the aiding or alleviating the material poverty of some groups in society, the restoration of certain environments, or research into aspects of society or environment' (p. 240). This definition uses criteria that limit volunteer tourism to those experiences located within the context of holidays or vacations. Others such as Uriely et al. (2003) take a more macro-approach and consider the more inclusive notion of volunteering in tourism as an 'expression of what is recognized in tourism literature as the "other" dimension of postmodern tourism, which emphasizes the growing appeal of concepts such as "alternative", "real", "ecological", and "responsible" forms of tourism' (p. 61). While specific definitions are used in some of the contributions to this book to frame individual case studies, we have resisted the temptation to offer an overarching definition of volunteer tourism for this volume. Instead we recognize volunteer tourism as a form of contested alternative tourism. This contestation is further explored later in this chapter.

Focus and Purpose: an International Case Studies Perspective

This book focuses upon the phenomenon of volunteer tourism, its sources and its development as a concept. In this book we have cast the net relatively widely and have sought out case studies that exemplify and capture the breadth of a phenomenon that continues to grow. In the case studies presented here we have attempted to engage critically with the ideas and ideals of volunteer tourism and recognize the transformative power of volunteer tourism. We feel the following chapters provide a balanced blend of theoretical, conceptual and empirical analysis while also providing rich descriptions of volunteer tourism as it manifests in diverse contexts. This book emphasizes micro-social elements that are fundamental to conceptualizations of the tourist and the tourist destination. This emphasis is often overlooked in the sociological analysis of the tourist experience, where the focus has generally been on more macro-social influences, impacts of tourism upon destinations, the quality of the tourist experience and industry construction of the experience. Drawing on concepts from interactionist and post-structural theories among others, this book critiques the ideas inherent in the paradigm of mass tourism that has dominated tourism research, where it is assumed that all tourists are escaping from the city, 'sightseeing' with 'authenticity' in a tourist destination offered as 'image' for the tourist 'gaze'.

These case studies not only demonstrate the impact this form of tourism can have on volunteers and host communities but also consider the broader social and political implications of these impacts. Part of the purpose of this book is to begin seeking answers to a number of questions that will advance critical understanding of this burgeoning area of alternative tourism. These questions include: What are the potential positive social and environmental benefits of volunteer tourism? What are the prerequisites for a successful experience? What is the nature of the experience? What messages does the visitor receive? What attitudes do they take away? In working with communities, what are the key issues leading to successful outcomes? Where has it worked and why? What are the key problems and issues to be overcome? How do host communities experience volunteers? What are the overlaps and synergies within other cognate areas of study? Not all of these questions are fully answered in these case studies; however, the ideas presented here are designed to start a dialogue that will help develop deeper understanding.

Background: the Rise of Alternatives

Tourism has long been hailed a significant and fast-growing global phenomenon worthy of critical analysis. Much of the initial sociological work on tourism was concerned with the individual tourist and the part that holidays and vacations play in establishing identity and a sense of self. This self was predominantly posited as a universal, and tourism, like leisure, was seen in a dialectical relationship with the 'workaday world'. Cohen and Taylor (1976), for example, drew on Goffman's (1959) concern with the presentation of self in everyday life, to argue that vacations are culturally sanctioned escape routes from paid work for Western travellers. One of the key challenges for the modern travel-ler, in this view, is to establish identity and a sense of personal individuality in the face of the anomic forces of a technological world. Holidays and vacations provide freedom to mentally and physically escape from the immediacy of the multiplicity of impinging pressures in technological society. According to Cohen and Taylor (1976), the tourist uses all aspects of the holiday/vacation for the manipulation of well-being.

However, while the examination of the self continued in the cognate area of leisure studies, in the tourist literature, these arguments became diverted into a debate about the authenticity or otherwise of this experience (cf. MacCannell, 1976; Cohen, 1988), serving to focus attention on the attractions of the tour-ist destination. Such a shift objectified the destination as place – a specific geographical site was presented to the tourists for their gaze (Urry, 1990). Thus, the manner of presentation became all important and its authenticity or otherwise the focus of classifying analysis: 'I categorised objects of the gaze in terms of romantic/collective, historical/modern, and authentic/unauthentic', says Urry (1990, p. 135). Tourists themselves became synonymous with the Baudelarian flaneur: '[T]he strolling flaneur was a forerunner of the twentieth century tourist' (Urry, 1990, p. 138). This flaneur was generally perceived as escaping from the workaday world for an 'ephemeral', 'fugitive' and 'contin-gent' leisure experience (cf. Rojek, 1993, p. 216). In such an analysis, tourism becomes a mass phenomenon predicated on ontological universal categories with sharply dichotomous conceptions utilized to account for the dynamic pro-cesses, interrelations and inherent divergences of tourism experiences.

Ensuing debates about tourism have critically linked the debates about authenticity to broader macro-social issues associated with the globalization of mass tourism. Increasingly there is recognition that in mass tourism mar-ginalized communities have rarely (if at all) had their voices heard. The host communities who are the recipients of mass tourism have little or no ability to influence its construction.

The complexity of cross-cultural issues inherent in the tourist experi-ence that was omitted in earlier analyses is beginning to emerge. Recognition of the increasing domination of the market by multinational corporations, and the increasing proliferation of 'cashed-up' but time-poor tourism consumers, has led governments, researchers and tourism bodies to view mass tourism as highly consumptive, which has had an irreversible impact upon a range of natu-ral and cultural environments globally. This analysis and critique of mass forms of global tourism has led to a search for, and growing interest in, alternatives. Alternate conceptualizations of tourism have been developed that provide addi-tional elements or dimensions to the current perspectives in current sociologi-cal analyses of the tourist phenomenon, which tend to continue to emphasize tourists and tourism as consumptive rather than alternative, productive and sustainable praxes.

It has been claimed that alternative tourism reconfigures the tourist destination as an interactive space where tourists become creative actors who engage in behaviours that are mutually beneficial to host communities, and to the cultural and social environment of those communities. From these alternative tourism interactions tourists take home an experience which is potentially life-changing and, at minimum, impacts on the self in some way (Butler, 1990; Wearing, 2002).

The 'alternative turn' in tourism first became most notably evident with the development of ecotourism, which has gone on to become a major player in the global tourism industry. However, some have suggested that ecotourism has undergone a process of commodification over the last two decades and is now little more than another niche product that can be developed and sold to the mass tourism market (Wearing *et al.*, 2005). Other forms of alternative tourism have also emerged in recent times but it is volunteer tourism that has become the new 'poster-child' for alternative tourism in the past few years.

Volunteer tourism is a term that has been used to describe a wide range of tourist behaviours and tourism products and services and is now one of the fastest-growing forms of alternative tourism. Indeed the definition and boundaries that constitute volunteer tourism are in flux as new and existing intersections between volunteers and travel stake a claim to the volunteer tourism brand. Volunteer tourism is increasingly viewed and marketed by governments, non-government agencies and private-commercial operators globally as a creative and non-consumptive solution to a wide range of social and environmental issues that manifest in diverse communities globally. However, this view is based on the often unchallenged belief in a symbiotic relationship between volunteering and tourism – in reality this relationship is complex and fraught with potential inequities and challenges. This complexity can be seen when observing the challenges faced by communities who host volunteer tourists and the role taken primarily (thus far) by non-governmental organizations (NGOs) who act as a conduit between volunteers and these communities. The remainder of this chapter explores the role of NGOs in volunteer tourism as a foundation and introduction to the chapters in Part I of this volume.

In particular, the following discussion presents and challenges a key argument raised in other work primarily by Wearing and associates (see Wearing, 2001; Wearing and McDonald, 2002; Wearing *et al.*, 2005) that the decommodified philosophy that underpins NGOs who provide volunteer tourism is essential for ensuring that the needs of host communities are placed before the bottom line of transnational corporations who have vested interest in commercializing volunteer tourism products.

NGOs and a Decommodification Agenda

NGOs have emerged in the last decade as one of the principal advocates and implementers of sustainable tourism (Wearing *et al.*, 2005). They have also played a major role in specific areas of tourism including volunteer tourism (Wearing, 2001). For NGOs tourism is not just an 'industry' or activity that serves the needs of those who desire a 'holiday' or an escape away from home – instead they view tourism with the intention of effecting new and positive attitudes, values and actions in the tourist and the host community (Wearing *et al.*, 2005).

NGOs look to assist communities by carrying out a range of activities and projects. Examples of this include environmental education, the fostering of attitudes and behaviours that are conducive to maintaining natural and social environments and empowering host communities to operate and maintain sustainable approaches to industry such as tourism (Wearing and McDonald, 2002). NGOs present the case that social ethics introduces notions of empowerment and control for local communities, as well as issues of equity regarding benefit and access.

Numerous studies have revealed the disempowerment that host communities feel as a consequence of tourism in their community. NGOs often engage in tourism with the aim of achieving socially appropriate tourism, which is defined as having community support and involving the host community in decision making (Hall, 1991). They aspire to benefit local (or host) communities directly and assist in providing real benefits that are ongoing within those communities and that can also be controlled at the local level.

Many NGOs are committed to specifically undertaking projects and programmes in developing nations. These programmes have evolved out of a tradition of overseas volunteer organizations that work on projects of community service, medical assistance and scientific discovery. A number of these organizations have recently begun to recognize how their programmes may be appealing to tourists as a form of personal development. Indeed NGOs who offer volunteer tourism opportunities have developed a niche within the tourism industry where the personal development of the tourist is atypical.

In many ways NGOs demonstrate best practice in alternative tourism, and volunteer tourism specifically. Most notably, NGOs place tourist development approaches that are inclusive of indigenous and/or host communities as a priority. They place a high priority on the quality of interactions between tourists and host communities and recognize that this interaction must move beyond superficiality (Wearing, 2001). These priorities are consistent with the decommodification agenda that underpins alternative tourism.

Conversely a corporate approach to supporting local communities through sustainable tourism development has emerged which embraces not only volunteer tourism but also alternative tourism in general, and is far from best practice (Wearing *et al.*, 2005). It has been argued that corporate philosophies and ideologies are fundamentally underpinned by capital accumulation logic of profit before people (Elliott, 2002).

In a free-market society many would argue that profit-for-shareholder philosophies are completely justified. Over the past few years, however, there has been a gradual change in corporate philosophies as they scramble to harness the growing market desire for global economic, social and environmental equality. Many corporations represent this growing societal movement by selling 'social responsibility' or 'sustainable' policies and programmes to their various markets. However, Elliott (2002) argues that corporations, particularly those that are transnational, are involved with many of the world's largest projects in developing nations around the world. These projects are carried out in partnerships with governments and other large corporate entities that effectively exclude the involvement of local communities. Elliott goes on to argue that, as a result, transnationals are responsible for extensive environmental degradation and resource depletion while they cast themselves as corporate environmentalists upon whom we can rely for the solutions to sustainable development. To ensure survival, corporations rely on investor confidence – which is naturally buoyed by profit earnings. Governance resides in the hands of a multitude of shareholders whose overriding motives are dividends, not environmental, social and economic responsibility.

In contrast, NGOs are funded by public memberships, public and private institutions and donations from philanthropic organizations that look to support the various missions that NGOs undertake, for example, poverty alleviation, education, health and environmental sustainability. UN-sponsored research has found that many corporations from the OECD flout their environmental responsibilities by paying an estimated $80 billion a year, in the form of bribes or cash donations, to governments of developing countries to win support for their so-called sustainable growth activities (Khan, 2002).

Liu (2003) argues that in less-developed countries poverty and social desperation necessitate a great need for the local community to benefit from tourism development. However, too often the inability of the host population to fully participate in the development process results in the lion's share of tourism income being taken away or 'leaked' out from the destination (Liu, 2003). These commodifying processes occur when the final outcome is defined as the economic use-value of a product or service.

Current trends in tourism continue to move towards the increasing commodification of tourism in the search for global profits. The negative impacts of such a trajectory on the tourism experience require decommodifying actions, best informed by alternative philosophies and theoretical perspectives that include feminism, ecocentrism, community development and post-structuralism. NGOs provide avenues to pursue decommodification in tourism as they move beyond the almost exclusive pursuit of industry profits and are able to place social, cultural and ecological value on local environments and communities. Sitting outside the mainstream commodified free-market process, NGOs are able to provide us with examples of policy strategies that may move the tourism industry towards more decommodified practice (Wearing and McDonald, 2002; Wearing et al., 2005).

Volunteer Tourism, Power and Host Communities

Clearly, the argument outlined above posits NGOs as 'all good' – and corporate and commercial interests as 'all bad'. However, this starkly dichotomous view does not account for the increasingly blurry and overlapping relationships that are beginning to emerge in volunteer tourism between NGOs and commercial operators (Lyons, 2003). In many cases NGOs contract out to commercial

providers components of the volunteer tour product and limit their involven
to negotiating suitable projects where host communities need volunteer labour.
Likewise, NGOs work directly with transnational developers towards outcomes
that may not have total support from all factions of affected local communities. The argument could be made that as NGOs begin to develop partnerships
with corporate entities, they run the risk of losing sight of their core activity of
supporting local communities at all costs and instead become engaged in the
gradual processes of the commodification of alternative – and by extension,
volunteer – tourism.

However, this view of the commodification process underestimates local
communities and the influential role they can play in maintaining the alternative frame of volunteer tourism. Wearing and McDonald (2002) demonstrate
that communities do not passively accept top–down direction. Rather they
assimilate 'knowledge' into day-to-day negotiations of the existing social order.
Instead of simplistically relegating local communities to a 'dominated' position – a
much accepted stereotype – it is crucial for volunteer tourism to turn the language of critique into a language of possibility in order to pay attention to the
actualities of the everyday struggles of people (Fagan, 1999, p. 180).

Foucault's philosophies on power/knowledge, discourse, subjectivity and
resistance have relevance here. His idea of 'disciplinary power' (Foucault, 1980,
p. 105) allows us to explore some of the issues around developing tourism in
these host communities. Foucault argues that power is exercised through concrete mechanisms and practices (Foucault, 1983); he explains: 'The problem
is to both distinguish the events, differentiate the networks and levels to which
they belong, and to reconstitute the threads which connect them and make
them give rise to one another' (Foucault, 1979, p. 33). Adopting Foucault's
advice would bring the two worlds of host community and volunteer together,
which would further provide a new way of thinking, and would challenge the
neocolonial approach to tourism where communities are exploited and seen as
'other'. In Foucault, people are never considered to be just victims. Although
they are constrained by subjectivities, normative sexuality and 'docile bodies'
constituted through powerful, normalizing discourses and self-surveillance,
they are 'free' in the sense that even given this they can choose to resist.
Foucault's idea of resistance allows for a more flexible and optimistic situation
grounded in the everyday experiences of individuals; in this case, host community members.

Conclusion

This introductory chapter has attempted to provide some foundational discussion that opens the way for detailed exploration of volunteer tourism through
the following case studies. In this chapter we have outlined some broader
debates about alternative tourism and the processes of power that underpin
it. In order to elaborate how volunteer tourism has the ability to move beyond
the simplistic oppression/emancipation dialectic, it is crucial for researchers
engaging in examining volunteer tourism to steer away from the dichotomous

view that power is exercised by dominant players (tourism operators) over oppressed actors (destination communities), and instead adopt an alternative analytical framework that suggests emancipation is immanent in daily power struggles, rather than simply standing in opposition to oppression.

The remaining chapters in Part I of this book demonstrate this approach, and include contributions from researchers who consider the political dimensions of volunteer tourism in-depth and examine theoretical and applied manifestations of power, empowerment and equity as it plays out in a wide range of cultural contexts.

References

Butler, R.W. (1990) Alternative tourism: pious hope or Trojan horse? *Journal of Travel Research* 28(3), 40–45.

Cohen, E. (1988) Authenticity and commoditization in tourism. *Annals of Tourism Research* 15, 371–386.

Cohen, S. and Taylor, L. (1976) *Escape Attempts*. Penguin, Harmondsworth, UK.

Elliott, L. (2002) Global environmental governance. In: Wilkinson, R. and Hughes, S. (eds) *Global Governance*. Routledge, London, pp. 57–74.

Fagan, G.H. (1999) Cultural politics and post development paradigms. In: Munik, R. and O'Hearn, D. (eds) *Critical Development Theory: Contributions to a New Paradigm*. Zed Books, London, pp. 178–195.

Foucault, M. (1979) *Michel Foucault: Power, Truth, Strategy*. Feral Publications, Sydney, Australia.

Foucault, M. (1980) *Power/ Knowledge: Selected Interviews and Other Writings 1972–77*. The Harvester Press, Brighton, UK.

Foucault, M. (1983) Afterword: the subject and power. In: Dreyfus, H.L. and Rabinow, P. (eds) *Michel Foucault: Beyond Structuralism and Hermeneutics*. University of Chicago Press, Chicago, Illinois, pp. i–iv.

Goffman, E. (1959) *The Presentation of Self in Everyday Life*. Anchor Books, New York.

Hall, C.M. (1991) *Introduction to Tourism in Australia: Impacts, Planning and Development*. Longman Cheshire, London.

Khan, S.A. (2002) Beyond the limits of sustainable growth: earth on the market. *Le Monde Diplomatique*, 8 December.

Liu, Z. (2003) Sustainable tourism development: a critique. *Journal of Sustainable Tourism* 11(6), 459–475.

Lyons, K.D. (2003) Ambiguities in volunteer tourism: a case study of Australians participating in a J-1 visitor exchange program. *Tourism Recreation Research* 28(3), 5–13.

MacCannell, D. (1976) *The Tourist: A New Theory of the Leisure Class*. Macmillan, London.

Rojek, C. (1993) *Ways of Escape: Modern Transformations in Leisure and Travel*. Macmillan, London.

Uriely, N., Reichel, A. and Ron, A. (2003) Volunteering in tourism: additional thinking. *Tourism Recreation Research* 28(3), 57–62.

Urry, J. (1990) *The Tourist Gaze*. Sage, London.

Wearing, S.L. (2001) *Volunteer Tourism: Seeking Experiences That Make a Difference*. CAB International, Wallingford, UK.

Wearing, S. (2002) Re-centering the self in volunteer tourism. In: Dann, G.S. (ed.) *The Tourist as a Metaphor of the Social World*. CAB International, Wallingford, UK, pp. 237–262.

Wearing, S. and McDonald, M. (2002) The development of community-based tourism: re-thinking the relationship between tour operators and development agents as intermediaries in rural and isolated area communities. *Journal of Sustainable Tourism* 10(2), 191–206.

Wearing, S.L., McDonald, M. and Ponting, J. (2005) Decommodifying tourism: the contribution of non-governmental organizations. *Journal of Sustainable Tourism* 13(5), 422–424.

2

'Pettin' the Critters': Exploring the Complex Relationship Between Volunteers and the Voluntoured in McDowell County, West Virginia, USA, and Tijuana, Mexico

N.G. McGehee[1] and K. Andereck[2]

[1]Virginia Polytechnic Institute and State University, Hospitality and Tourism Management, Blacksburg, Virginia, USA; [2]Department of Recreation and Tourism Management, Arizona State University, Phoenix, Arizona, USA

This is a story about the relationship between the residents of two volunteer tourism host communities and the volunteer tourists who visit them. One is a declining rural community located in the Appalachian mountains of the USA. The other is in a rapidly expanding urban area in Baja California, Mexico. Both are suffering from a lack of affordable health care, with minimal access to quality public education and healthy food and drinking water. Both are populated by men and women of great strength and abilities, overcoming day-to-day trials with grace and dignity. Both are experiencing the benefits and the challenges of receiving large numbers of volunteer tourists each year. This is an attempt to illuminate the perspective of the men and women in these two communities and to recognize the complexity of the relationships between and among volunteer tourists and the voluntoured.

A steadily growing body of work exists in the area of volunteer tourism. Volunteer tourism (also known as voluntourism) is defined by the industry as 'a seamlessly integrated combination of voluntary service to a destination along with the best, traditional elements of travel – arts, culture, geography, and history – in that destination' (VolunTourism International, 1999). In the area of academic research, McGehee and Santos (2005, p. 760) define volunteer tourism as 'utilizing discretionary time and income to travel out of the sphere of regular activity to assist others in need'.

Most of the research in this area has concentrated on the volunteer tourist (Brown and Morrison, 2003; Stoddart and Rogerson, 2004; Wearing, 2004; McGehee and Santos, 2005; Mustonen, 2005), as opposed to people in the local community who host the volunteers. For example, Brown and Morrison

(2003) focused on the receptivity of group tourists to an extension of their tour packages that would include a mini-mission or short-term opportunity. Others have studied those already involved in voluntourism. McGehee and Santos (2005) examined the relationship between participation in volunteer tourism (as a tourist) and social movement participation, while Stoddart and Rogerson (2004) profiled volunteer tourists in South Africa who were participating in a Habitat for Humanity project.

Some have focused on the organizations surrounding volunteer tourism. Wearing (2004) examined conservation-based volunteer tourism and its potential as a less-commodified alternative to mainstream tourism. Wearing *et al.* (2005) examined the role of NGOs as links between volunteer tourists and the host communities and as key to success. The only research to date that has focused directly on the host community is that of Higgins-Desboilles (2003), Singh (2002, 2004) and Broad (2003). Higgins-Desboilles (2003) focused on volunteer tourism as a potential form of reconciliation between divided societies, in particular the relationship between aboriginal Australians and Australians of European descent. Singh (2002, 2004) reported a case study in the Himalayas that highlighted the person-to-person relationships developed between members of the host communities and their volunteer tourism guests, and Broad (2003) conducted a participant observation case study that included examination of the informal yet valuable cultural exchange component of volunteer tourism that took place in the Gibbon Rehabilitation Project on the island of Phuket. For the most part, the research to date has been primarily descriptive and uncritically posits volunteer tourism as a positive alternative to mass tourism. The purpose of this chapter is to illuminate some of the complex issues that exist in the relationship between volunteer tourists and the voluntoured.

Methodological Approach

This case study research is in line with Jennings' description of the 'interpretivist paradigm, which holds an ontology (worldview) that recognizes multiple perspectives in regard to the research focus, an epistemological stance that is subjective in nature and a methodology which is predicated on qualitative principles' (2005, p. 104). In our attempt to capture a number of different perspectives on the relationship between volunteer tourists and the voluntoured in ways that could not be anticipated using strictly quantitative research, a mixed method approach was utilized. This method, as identified by Beeton (2005) and DeCrop (2004), is crucial to gathering meaningful data about a case or cases.

Table 2.1 lists the various methods utilized for the project. In-depth interviews were conducted with volunteer tourism organization administrators and full-time volunteer interns. Informal interviews were conducted with Promotoras (local trainers) and local residents in the two communities. As there were some language barrier issues between us as English-speaking researchers and our Spanish-speaking informants, survey research was conducted with some residents in Tijuana using an instrument that had been carefully translated into 'Tijuanan' Spanish and pilot-tested. The open-ended results were translated back by one of us who reads and

Table 2.1. Research methods utilized.

Tijuana, Mexico	Method	McDowell County, WV
Los Niños Administrators	In-depth interviews	McDowell Mission administrators
Los Niños Interns	In-depth interviews	Mustard Seeds and Mountains administrators
Los Niños Promotoras/Residents	Informal interviews	McDowell Mission employees/residents
Los Niños Promotoras/Residents	Self-completed convenience questionnaires	
Esperanza Administrators	Informal interviews	
Esperanza Promotoras/Residents	Self-completed convenience questionnaires	
Los Niños	Web site content	McDowell Mission
Esperanza	analysis	Mustard Seeds and Mountains
Los Niños	Participant observation	McDowell Mission

speaks Spanish with assistance from a native Mexican Spanish language instructor. While efforts were made to include a variety of voices in this research, our previous relationships with the volunteer tourism organizations resulted in greater representation from this group. It is very important, however, to note that many of these organizations are community-run and resident-driven. In other words, those who run the organizations are often also those who are the voluntoured.

Web sites operated by volunteer tourism organizations that target McDowell County and Tijuana, Mexico, were also content-analysed. Finally, participant observation was implemented intermittently over a 2-year period. The data collected from the various sources were transcribed and coded. Themes and patterns emerged from textual analysis of the coded data, all with an eye for the examination of the complex relationships that exist between the volunteer tourists and the voluntoured.

Critics of the case study approach often argue that the bias of the researcher influences the findings (Beeton, 2005). We argue that all research is vulnerable to bias; the research design of any project must be such that bias is both recognized and limited through the use of time-honoured methodological techniques. Specifically, DeCrop (2004) outlines four criteria of trustworthiness for qualitative inquiry: credibility, transferability, dependability and confirmability (DeCrop, 2004). For this study, we addressed credibility using techniques of prolonged engagement (the researchers have been working in the two communities intermittently for 2 years), persistent observation (adding emerging data sources as the study progressed) and referential adequacy (contextualizing the findings). We incorporated transferability via the development of thick descriptions. Prolonged engagement and a specific but flexible research plan were used to increase dependability. Finally, we assessed confirmability using investigator triangulation.

The following is not an exhaustive report of the findings from the cases. As is common with case studies, page limitations prevent a full disclosure of the data. Instead, we have focused on two emergent themes that appeared surrounding the relationship between volunteers and the voluntoured: the issues related to dependency and the role of organized religion. Discussion of these two themes follows after a description of each of the volunteer tourism host communities. Additional illustrative comments derived from other volunteer tourism organizations outside the two case communities will also be used as clarification for the concepts presented.

McDowell County, West Virginia, USA

McDowell County is located in south-western West Virginia (WV), nestled in the Appalachian mountains of the USA. This area has been the site of ecological bounty through its rich coal veins and dense hardwood forests as well as the location of some of the greatest hardship for its people, with low per capita income, limited educational opportunities and geographic isolation. The 2000 US census indicates that the unemployment rate exceeds 10% in McDowell County, compared to a national unemployment rate of 4.7%. The median household income is US$16,931 in McDowell County, compared to a national median income of US$43,318 (US Census Bureau, 2005).

Through the years, various private, political and governmental entities have attempted to improve the region and the circumstances of its inhabitants. In the 1930s, President Franklin D. Roosevelt and his wife Eleanor spent a great deal of time in McDowell County promoting his 'New Deal' programme that resulted, among other things, in the advent of a national social security system, and in the 1960s, President John F. Kennedy again identified Appalachia as an area of great poverty and need. With the development of advanced extraction technology, the coal boom became the coal bust, plastics began replacing the market for wood and other forest products, and young people continued to leave the region searching for job opportunities elsewhere. Volunteers In Service To America (VISTA), a kind of domestic Peace Corps, began coming into the region in 1965 (AmeriCorps, 2006). Most likely they did not see themselves as such, but VISTA volunteers created the first wave of volunteer tourists to McDowell County, WV.

VISTA volunteers were closely followed by the beginnings of what have been legions of volunteers from all over the USA, coming as part of high school-aged church mission groups, college students conducting service projects or young retirees hoping to give back with the skill sets that come from a lifetime of experience. Randy Wallace is Team Leader of Mustard Seeds and Mountains (Mustard Seeds and Mountains, 2001), a Christian relief and development agency. He estimates that upwards of 10,000 volunteers come to the county per year, numbering over one-third of the county's own population of 27,329 (R. Wallace, Princeton, West Virginia, 2006, personal communication). There is no governmental regulation of volunteer tourism organizations in McDowell County; nor is there a method of tracking how many organizations are located in the county. Volunteers involved with both Randy's organization and many others participate in home building, home improvement, school and/or community centre repair, educational assistance through bookmobiles and after-school/summer school programmes, and many other types of volunteer programmes. At first blush, this may appear to be a positive contribution to the community. However, upon deeper examination, the contribution is still viable, but the resulting impacts are more complex.

The McDowell County Mission is an entity sponsored by the West Virginia Conference of the United Methodist Church 'to meet the needs of the southern West Virginia coalfields of McDowell, Wyoming, Mercer, Mingo, and Logan counties' (McDowell Mission, 2001). According to Jay Wilson, director of the McDowell County Mission, the organization's primary aim is to provide Christian spiritual guidance and opportunities for worship to the community, but a secondary part of the mission's operation involves the logistical coordination of the church and school-related groups who come to volunteer in McDowell County every year, specifically to participate in home repair and assist with a summer vacation bible school programme and/or the bookmobile travelling library (J. Wilson, Welch, West Virginia, 2007, personal communication). While there are many groups involved in coordinating volunteer efforts, the McDowell Mission is perhaps the organization that has the greatest visibility and presence in McDowell County. The mission is based in Welch, WV, the county seat, and all the employees live in the county year-round. This creates a rather unique situation in that many of the employees of the McDowell Mission are also recipients of the assistance offered by volunteers. In addition, due to the rural nature of the county, even those who are not direct recipients are in fact impacted by, and very aware of, the presence of volunteer tourists in the community. Over 1800 junior high school, high school and college students, families and individuals travel to McDowell County and work directly through the mission each year, with an additional 2500 working with them indirectly. Volunteers spend between a 3-day weekend and a 7-day week in McDowell County. In the case of home repair assistance, residents qualify as a result of a fairly detailed application process conducted by the McDowell County Mission. Once they qualify, they are required to be present during the home improvements and if they are physically able, they work side by side with volunteers. Types of home repair range from basic painting and cosmetic improvements to more complex carpentry, plumbing and electrical projects. It is the policy of the McDowell County Mission to complete a variety of projects on one residence and all the necessary improvements within that house rather than to perform basic projects on a large number of homes.

In addition to Mustard Seeds and Mountains and the McDowell County Mission, there are a number of other organizations involved in volunteer tourism to the region that do not have a permanent office in the county. For example, Adventures in Missions (AIM) is an entity located in Gainesville, Georgia, 350 miles (approximately 563 km) south of McDowell County (Adventures in Missions, 2006). This group coordinates 1-week motor coach tours in spring and summer that consist primarily of high school and college students who come into the county and perform small repair projects, as well as painting or cleaning to renovate and renew community meeting places, private homes and churches. AIM also conducts what they refer to as 'outreach activities, door-to-door evangelism, including sports outreach (particularly basketball), singings, nursing home programs, dramas, helping at the food bank, and visitations to private homes' (Adventures in Missions, 2006).

Tijuana, Mexico

In great contrast to McDowell County, WV, the city of Tijuana, Mexico, is growing by eight city blocks per day (J.C. Ramos, Tijuana, Mexico, 2006, personal communication). Tijuana is the busiest border city in the world; as a result, many rural Mexicans migrate there with the hopes of finding better economic opportunities. The humble and tidy houses of these immigrants are often built of recycled material such as garage doors, scrap corrugated aluminum or wood discarded from construction sites. Homes seem to spring up overnight on the hillsides surrounding the cities, often without basic public services. At first glance, these Tijuanan communities (*colonias*) made up of simple housing may appear to provide a bleak existence. However, if you take the time to look more closely, what you will find are lively, bustling communities, filled with families who have hopes, dreams and desires for a better life.

Due to a number of factors, including proximity to the USA, Tijuana is a highly 'voluntoured' city. As with McDowell County, WV, there is no governmental regulation of volunteer tourism organizations in Tijuana, and there is no method of tracking how many organizations are located in the city. Los Niños is one of the many non-profit organizations that coordinate volunteer tourism activities primarily between American college students and communities within Tijuana. In particular, Los Niños is involved in the Promotoras programme, which utilizes a train-the-trainers approach in leadership, organizing and community education targeting residents of communities within Tijuana. Approximately 60 resident Promotoras work with upwards of 19,000 Mexican families per year, disseminating information on nutrition and ecology and exploring other ways to improve the quality of life for their friends and neighbours. In cooperation and collaboration with the resident Promotoras and Los Niños administrators, volunteer tourists spend an average of 1 week working on community-directed basic construction projects, most often targeting elementary schools. Due to the extremely rapid growth of Tijuana and the low tax base from which the government operates, financial support for the construction of school facilities is nearly non-existent, particularly in low-income neighbourhoods. Often children attend classes in buildings made of scrap corrugated aluminum or abandoned garage doors. Los Niños coordinates activities between the local residents and the volunteer tourists. Volunteers pay for their own housing, food and transportation, as well as purchasing all of the construction materials and equipment necessary for their projects. Local residents work side by side on the construction projects with the volunteer tourists.

Esperanza is a very similar non-profit organization located in Tijuana, in that it is the same size as Los Niños and operates with the Promotora system as well.

It is different from Los Niños in that its primary goal is to provide micro-credit towards home building and ownership and to utilize volunteer tourists for labour. Community associations, composed primarily of women, form small micro-credit organizations. Members vote on applications and proposals for the purchase of the materials that are presented by their fellow members at weekly meetings based on demonstrated ability to pay, primarily through existing savings accounts and steady employment. Members whose applications are approved are then placed on a waiting list and their homes are completed as volunteer groups become available. The queue is primarily determined according to first-approved, first-served, but sometimes other issues come into play based on the social norms and morals of the group. For example, one member's position on the waiting list was raised considerably as her terminal illness became worse. The goal was to make sure that her home would be completed and her two teenaged sons would have a permanent residence before her death. Once a home-building project comes to the top of the list, members and volunteers work side by side to actually make the concrete blocks by hand and to build the homes from the ground up.

'Pettin' the Critters': Dependency, Othering and Coping Strategies of the Voluntoured

During interviews at the offices of the McDowell County Mission, Norma McKinney, Director of Development (and also a lifelong resident of McDowell County), told a story that illustrated a major issue within volunteer tourism: dependency (N. McKinney, Welch, West Virginia, 2006, personal communication). She recalled a phone call she had recently received. An organization was interested in bringing a truckload of used clothing to the mission so that they could distribute it directly to local families. She politely thanked them for their interest, and then explained that the mission did not support any kind of free handouts of items. She offered to take the clothing and sell it at a very inexpensive price at their local thrift store; this way it would preserve the dignity of local residents and reduce dependency on outside sources. The response from the organizers on the other end was adamant: they wanted to set up a table with the truck and 'personally hand the clothing to the needy folks'. At that point, Norma explained to me, she knew the phone call was yet another from people who wanted to, in her classic use of the local vernacular, 'pet the critters'. Cases abound of organizations that may have the best of intentions but a total lack of understanding of how their actions affect the dignity of local residents, both in McDowell County, WV, and Tijuana, Mexico, and countless other volunteer tourism destinations throughout the world. This is a classic example where cultural and geographic distance and difference create an atmosphere ripe for the 'othering' of the voluntoured by the volunteer tourists. Obviously, Norma McKinney as well as other residents in the community have developed coping strategies to deal with such othering. Simply by inventing a term for it, e.g. 'pettin' the critters', they had defined and exposed these kinds of volunteer tourist activities from their perspective. While this type of coping strategy has been identified in a variety of cultures, particularly Sweet's (1989) work exploring the practice of Pueblo Indians burlesquing the behaviour of visiting tourists, to date it has not been identified among the voluntoured.

Of course, not all of these types of potentially damaging volunteer tourism activities get channelled through the McDowell Mission. Because of a lack of organized policy and local oversight, any organization that wishes may 'pet the critters': bring a truckload of discarded clothing into the community, set up a table and post a 'Free Clothing' sign along the road, waiting for takers. Often quite unwittingly volunteer tourists of all types seek to give, but they also want to receive – they want to be thanked for their efforts and to feel good about what they have done. The face-to-face interaction with members of the community provides volunteers with a sense of self-affirmation they may not otherwise experience.

The dependency issue is also addressed by Los Niños and Esperanza (E. Sabatini, San Diego, California, 2006, personal communication). They have developed specific policies and stressed these to their volunteers, including a 'no handouts' rule. Those who come to help make concrete blocks and build homes or work on school improvement projects in Tijuana are explicitly told *not* to bring used clothing. However, in an example of the complexity of the relationship between volunteer tourists and the voluntoured, this rule is often circumvented. The relationships built between volunteers and the voluntoured are often strong and enduring. The effect of working side by side for many days in less than ideal conditions can forge lifelong bonds between people. At this point, after the relationships are established, the sharing of used clothing becomes more like a family exchange, e.g. a sister sharing a blouse with her sibling because she knows the colour would be perfect on her, or a pair of pants because she knows she will never really lose that 10 lb she thought she could when she originally purchased the pants. As a result, methods of resistance occur when volunteers send clothing in the mail after they come home from their volunteer experience, or they send clothing with friends who are making the trip with instructions to deliver the goods when organizational administrators 'are looking the other way'. We witnessed one of these 'subversive exchanges' with an organization that will remain nameless (to protect the participants), and it was a joyous and equitable experience, not unlike our personal experiences exchanging clothing with other female friends and relatives, or handing down our children's gently used clothes to friends who have younger children. Because of the personal relationships established between volunteer and the voluntoured, the sense of 'othering' did not exist. Residents explained (through an interpreter) that receiving the clothing brought back memories of the friendships forged while working beside volunteers.

Another volunteer tourism organization (not located at either of the case study sites) addresses the challenge of othering quite differently. Dan Nesbitt, Construction Program Director with the United Methodist Relief Center (UMRC), an organization that focuses on home building in Charleston, South Carolina, USA, explains that their organization has adopted a policy whereby the volunteers do not meet the people for whom they are building their homes. 'When groups make the request to meet the homeowners, I first ask them why they are eager to meet them. Is it so they will thank you? If so, do you realize the position you are putting the residents in?' (D. Nesbitt, Charleston, South Carolina, 2006, personal communication). Nesbitt feels strongly that volunteers should be motivated internally and spiritually to assist those in need.

In contrast, many volunteer tourism organizations cite the interactions between volunteers and their hosts as perhaps the most vital component of the volunteer tourism experience for both parties. David Clemmons, Director of the Volunteerism Program with Los Niños, firmly believes that the relationships developed between host and volunteer is the most vital component of the volunteer tourism experience and actively maximizes opportunities for interaction (D. Clemmons, San Diego, California, 2006, personal communication). Amanda Kelly, a graduate student who conducted interviews of participants in the Alternative Spring Break Program at Virginia Tech in Blacksburg, Virginia, USA, recounted the story of one volunteer's experience in New Orleans, Louisiana, in spring 2006 that exemplifies the best of what can happen as a result of these interactions (A. Kelly, Blacksburg, Virginia, 2006, personal communication). The group was assisting a woman in cleaning out her house, which had been severely damaged by flooding that resulted from the severe hurricane season that damaged much of the city. The team worked side by side with the woman. At one point, a volunteer found an album filled with family photos that were precious to the homeowner. Tragically, as the photos were drying, they were also disappearing. Thinking quickly, the volunteer used a digital video camera to record the pictures before they faded and, as she did, the homeowner narrated, providing a valuable oral history to complement the photos being recorded. Had there been no volunteer–homeowner interaction, the photos still may have been recognized for what they were, and the recording still may have occurred, but without the priceless narration of the homeowner. The resulting final product not only preserved valuable memories of the past, but created a new memory of hope for the homeowner and the value of service for the volunteer. Again, the complexity of the relationship between volunteer and voluntoured is revealed.

The 'R Word': Organized Religion and Volunteer Tourism

The role of organized religion in volunteer tourism often seems to be the 'elephant in the living room' that no one wishes to discuss. Of course there are many secular volunteer tourism organizations with no connection to organized religion, and there are many volunteers who practise any of a great number of religions, but if we were to trace the roots of volunteer tourism, what we would likely find would be some form of the early mission and relief work of both the Catholic and Protestant Christian churches.

The relationship between the voluntoured and volunteer tourists is complex when it comes to the subject of religion. Sometimes the relationship appears to be contradictory, as in the case of the two communities of McDowell County and Tijuana. Census statistics report low church attendance or association with organized religion in McDowell County (US Census Bureau, 2005), but interviews with residents reveal support for the church-based volunteers who work through local religious-based organizations like the McDowell Mission. One resident reported that he could 'trust the church groups more than groups like the Red Cross'. This perspective also comes out of previous negative experiences with NGOs after flooding that occurred in the 1990s. Conversely, in the survey conducted in Tijuana, a culture known for high rates of church attendance and affiliation, respondents were asked to rank their preferences for the type of volunteers they would like to see in their community. While it is important to note that all categories were ranked favourably, 'faith-based organizations' were ranked last, after college students, corporate teams, fellow Mexicans and senior citizens. During interviews with Tijuana residents, many referred to getting 'the God talk'; e.g. asking 'when are we going to get the God talk?' as if this is an expected price that they will pay in exchange for the volunteer work. Residents expect this from certain church-related organizations, particularly those associated with Protestant Christian church groups who are more known for their prostheletizing. Interestingly, their lack of enthusiasm for volunteer tourists associated with organized religion does not spill over to many of the volunteer organizations that are well established within the communities but lack a prostheletizing component. For example, Los Niños and Esperanza both have roots in organized religion, but the Tijuana residents with whom they work do not associate these groups with organized religion, and they express high degrees of support and appreciation towards them. The common thread between the reactions of hosts from both communities may be found in the fact that both organizations have permanent offices and full-time employees who live in the community.

The Future of Volunteer Tourism

As indicated at the beginning of this chapter, this has been a story of two communities heavily involved with volunteer tourism. The experiences of these communities were used to illustrate some of the issues and complexities surrounding the relationships between volunteer tourists and the voluntoured. Perhaps the most telling testimonial to the complexity of the relationship may be exemplified through the countless conversations with people heavily involved in volunteer tourism. After discussing the various positive and negative impacts of volunteer tourism upon the community (Table 2.2), invariably, the conversation would boil down to one basic (and some would argue decidedly un-academic) question: 'Is volunteer tourism a good thing?' As expected, the answer was never simple. The commonality that existed was the deep struggle each person had with the question. Jay Wilson, Executive Director of McDowell Mission, exemplified the thoughts of many when he shared that he had been wrestling with the question for 2 years. 'Volunteers have been coming to this part of the country for thirty years, I have been here for six years, and while I am sure that the volunteers reap benefits from the experience, I honestly don't see a change in the community' (J. Wilson, Welch, West Virginia, 2007, personal communication).

Table 2.2. Potential positive and negative impacts of volunteer tourism on the community.

Positive impacts	Negative impacts
• Cross-cultural interaction between volunteer tourists and the voluntoured can result in increased understanding for both groups • Volunteer tourists may better see the connection between local actions and global effects • Volunteer tourists may increase their understanding of international issues by seeing them directly (border issues, environmental issues, etc.) • Volunteer tourists may return home inspired to get more involved in environmental or social issue organizations • Improvement of the quality of life for targeted individuals and host communities • Volunteer tourists may have a more positive economic impact on host communities than mass tourists through more direct injections of resources into communities and less leakage • Volunteer tourists are able to subsidize social programmes in areas with minimal government and private financial resources • Volunteer tourists provide services in areas that do not have a culture of volunteerism among local residents	• If individuals stay home and volunteer, they can save the travel costs and put those resources (both time and money) towards local volunteer efforts as well as eliminate the environmental impact of travel • Volunteer tourists may drain valuable resources that might otherwise go to local residents • If not properly briefed before visiting, the behaviour of volunteer tourists can negatively impact the culture of local communities and offend residents • As with mass tourism, if carrying capacity is exceeded, environmental damage may occur • Volunteer tourist activities may be conducted in a way that undermines the dignity of local residents • An environment of dependency may arise as residents begin to rely on volunteer tourists to provide economic support for their communities • Volunteer tourism may negatively influence perceived dignity and self-esteem among residents • The environment of dependency and despondency may be transferred to the next generation thereby perpetuating the problem

But this is not to say that organizers wanted to throw the proverbial baby out with the bathwater. For example, Randy Wallace of Mustard Seeds and Mountains had very concrete ideas about improving volunteer tourism in McDowell County (R. Wallace, Princeton, West Virginia, 2006, personal communication). As with many who support the concepts of sustainable tourism, he argues for a 'less is more' approach to volunteer tourism: reduce the number of volunteer tourists and be more selective in terms of matching the skill set each possesses with the particular needs of the community. A recurring theme that emerged among the volunteer tourism administrators interviewed was an interest in furthering development of regulation of volunteer tourism in a way that would first track patterns of volunteer tourism to the community, second exercise some control over who comes, how many come and the type of activities in which they engage, and finally better match the skills and interests of volunteer tourists with the needs of the community or, even more particularly, various neighbourhoods within the community.

To use Tijuana as an example, Los Niños administrators estimate that over one million volunteer tourists visit Tijuana annually, but there is no method of tracking this resource. There is also no control – any organization can enter a community and proceed to conduct any type of volunteer tourism it wishes. Clothing giveaways and other forms of 'pettin' the critters' can occur without governmental clearance or oversight. Perhaps most importantly, there is no overarching method of matching community needs with each volunteer tourism organization's skills or projects. In other words, there is no way to determine if an organization that specializes in providing health care is getting to the communities who most need it due to exposure to hazardous waste or industrial pollution, or if another community is being inundated with school repair groups but would better benefit from assistance to its senior citizens. Given recent advances in geospatial technology, the development of a tracking system that matches community needs with the skills, abilities and interests of volunteers is not out of the question.

Finally, it is not the intention or presumption of this chapter to attempt to solve the debate over the role of religion in volunteer tourism, but merely to introduce it as an often overlooked issue. There is an undeniable logic that any organized religious doctrine that calls for environmental stewardship, social justice or caring for fellow human beings may inevitably turn to volunteer tourism as a possible way to support its doctrine on a global scale. The question that must be explored is 'How?' How should the phenomenon of volunteer tourism proceed and develop in a way that, just as with sustainable mainstream tourism, maximizes the positive impacts while minimizing the negative impacts? As indicated previously, of course not all volunteer tourism has a relationship with organized religion. But to best answer this question, the role of organized religion must be considered.

Acknowledgements

There are numerous acknowledgements that we would like to make. First and foremost, we would like to express our appreciation to the many residents of both Tijuana, Mexico, and McDowell County, WV, who shared their opinions, homes and meals with us as we attempted to explore this phenomenon of volunteer tourism. This includes all the wonderful Promotoras of Los Niños and Esperenza, interns Chrissy Phillips and Elizabeth Burpee of Los Niños, as well as numerous volunteers and employees of the McDowell Mission. We also appreciate the countless hours of discussions between ourselves and the administrators of these organizations. Specifically, Jay Wilson, Executive Director of McDowell Mission; Randy Wallace, Team Leader of Mustard Seeds and Mountains, also located in McDowell County; Elisa Sabatini, Executive Director, David Clemmons, Director of Volunteerism Program and Rigoberto Reyes, Director, Community Leadership Education Program, all of Los Niños International; and Graciela Lara of Esperenza. These are remarkable people born with extra-large hearts and clarity of vision that is inspiring.

References

Adventures in Missions (2006) Homepage. Available at: http://www.adventures.org

AmeriCorps (2006) AmeriCorps*VISTA. Available at: http://www.americorps.org/about/programs/vista.asp

Beeton, S. (2005) The case study in tourism research: a multi-method case study approach. In: Ritchie, B.W., Burns, P. and Palmer, C. (eds) *Tourism Research Methods: Integrating Theory with Practice*. CAB International, Wallingford, UK, pp. 37–48.

Broad, S. (2003) Living the Thai life – A case study of volunteer tourism at the Gibbon rehabilitation project, Thailand. *Tourism Recreation Research* 28, 63–72.

Brown, S. and Morrison, A. (2003) Expanding volunteer vacation participation: an exploratory study on the mini-mission concept. *Tourism Recreation Research* 28, 73–82.

DeCrop, A. (2004) Trustworthiness in qualitative tourism research. In: Phillimore, J. and Goodson, L. (eds) *Qualitative Research in Tourism: Ontologies, Epistemologies, and Methodologies*. Routledge, London, pp. 156–169.

Higgins-Desboilles, F. (2003) Reconciliation tourism: tourism healing divided societies! *Tourism Recreation Research* 28, 35–44.

Jennings, G.R. (2005) Interviewing: a focus on qualitative techniques. In: Ritchie, B.W., Burns, P. and Palmer, C. (eds) *Tourism Research Methods: Integrating Theory with Practice*. CAB International, Wallingford, UK, pp. 99–118.

McDowell Mission (2001) Homepage. Available at: http://www.mcdowellmission.org

McGehee, N.G. and Santos, C.A. (2005) Social change, discourse and volunteer tourism. *Annals of Tourism Research* 32, 760–779.

Mustard Seeds and Mountains (2001) Homepage. Available at: http://www.mustardseeds.org

Mustonen, P. (2005) Volunteer tourism: postmodern pilgrimage? *Journal of Tourism and Cultural Change* 3, 160–177.

Singh, T.V. (2002) Altruistic tourism: another shade of sustainable tourism. The case of Kanda community. *Tourism (Zagreb)* 50, 361–370.

Singh, T.V. (2004) *New Horizons in Tourism: Strange Experiences and Stranger Practices*. CAB International, Wallingford, UK.

Stoddart, H. and Rogerson, C. (2004) Volunteer tourism: the case of Habitat for Humanity South Africa. *GeoJournal* 60, 311–318.

Sweet, J.D. (1989) Burlesquing 'the other' in Pueblo performance. *Annals of Tourism Research* 16, 62–75.

US Census Bureau (2005) McDowell County Quick Facts. Available at: http://quickfacts.census.gov/qfd/states/54/54047.html

VolunTourism International (1999) VolunTourism. Avialable at: http://www.voluntourism.org/index.html

Wearing, S. (2004) Examining best practice in volunteer tourism. In: Stebbins, R. and Graham, M. (eds) *Volunteering as Leisure, Leisure as Volunteering: An International Assessment*. CAB International, Wallingford, UK, pp. 209–224.

Wearing, S., McDonald, M. and Ponting, J. (2005) Building a decommodified research paradigm in tourism: the contribution of NGOs. *Journal of Sustainable Tourism* 13, 424–439.

3 Volunteering Tourism Knowledge: a Case from the United Nations World Tourism Organization

L. Ruhanen,[1] C. Cooper[1] and E. Fayos-Solá[2]

[1]*The School of Tourism, The University of Queensland, Ipswich, Australia;* [2]*Education and Knowledge Management, Department of World Tourism Organization, Madrid, Spain*

Tourism activity has long been considered an agent for economic development and social revitalization, with more recent attention focused on the ability of tourism to generate opportunities for the least-developed countries of the world (Sofield *et al.*, 2004). Much of this focus has emanated from the 2000 United Nations (UN) Millennium Development Goals, which brought widespread attention to the issue of sustainable development. Tourism has been identified as one industry which can contribute to the Millennium Development Goals due to its ability to generate revenues, affect a favourable balance of trade, benefit the poor and create employment (Downes, 2006). Indeed, in the 49 least-developed countries of the world, tourism (after the oil industry) has become the main source of foreign exchange (Frangialli, 2004). However, for tourism to make a significant contribution to the Millennium Development Goals, achievement will, in part, require sustainable development practices and management systems with legitimate cooperation between the local community, the public and private sectors and intergovernmental organizations. The United Nations World Tourism Organization (UNWTO), as a specialized agency of the UN, is focusing many of its initiatives towards sustainable tourism development as a tool for poverty alleviation. As part of this effort, the UNWTO has embraced the concept of volunteering through its UNWTO TedQual Volunteers Programme.

The UN has long supported the concept of volunteerism, specifically through its dedicated division, the United Nations Volunteers (UNV). The UNV, administered by the UN Development Programme, was established in 1970 to serve as an operational partner in development cooperation at the request of UN member states (United Nations Volunteers, 2006). Their mission is to 'support sustainable human development globally through the promotion of volunteerism, including the mobilization of volunteers....It values free will, commitment, engagement and solidarity, which are the foundations of volunteerism' (United

Nations Volunteers, 2006). At the launch of the International Year of Volunteers in 2001, former UN Secretary General Kofi Annan stated: '[A]t the heart of volunteerism are the ideals of service and solidarity and the belief that together we can make the world a better place. In that sense, we can say that volunteerism is the ultimate expression of what the United Nations is all about'.

In 2005, the UNWTO implemented the UNWTO TedQual Volunteers Programme through its Education and Knowledge Management Department (UNWTO EKM) and the affiliated body of tourism education institutions, the UNWTO Education Council (UNWTO EdC). With the shared mandate of promoting the development of knowledge for the advancement of sustainable tourism worldwide, the UNWTO TedQual Volunteers Programme was designed to assist developing countries achieve a sustainable and more competitive tourism sector through the hands-on dissemination of knowledge via education, training and research. This knowledge transfer is achieved by leveraging the expertise of UNWTO EdC member institutions to assist developing countries plan for positive development outcomes. This chapter introduces the rationale and objectives of the UNWTO TedQual Volunteers Programme, highlighting the role of knowledge management and specifically knowledge transfer and knowledge-sharing in assisting developing countries and destinations to create a sustainable tourism sector. Case studies from several of the previously undertaken volunteer projects are also presented.

Knowledge Transfer Through Volunteer Experiences

As the chapters in this volume demonstrate, volunteering generates benefits not only to the individual volunteer, but also, importantly, contributes to the broader economic and social goals of society. Research on the motivations of volunteers has found that individuals primarily volunteer for altruistic and self-interest reasons (Stebbins, 1982; Clary and Snyder, 1991). However, research conducted on the George Washington University volunteer programme (which the UNWTO TedQual Volunteers concept is based upon) showed that volunteers favoured the experience because the concepts learned through the volunteer project would benefit their future study and/or work. Further, the fact that the volunteer experience took place in a foreign country was also seen as a benefit of volunteering through the programme (Hawkins and Weiss, 2004). The motivation to volunteer in this case is more focused on skill development for personal professional gain through an experiential learning activity, as opposed to overriding philanthropic goals, suggesting that volunteers in the programme are motivated more by the material incentives or 'perks' of volunteering (Caldwell and Andereck, 1994). This notion of volunteering for an educational experience is in contrast to studies such as Farrell *et al.*'s (1998) investigation of sport event volunteers who ranked obtaining an educational experience as one of the least motivating factors for volunteering relative to making the event a success and creating a better society by doing something worthwhile for the community. Hawkins and Weiss's (2004) study further highlighted the importance of the travel experience to the volunteers. While the volunteers are not vacationing at the destination and so could not be classed as volunteer 'vacationers' or 'tourists' (Brown, 2005), they are motivated to volunteer to enjoy some of the associated privileges of travelling to an overseas country including sightseeing and experiencing foreign cultures and places.

Volunteer work is widely recognized as contributing to the 'greater good' of society (United Nations Volunteers, 2006). Indeed, the underlying objective of the UNWTO TedQual Volunteers Programme is to enhance the opportunities of developing countries through the development of a tourism sector that is economically, socially and environmentally sustainable and competitive. Ralston *et al*. (2005) actually claim that the voluntary sector is now recognized as an important stakeholder in achieving such tourism policy goals. The focus of the UNWTO TedQual Volunteers Programme, however, is situated within a knowledge management framework, with knowledge transfer and knowledge-sharing employed as a means of enhancing the opportunities for developing countries and regions and benefiting stakeholders. The importance of knowledge is identified in the World Bank's (1998) report on development practices and the role of aid in developing countries where it is claimed that knowledge is one of the most essential best practices. In fact, the report notes that 'foreign aid is as much about knowledge as it is about money', and that it is the local knowledge capacity created through aid projects which remains after the money has been spent (World Bank, 1998, p. ix). Similarly, Article 14(c) of the UNWTO Declaration on the Millennium Development Goals (2005) identifies the need to

> [h]arness the human resource potential of poor people in the delivery of quality services through the tourism value chain. There is a pressing need for capacity building at the local destination level, including . . . dissemination of know-how and good practices through enhanced knowledge management systems.

The UNWTO TedQual Volunteers concept is firmly underpinned and situated within a knowledge management framework. In this case, knowledge is transferred to, and between, volunteer participants from universities and other education institutions in the developed and developing worlds, governments and civil society in the country which hosts the programme (Nikolova and Weiss, 2005). This knowledge management approach to volunteering sees the cumulative knowledge and expertise of the UNWTO and tourism education institutions channelled to governments, tourism organizations, education institutions and civil society in the developing world as a means of enhancing the country's knowledge capacity and, in turn, facilitating their sustainable development efforts.

The knowledge transfer and knowledge-sharing aspects of the UNWTO TedQual programme are where this volunteering scheme differs from others. The UNWTO programme and its methodology reflect the growing importance placed on knowledge management in the tourism sector and by international organizations such as the UN (Cooper, 2006; Xiao, 2006). The notion that future economic prosperity and growth is attached solely to traditional commodities and physical resources is increasingly being recognized as an outmoded concept. The recognition that the 'one sure source of lasting competitive advantage is knowledge' (Nonaka, 1991, p. 96), and that it is knowledge which will be the key competitive tool for the private sector and a determinant of economic growth for governments, has gained prominence. That is, a nation's competitiveness in the global marketplace will be reliant on its ability to capitalize on its knowledge-based commodities (Ruhanen and Cooper, 2004). This realization has led to considerable advances since the 1980s, both in academia and industry, in the field of knowledge management (Wiig, 1999; Bahra, 2001; Ahmed *et al.*, 2002), highlighting the need for a structured and conscious approach to generating, identifying and managing learning and knowledge, in order to achieve competitive advantages (Drucker, 2000).

However, communication is a crucial component of knowledge management and transfer. Beesley and Cooper (2007) note that, consistent with psychological perspectives of knowledge management, knowledge transfer is the process by which individuals create and share information with one another so as to attain mutual understanding. This occurs through the interconnectivity of individual world views which become apparent through mutual understanding, with social relationships acting as conduits for knowledge transfer to take place (Beesley and Cooper, 2007). As such, the UNWTO Volunteer programme, through its partnership and collaborative approaches between stakeholders (discussed below), aims to transfer and diffuse the knowledge that resides within UNWTO, universities and similar organizations to assist those 'on the ground' in developing countries plan for positive development outcomes.

Beesley and Cooper (2007) discuss the fact that, currently, preferred knowledge dissemination techniques (publication of research or presentations by researchers) employ a single-loop learning strategy. They note that such one-way communication, at best, will result in an adjustment of existing knowledge structures, with receptivity limited by the strength of the intent to learn. Conversely, double-loop learning, such as that seen in the UNWTO Volunteers approach, aims to facilitate continual education and training experiences as both parties gain an appreciation of each other's cognitive processes and then build and broaden their own. This results in generative learning, a process in which the learner can develop new concepts and attitudes, cognitively recode existing classifications and amend standards of judgment (Beesley and Cooper, 2007).

The UNWTO TedQual Volunteers Programme

Adapted from the consulting practicum model developed by the George Washington University discussed previously, the rationale of the UNWTO TedQual Volunteers Programme is to utilize the collective pool of knowledge and expertise of the UNWTO, together with faculty members and postgraduate tourism students from UNWTO member educational institutions, to undertake a tourism development project for a region or destination in a developing country.

In collaboration with local stakeholders, including local tourism education institutions, the volunteer group will undertake a project in an area identified by the destination to be important for its sustainable tourism development efforts. As noted, the primary objective of the programme is to transfer the knowledge and expertise possessed by the UNWTO and UNWTO educational institutions for the benefit of developing countries with the specific aims of:

- Providing developing countries with knowledge for both technical assistance and tangible tourism products;
- Stimulating community-based and pro-poor tourism efforts, while ensuring that sustainability philosophies underpin tourism product development;
- Contributing, through mentoring, to the development of quality knowledge assets for the developing nations' educational institutions;
- Training the next generation of sustainable tourism development practitioners, from both developed and developing countries;
- Ensuring that sustainable development principles are not only taught in the classroom, but also practised in the field;
- Strengthening links among developing world tourism government organizations, UNWTO and its member education institutions, and development assistance agencies.

Following the identification of a country/destination (the host country) and a suitable project, the UNWTO TedQual programme involves four phases: (i) planning, preparatory coursework and research; (ii) fieldwork; (iii) submission of final report with conclusions and recommendations for future action; and (iv) additional projects and research at the request of the host government and other stakeholders. In the first phase, the student volunteers undertake a programme of coursework covering the scope of the project and methodology, design a statement of work (specifying the type of activity, the focus of the activity and the exact location/area of the project) and develop the specific work plan and logistics of the fieldwork. Importantly, it is during this phase that much of the background research is carried out that will supplement the primary research undertaken during the fieldwork. The student volunteers will spend up to 12 weeks completing extensive desk-based research on tourism in the chosen country including an analysis of general tourism trends for both the country and the broader region including visitor arrival data and traveller profiles, competitive benchmark analysis and assessments of current branding, image and marketing strategies.

The objective of undertaking such a thorough research phase is so that by the time the fieldwork phase commences, the volunteers are well prepared in terms of the aims of the project, the research methodology and processes and the current and future inhibitors and facilitators to tourism development in the host country and region. This enables the volunteer team to take full advantage of the limited fieldwork time (generally 2–3 weeks) in the country during which they will undertake the primary research. The UNWTO, the education institution and the host country government will have previously agreed to the scope, nature and deliverables of the project. The chosen project should be one that is important to the sustainable tourism development efforts of the country with possible areas of focus including marketing strategies, product assessment, development plans, business plan creation, development of community-based tourism plans, interpretation strategies and the development of pro-poor tourism strategies. Depending on the nature of the specific project, the fieldwork research tasks may include an internal analysis of the attractors, resources and support systems of the tourism industry in the country or specific area of the country, visits to tourism sites and/or to determine potential sites for tourism products, and interviews and workshops with relevant stakeholders including the government, industry and local community to ensure broad-based participation in the project. Upon completing the fieldwork, the volunteers present their preliminary conclusions and recommendations to the stakeholder groups from the public and private sectors and civil society. This forum is designed to generate further discussion of the findings and ensure that the key stakeholder groups, which will ultimately be responsible for implementation and long-term monitoring, have participated in the decision-making process and have ownership of the project directions and outcomes. The volunteer students and staff from the local educational institution also play a key role in the fieldwork phase with both logistical support and destination knowledge, but more importantly in working with other stakeholders in the implementation and monitoring phases of the project once the volunteer team has completed the project and departed.

The reporting phase of the UNWTO TedQual programme occurs over the 2- to 3-month period following the completion of the fieldwork. It is during this stage that the final report is presented to the government and stakeholders of the host country. The final report provides the detailed analysis, recommendations and follow-up action points arising from the project. The fourth and final stage, follow-up and implementation, is considered essential to ensure the longer-term success of the project. During this phase, at the country's request, volunteer team members with the support of local stakeholders can assist in facilitating the implementation of suggested actions. Other UNWTO programmes such as the UNWTO Sbest or the new UNWTO Young Entrepreneurs for Development may be engaged during this phase.

The UNWTO TedQual Volunteers Programme is designed to generate benefits for all stakeholder groups. The host country receives high-level consulting at little or no cost; the only expense, which may be assumed by a partnering development agency, will be in-country transport and accommodation for the volunteers. The UNWTO TedQual student volunteers gain important tourism development field experience, with their only expenses being airfares and in-country sundries. Further benefits accrue for the UNWTO member tourism education institution and their in-country institutional partner who have the opportunity to learn through collaboration with one another. From the UNWTO perspective, the programme provides the opportunity to disseminate knowledge to developing countries through education, training and research, with the aim of producing directions and strategies for sustainable tourism development. The benefits, expectations and requirements for each of the participating stakeholder groups are detailed in Table 3.1.

Table 3.1. UNWTO TedQual programme benefits and requirements.

UNWTO TedQual institutions	UNWTO TedQual student volunteers	UNWTO member host country and institution
BENEFITS		
Attractor for top tourism students	Application of theory to practice	Access to top institutions and latest tourism knowledge
Important contacts with host countries, development agencies	Developing teamwork and problem-solving skills	Project reports and tangible outcomes
Possible follow-up work with country	International consulting experience	No consulting fees only in-country expenses
Learning through cooperation with other educational institutions	Improved career options Possible follow-up work	Emphasis on sustainability
More knowledgeable and experienced student body	Contacts (clients, students from partner institutions)	Transfer of knowledge to country's education institutions
		Strengthened contacts with UNWTO, academic institutions, development agencies
REQUIREMENTS		
UNWTO TedQual certified Implement the course into curriculum	Strong academic performance and professional experience	UNWTO member nation
Fully dedicated faculty member experienced in international tourism development who will attend any necessary training and will lead the fieldwork project	Language abilities (in some cases) Undertake 2–3 weeks fieldwork in-country Active participation in pre- and post-fieldwork research	Dedicated officer to liaise with UNWTO and institutions, make necessary arrangements and accompany research teams during fieldwork
Highly qualified graduate student body		Payment of in-country expenses including accommodation, in-country transportation and work space for research teams

Applications of the UNWTO TedQual Volunteers Programme

Armenia

In January 2007, a student volunteer team, together with an UNWTO expert, undertook an analysis of Armenia's current tourism policies and resources with the objective of improving the country's tourism governance by reformu-lating the tourism development plan of the Municipality of Armenia. Following an extensive programme of research and fieldwork, the final report was presented to the Armenian government. The report included plans and recommendations for both the public and private sectors designed to provide Armenia with more efficient tourism governance standards and competitiveness strategies.

Province of Cabo Delgado, Mozambique

A UNWTO TedQual Volunteers Programme was undertaken in 2006 for the Cabo Delgado Province of Mozambique. The focus of this volunteer project was to plan tourist routes and make recommendations regarding product development initiatives. A further objective of the project was to design a tourism management information system (TMIS) to enable the local tourism industry to have a better understanding of visitor demographics and activities, the economic impacts of tourism and the effectiveness of marketing programmes. This project involved 17 students and three faculty members from the University of Pretoria and 15 students and three faculty members from the Universidade Católica de Moçambique. The project was organized in conjunction with UNWTO by the Ministry of Mozambique, George Washington University and the University of Pretoria within the framework of the USAID 3-year Northern Mozambique Tourism Project. The project outcomes provided insights into the value chain involved in providing service to tourists from their point of origin to the destination, with further recommendations to the destination stakeholders for implementing the TMIS at national, regional and provincial levels.

Provinces of Imbabura, Pichincha, Cotopaxi, Tungurahua and Chimborazo, Ecuador

Carried out in the Sierra Interandina of Ecuador, this project was designed to provide a proposal for local governance in Ecuador and develop new tourism products through collaborative efforts between the public and private sectors and civil society of the involved provinces. Seventeen student volunteers from eight countries participated in the project. The research and fieldwork resulted in a tourism competitiveness plan which included the following recommendations: (i) to build public–private partnerships for tourism development; (ii) to establish parameters and criteria for tourism products; (iii) to design and implement quality management systems for tourism services; (iv) to develop/introduce a system for knowledge management in tourism for all stakeholders; and (v) to stimulate a business plan and positioning strategy for tourism. The volunteers project was organized by the Government of Ecuador, the UNWTO specialized office in Andorra, the Government of Andorra, the Municipality of Ibarra, Haciendas of Ecuador, the universities of the Balearic Islands (Spain), ESADE (Spain) and Antonio de Nebrija (Spain).

Montenegro

In June 2006, a group of 15 graduate student volunteers from George Washington University and eight students from two universities in Montenegro participated in a project focused on identifying opportunities for nature-based tourism development in the area of Durmitor National Park in Northern Montenegro. The outcome of the project was a preliminary strategy to realize the potential of the Durmitor National Park as a world-class nature-based tourism destination, including: (i) implementing an integrated destination management approach; (ii) building the capacity of local businesses, entrepreneurs and community members through training and education in tourism; and (iii) the implementation of three sustainable tourism business concepts. With the support of the UNWTO this project was organized by the Ministry of Tourism of the Republic of Montenegro, the United Nations Development Programme and George Washington University.

Tabasco, Mexico

In December 2005, the UNWTO TedQual Volunteers Programme undertook a project in Tabasco, Mexico, to develop a competitiveness plan for the state, and a tourism vision for the year 2020. The volunteer project team comprised faculty and graduate students from UNWTO TedQual certified universities in Spain, Colombia and a local Mexican institution. Following the coursework programme, the volunteer team undertook a 2-week fieldwork trip and were accompanied by UNWTO officials and experts, as well as officials from the tourism administrations of Tabasco and Mexico. The volunteer team undertook benchmarking studies, interviews, workshops, surveys and an inventory and analysis of tourism resources. The importance of consultation and involving the local community in the project was a primary consideration and during the course of the trip over 700 people were consulted in more than 65 interviews and workshops with representatives from municipal governments, the private sector and civil society. The project was organized by the Government of Mexico, the Government of the State of Tabasco, the UNWTO and the University del Valle (Mexico).

Panama

The UNWTO TedQual Volunteer's project was undertaken in Panama in June 2005. Led by George Washington University, a group of graduate students and faculty members undertook an assessment of the Soberania National Park and assessed its potential to stimulate economic development through sustainable tourism. The research resulted in a number of major outcomes for the host country government and stakeholders including park visitor management systems, site linkages, marketing of the park and related attractions, the web site, promotional events and small and micro-business development.

Conclusion

The UNWTO TedQual Volunteer Programme represents a contemporary approach to volunteering, utilizing a knowledge transfer approach and delivering benefits to all stakeholders. As the programme moves forward, there are two key issues that have merged.

First, operating the programme has thrown up a range of challenges, mainly focused on the stakeholders and their management. These include the logistical difficulties of organizing a volunteering scheme in a developing country, often at a considerable distance from the host institution; the need to ensure that the goals of the programme align with those of the host country; and the danger of inflated expectations of the results from the host country. Each of these challenges can be overcome by the disciplined and enlightened management of the volunteers programme and the host country stakeholders. As the programme moves forward, good management will be key to the success of this variant of volunteering.

Second, the programme is based upon the concept of knowledge management and in particular that of knowledge transfer. The World Bank (1998) identified knowledge as one of the most important factors in development project success. The notion of knowledge-based aid is central to this volunteering programme, not only by transferring knowledge, but also by working with selected host institutions in-country, effecting a transfer of the *ownership* of knowledge. This approach facilitates capacity in the tourism sector of the developing world sharing best practice, lessons and techniques with respect to sustainable tourism. Of course, there are challenges in this process, not the least that of ensuring the transfer of knowledge, but also the use and adoption of the knowledge when the volunteers have departed. In summary, the UNWTO TedQual programme is an enlightened approach to volunteers, takes the participants on a true journey of discovery, delivers benefits to all involved and provides a glimpse into the future of volunteering as a development tool.

References

Ahmed, P.K., Lim, K.K. and Loh, A.Y.E. (2002) *Learning Through Knowledge Management*. Butterworth-Heinemann, Oxford, UK.

Bahra, N. (2001) *Competitive Knowledge Management*. Palgrave, Basingstoke, UK.

Beesley, L.G.A. and Cooper, C. (2007) A framework for defining knowledge management practices within the tourism sector. *Proceedings of the CAUTHE 2007 Conference*. Manly, Australia.

Brown, S. (2005) Travelling with a purpose: understanding the motives and benefits of volunteer vacationers. *Current Issues in Tourism* 8, 479–496.

Caldwell, L.L. and Andereck, K.L. (1994) Motives for initiating and continuing membership in a recreation-related voluntary association. *Leisure Studies* 16, 33–44.

Clary, E. and Snyder, M. (1991) A functional analysis of altruism and prosocial behavior. In: Clark, M. (ed.) *Prosocial Behavior*. Sage, Thousand Oaks, California, pp. 119–148.

Cooper, C. (2006) Knowledge management and tourism. *Annals of Tourism Research* 33, 47–64.

Downes, J. (2006) *Tourism Legislation and the Millennium Development Goals*. Sustainable Tourism Cooperative Research Centre, Gold Coast, Australia.

Drucker, P. (2000) Putting more now into knowledge. *Forbes Global*. May 15, 93–95.

Farrell, J.M., Johnstone, M.E. and Twynam, G.D. (1998) Volunteer motivation, satisfaction, and management at an elite sporting competition. *Journal of Sport Management* 12, 288–300.

Frangialli, F. (2004) *Address to the High-level Segment and Investment Promotion Forum ECOSOC*. New York, 29 June 2004.

Hawkins, D.E. and Weiss, B. (2004) Experiential education in graduate tourism studies: an international consulting practicum. *Journal of Teaching in Travel and Tourism* 4, 1–29.

Nikolova, M.S. and Weiss, B. (2005) *WTO TedQual Volunteers Program Manual*. World Tourism Organization, Madrid, Spain.

Nonaka, I. (1991) The knowledge creating company. *Harvard Business Review* November/December, 96–104.

Ralston, R., Lumsdon, L. and Downward, P. (2005) The third force in events tourism: volunteers at the XVII Commonwealth Games. *Journal of Sustainable Tourism* 13, 504–519.

Ruhanen, L. and Cooper, C. (2004) Applying a knowledge management framework to tourism research. *Tourism Recreation Research* 29, 83–89.

Sofield, T., Bauer, J., De Lacy, T., Lipman, G. and Daugherty, S. (2004) *Sustainable Tourism – Eliminating Poverty (ST-EP): An Overview*. Sustainable Tourism Cooperative Research Centre, Gold Coast, Australia.

Stebbins, R.A. (1982) Serious leisure: a conceptual statement. *Pacific Sociological Review* 25, 251–272.

United Nations Volunteers (2006) UN Volunteers Mission Statement. Available at: http://www.unvolunteers.org/about/03_11_07DEU_mission.htm

United Nations World Tourism Organization (2005) *UNWTO Declaration on the Millennium Development Goals*. Madrid, Spain, UNWTO.

Wiig, K.M. (1999) Introducing knowledge management in the enterprise. In: Liebowitz, J. (ed.) *Knowledge Management Handbook*. CRC Press, Boca Raton, Florida, pp. 3.1–3.41.

World Bank (1998) *Assessing Aid: What Works, What Doesn't, and Why*. Oxford University Press, New York.

Xiao, H. (2006) Towards a research agenda for knowledge management in tourism. *Tourism and Hospitality Planning & Development* 3, 143–157.

4   Lessons from Cuba: a Volunteer Army of Ambassadors

R. Spencer

Centre for Research on Social Inclusion, Macquarie University, Sydney, Australia

Cuba is a country of beguiling beauty which attracts many tourists. It is also a poor country suffering the combined effects of the collapse of the Soviet Union and the constraints of the US embargo. However, the only crises most tourists will confront are a barman who runs out of the *hierba buena* variety of mint that makes for a perfect mojito; or a driver whose 1950s Chevrolet *maquina* (taxi) chugs and bounces along Havana's heavily potholed roads. There is, however, a kind of tourist who visits Cuba expressly to learn about the development challenges and accomplishments of its tenacious communist revolution. Study tours operated by non-government organizations (NGOs) comprise small groups of people travelling through the provinces once or twice a month. These tours include seminars on development issues in association with visits to community projects. In providing participants with an insight into daily life in Cuba, they aim to show the positive sustainable development initiatives being undertaken by ordinary people. These NGO study tours, thus, inspire participants to become more socially and environmentally active in regards to Cuba and/or international development on their return to their own countries. Focusing on development, these tours discuss the merits, failures and challenges of Cuban socialism in this age of globalization and neo-liberalism, offering very particular insights into alternative models. By looking at the moral imperatives underpinning the conjunction between this particular form of tourism and development, I examine how an educational engagement that embodies a particularly powerful experience for tourists leads to a process whereby tourists become actual agents of development. Thus, NGO study tours in Cuba shed light on the instrumental outcomes of tourism as a tool for development. I theorize this encounter within the parameters of rights-based development and label it 'rights-based tourism'. As we face a changing world where almost everything has become more global and this 'world-in-motion' produces disjunctures, disconnections and exclusions (Appadurai, 1996), the convergence of particular styles of tourism and development might offer new ways towards social inclusion.

I lived in Cuba as an anthropologist in the early 2000s at the time when the country was emerging from a decade-long depression. Tourism was at the forefront of Cuba's development policy. For the Cuban government, it was a critical and vulnerable time balancing the introduction of some capitalist tools with long-term imbedded socialist ideologies. It provided an anthropologist with fertile ground to investigate convergences between tourism and development in the unique context that Cuba is. This chapter is based on my research during this period.

My research reflects what Marcus (1995, p. 95) referred to as multi-sited ethnography: 'an emergent methodological trend in anthropological research [where]...Ethnography moves from its conventional single-site location...to multiple sites of observation and participation that cross-cut dichotomies such as the "local" and the "global" '. I tracked the progress of NGO study tours and the meetings and projects they encountered by travelling with them as they moved from place to place. Throughout I adopted a qualitative approach in order to gain an in-depth insight into the experiences of the participants as they perceived them (Sarantakos, 1993). The research included seven study tours conducted by ancillary arms of an international development agency and a human rights organization. Approximately 100 people participated in the tours and 28 of those participated in interviews and follow-up questionnaires. The research involved the use of different methods by combining formal recorded interviews, direct participation and observation, literature and document analysis, qualitative follow-up e-mail questionnaires, informal conversations and introspection. My adoption of these methods reflects the particular empirical objective of the study to understand the experiences of learning about development in Cuba within a tourism context. The ethnographic data collected among NGO study tourists is not isolated from other information sources; rather it is linked with data collected from the grass-roots and development organizations and government agency authorities that we met with in Cuba.

Moral Imperatives Within Tourism and Development

A culture of concern and the notion of 'moral responsibility' underpin new emerging trends of tourism and development. This is evidenced by NGO study tours and rights-based development, the latest manifestations of the moral imperative driving development and tourism practices. Based on their conjunction we can conceive of it as a rights-based tourism.

Rights-based development is the incorporation of human rights into development discourses and practices. It aims to ensure that people have moral and legal entitlements that pertain specifically to basic well-being and dignity (Ljumgman, 2005). In the context of tourism, the notion of morals has emerged from changing attitudes in the West around notions of sustainability (Mowforth and Munt, 2003). In the case of NGO study tours in Cuba, tour participants take a stance on tourism issues, which rest on minimizing harm to culture and the environment, and incorporate an educational agenda to learn about development issues.

NGO study tours are a form of tourism that is based on a moral imperative to be contributing something 'good' to the communities visited. This imperative encompasses ethical considerations insofar as 'ethical' stresses idealistic standards of right and wrong, such as codes of conduct within tourism. I use the term 'moral' to envisage the underpinnings of the convergence between development and tourism because it includes notions of ethics, right, virtuous and good. Such ideas of improvement (or at least careful avoidance of harm) correlate with rights-based development. NGO study tours are positioned as morally better than mainstream tours because they engage with local culture through an explicit educational agenda and because part of the cost of their tours goes towards supporting aid projects. Through a programme of visits to community projects and meetings with local people to discuss the nuances of social development in Cuba, people can feel they are engaging in a more judicious form of tourism. Such development-oriented tours allow people to enact their moral choice as responsible alternative tourists.

I challenge Butcher's (2003) critique of the increasing 'moral proscription and critical self awareness' in tourism, where he argues the attempt to do something good in fact does the opposite as it creates new barriers between people and has a negative impact in the field of development. Butcher positions new moral tourisms as 'a vessel into which we are encouraged to pour environmental angst and fears of globalization. New moral tourists travel with a sense of personal mission, as tourism is recast as philanthropy towards the hosts and a "unique experience" for the tourist' (2003, p. 139). I argue that moral intentions and critical self-awareness do not create barriers between people but facilitate and lead to the creation of global networks. Global Exchange's Reality Tours (GERT) and Oxfam's former Community Aid Abroad Tours (OCAAT) are examples of NGOs offering tours with a development focus. They demonstrate the values and characteristics associated with the moralization of tourism that Butcher (2003) critiques. Where he challenges the positive assumptions of moral tourism niches, I reveal its complexity as a culture of concern that promulgates connections between people; a social process akin to new social movements that has positive impacts in the field of development.

Although forms of 'new' tourism (Poon, 1989) are relatively minor when compared with all forms of holiday travel to developing countries, they are highly significant in terms of their presence as indications of contemporary change both in their mode of emergence and in their style of operation (Mowforth and Munt, 2003). They forecast an increasing connection between globalized social movements and consumer engagement in social change and endogenous development endeavours.

Attaching a universalistic moral framework to social practices as diverse as tourism is multifarious in nature. For example, how do we precisely assess what is good and what is bad or what is appropriate or inappropriate in a context of relative values and cultural norms? Nevertheless a moral framework is clearly a facet of this development–tourism convergence. To ignore it is to miss an important concern for subaltern rights. Arguably, people who travel with NGOs consider the capacity of tourism to impact on people's rights. It is this concern that underpins people's choices to embrace 'responsible' tourism and reproduces aspects of well-being and dignity in rights-based development.

Underpinning NGO study tours is a programme to learn about other cultures and their development issues. The development-focused meetings and project visits are the key point of difference from mainstream tourism because they provide opportunities to learn from grass-roots perspectives. While it is typical to accentuate positive experiences after a holiday, it is the underlying sensibility of education and interconnection expressed by NGO study tourists that offers key insights into the potential for agency and solidarity. Gertrude, an Oxfam participant, explained that 'these aspects were very important; I would not have had access to meetings with local people, which for me brought the trip alive'. Amelia from a GERT tour told me, 'without the visits and seminars it might otherwise have been just another holiday tour, but we connected with local people over really important issues'. Tour participants also experienced more impromptu encounters with local people, such as Oscar's spontaneous drumming lesson in the house of a local Cuban man in Santiago de Cuba:

> The private drum lesson in a man's home was a real highlight. He solicited me on the street. I declined but we continued to talk. He asked again and I agreed. He is an unemployed percussion instructor and my connection with him was deep. . . .

External Participation in Global Social Movements

This form of tourism is a burgeoning niche that potentially has positive implications for the tourist, their home society and development generally. Opportunities to connect with local people and with other tour participants who share common interests resonates with social movement theory about the creation of network ties as an important indicator of new social movement participation.

As part of the mosaic of global new social movements, some NGOs utilize tourism as a means of educating tourists to become more active in campaigning on issues of international concern. Likewise, the Cuban government clearly views international tourists as political agents who can give 'first-hand' accounts of the country and its achievements. These tourists are considered valued friends who witness first-hand the positive achievements of Fidel Castro's revolution and who return home, as a volunteer army of ambassadors to spread the good word about how Cuba is forging a radical alternative to neo-liberalism and capitalism.

GERT and OCAAT are by virtue of their educational itineraries agents of network building. Their tours often serve as a catalyst for increased social movement participation. In this way, these NGOs hope to harness the power and influence of educational development-oriented tourism for its ability to facilitate motivation and mobilization efforts.

Such tours forecast an increasing interest between globalized social movements, tourist engagement in social change and endogenous development. Identifying these conjunctions entails exploring beyond the membership of new social movements because belonging to an organization can manifest in a manifold of distinctive ways (Barkan *et al.*, 1995).

In analysing social movements, Knoke (1988) tells us that it is necessary to include external and internal forms of participation. Typically studies of social movement participation analyse internal forms such as membership, volunteering in the administrative procedures, voting or running in elections and the provision of resources. In the case of Cuba, external participation in social movements can have far-reaching effects in their mobilization against the US-dominated world system. External forms of participation include lobbying to politicians, writing letters to them, attending rallies, and I argue, participating in NGO study tours. These tours evidence a 'movement of movements' (Klein, 2004, p. 220) precisely because of their international reach, because the people who participate in them represent a mosaic of interests that concern new social movements, and because of the new networks created during these tours.

In discussing what she has mostly learnt about and felt impacted by, Henrietta, an elderly American woman on a Cuba at the Crossroads tour says:

> I have a much more concrete sense now of how, and how much, the embargo hurts Cubans, the mechanics by which it does so, and what the Cuban government and people have done in response. I will be writing to my political reps about ending the embargo and I do hope to work something of the Cuban experience into my healthcare talks. Meanwhile I've been mainly talking to friends and even clients about the insanity and destructiveness of the embargo.

Her account of how her tour has impacted on her is a striking example of the power of this form of tourism to positively affect external participation in new social movements (Knoke, 1988). Not only is she intending to write to her politicians, but she intends to incorporate information about Cuba in a professional capacity and has already been sharing information within her social network. McGehee (2002) tells us individuals are likely to participate in social movements if their family, friends or colleagues support their goals. This reinforces the potential instrumental benefits of participating in an NGO study tour for development.

Typically, NGO tour participants demonstrate a strong involvement in new social movement participation prior to joining a tour. Their level of support in such movements through charities, development agencies or conservation groups indicates their commitment to and involvement with global development issues. One member may make regular financial contributions and receive a newsletter while another participates in activism and campaigning. Indeed my research indicates that many participants are motivated to join an NGO study tour as a means to financially support projects and facilitate connections with other like-minded people and local Cuban people.

The creation of networks is an important aspect of social movements and this is key to NGO study tours in Cuba. Following Deleuze and Guattari's (1988) description of new social movements as rhizomic, we see how NGO tours can establish unexpected connections thus assuming diverse forms, across various dimensions such as the family, the neighbourhood and different issues. Individuals and organizations that are linked together through one or more social relationships become networks, which are an important element of social movement participation and potentially reinforce activism support (Klandermans and Oegema, 1987; McAdam and Rucht, 1993; McGehee, 2002). For example, our ties to family and friends or work colleagues can influence our world view and our support for political and social issues. Informal ties that form our social networks are important reference points that are vital to network development, participation and commitment to social movements (Pfaff, 1995; Lichterman, 1996). This is fundamental to the success of NGO study tours in mobilizing support because the people who participate in a tour each have their own social networks to which they disseminate information about their experiences in Cuba.

This style of tourism is of an active participatory and educational nature. It is these distinctive qualities that explain why participation in an NGO study tour can increase network ties. By interaction with fellow tour participants, local officials and local people, the establishment of network ties is facilitated. Despite the short immersion of only several weeks, my research indicates that the experience is educational and intense enough to have an impact on the tourists. The tours allow participants many opportunities to exchange information and to develop ties that might not occur otherwise. Tours of this kind would be expected to draw together like-minded people and it thus makes sense that tours enable the exchange of ideas and establishment of network ties between the tourists themselves. Many tour participants concede that NGO tours implicitly promote support for developing world development. Hence, by virtue of their intense social and learning experience, NGO tours lead to the creation of support networks for development in developing countries.

Development-oriented tours aim to move beyond typical touristic presentations of Cuba and counter the anti-Cuba rhetoric stemming from the US government and Cuban diasporas. Cuba is often represented by discourses that shift between diverse idealistic visionary representations of a bastion of socialism fighting against consumerism and capitalism to dystopic representations of a socialist victim of the cold war frozen in the 1950s. NGO study tours do more than feed into discourses of representation by providing Western tourists with opportunities to gain nuanced understandings of Cuban realities, both positive and negative. Often their experiences lead to a more informed understanding of Cuba and the role of development processes. This facilitates a transformation from tour participant to agent of development, which occurs both within their exchanges with local people and on their return home as they disseminate information about Cuba and its social development. This being the case, therefore requires unpacking the terms of transformation and the ways tourists acquire agency through experiential learning.

Transformative Learning Through Tourism Experiences

The anthropology of tourism perspective has long addressed transformation from one state to another. However, in order to capture the complexity of transformation, I reframe it in terms of social and cultural change. Notions of personal transition within tourism are not straightforward shifts but are nuanced and complex. One important dimension is the way tourists and their engagement facilitate the networking of new social movements, as discussed above. Accordingly, education provides the platform for subsequent action where the notion of 'meaningful' experiences has instrumental outcomes. Exploring such experiences highlights that there is resonance beyond the tour itself. To understand this broader picture we need to consider levels of agency that go beyond self-interest.

The transformation that takes place is an increased commitment specifically to Cuban issues through solidarity efforts. NGO tour participants are
typically politicized people, hence their existing interest in development and
human rights issues. Many of them return home from tours and write letters to
their politicians, write articles in their local newspapers and community news-
letters, give presentations, talk to friends, family and colleagues disseminating
what they have learnt about Cuba, often they even join their national Cuba
Friendship Society. For example:

> I believe the Cuba at the Crossroads tour introduced us to important movements
> in Cuban culture and politics. The tour made us aware of the difficulties facing
> the Cuban people and government and sent us home determined to help in their
> struggle. The Global Exchange tours are helping to educate Americans about Cuba.
>   (Henrietta)

Many participants on NGO study tours comment about meeting local people
and making deep connections, and importantly, the opportunities to undergo
these experiences with like-minded travellers. 'The exchange of ideas and
thoughts and friendships with local persons and with each other are extremely
satisfying to the tourists and I think the local people' (Innes – Oxfam Tour).
Thus, it is the combination of educational, intellectual and affective exchanges
with other participants and local people that are significant aspects – a process
analogous to normative communitas (Turner, 1977).

Exchanges that occur in a tourism development context, arguably improve
the social and cultural environment for the local people because it empowers
them to create global networks through these touristic exchanges that celebrate
their cultural, agricultural and political diversity. Arguably, the impact of such
experiences could be seen to transform tourists into nascent agents of rights-
based development because of the overall sense of well-being for local people
that such exchanges facilitate and the solidarity links it cultivates.

Notions of transformation are complex and cannot be understood merely
as a direct transition from one state to another. While most NGO tour participants already contribute to development efforts through financial support,
activism and fund-raising, greater commitments are made typically after participating in an NGO study tour.

Arguably, NGO tourists are not just interested in meeting the exotic 'Other'
as objects to be viewed, but rather they are engaged in what they perceive to be
meaningful contact with local people in order to exchange ideas and information about development issues. They can disseminate this information on their
return home in an act of solidarity and contribute to the development efforts of
the organizing NGO. Thus, NGO tours offer people enriched experiences of
Cuba through a lens of development. For Ruby: '[M]y trip has affected me tre-
mendously. I understand Cuba much better than I ever thought I would. I think
the trip was so affective because I was not just a tourist in Cuba; I was being
educated along the way'.

For participants in my research in Cuba, NGO tours provide educational
and intellectual experiences that transform their prior perceptions of Cuba.
Ruben exclaimed: '[I]t is such a great experience because it affects you and you

have to change'. Sebastian said to me, 'I want to be involved in development and community development issues and become more of an activist now' and for Wilhemena:

> [T]he lasting effect for me is that I will be engaged in Cuban politics and human rights from now on. I think Cuba/US relations are a fascinating story and I think that from now on Cuba news/culture/politics will be a hobby of mine. The trip has inspired me to grow my own vegetables – this is certainly a lifestyle change. I am inspired to spread the word about urban agriculture in Cuba and to encourage people to visit. I recently held a slide show on Cuba and will present another one next month at the University of Michigan. I also hope to write an article to further disseminate information of Cuba's unique model of relieving food crises through urban agriculture.

As I mentioned earlier, many NGO tour participants are mostly already committed to supporting development aid efforts, which suggests that tourist experiences involve complex negotiations that cultivate cultural change rather than an utter transformation per se. This cultural change is most likely because they are already interested in interculturality, international issues and development.

Cultural change occurs then, in terms of transformative learning, horizons are extended for some tourists, the individual dignity of local Cuban people they met with is valued, and the trust and solidarity that the groups create through sharing histories, difficulties or goals *potentially* feeds into giving local Cuban people some degree of support in their attempts to reinvent themselves as more active subjects in their communities. For the tourists, the high levels of interaction with other tour participants, local officials and local residents facilitate the establishment of network ties that are so important to the success of new social movements (McGehee, 2002) and can lead to them becoming more active subjects in their own communities too.

For many participants their experiences in Cuba have reinforced their commitment to supporting causes both at home and abroad. For example, Ingaberg from a GERT sustainable agriculture tour has experienced 'an awakened interest in gardening and a reinforced notion that organic agriculture is something that the West could embrace more fully. As a whole the trip solidified ideas that were brewing in my head'. Likewise, Valmia says her Cuba at the Crossroads tour reinforced her 'will to continue supporting as many environmental, family planning, and civil rights organizations that I can afford. I've always been an activist and will now contribute and disseminate pertinent information and lobby congressional members about our foreign policy towards Cuba'. These statements highlight the politicized commitment of tour participants and the opportunities provided by the tours to exchange information about networks and to develop ties.

The experiences tourists have engage them at a particular level of action that enables them to feel they are doing something positive and there is a level of change in the participants' behaviour in the form of increased solidarity efforts on their return home. At the very least, new relationships are established that allow for the creation of networks between the tourists and local people they meet and also between the tourists themselves. Thus, this convergence of tourism and development aims to create new kinds of solidarity and transnational connections. It is a form of interaction that is moralistic, but more importantly, didactic and provides experiences with local Cuban people that is productive because of the creation of networks. The dissemination of ideas and activities on a global scale occurs through such networks (McAdam and Rucht, 1993).

Agency and Solidarity

Solidarity through tourism, in whatever form this emerges, can be considered an important tool for development agencies, social movements and NGOs in terms of new and explicit ways of promulgating issues of rights, social justice and good governance. Solidarity, thus, connects directly with rights-based development; it becomes important in the NGO tourism context because it is implicitly expressed as an objective of NGOs and explicitly expressed by tourists as a key outcome of participating in NGO study tours. Likewise it is clearly a political and developmental goal of the Cuban government. We can effectively envisage solidarity as a means for tourists to participate and act as agents of change in the development process. Indeed, it is a novel means through which Cuba has developed a way to partially transcend the economic and social constraints of the blockade. It acts as a new form of global coalition and interconnectedness that builds on previous alliances that have since dissolved, as was the case with the former Soviet Union where Cuba engaged in cultural exchanges with nations who were politically sympathetic.

The ethnographic material this chapter is based on suggests that participants are very keen to engage with Cuban people and learn about their development initiatives. This indicates a level of agency achieved through solidarity activities mentioned above. Post-tour actions illuminate individual tourist expressions of 'desire' (Kapoor, 2005) insofar as the tourists aim to be part of development activities and social movements. It could even be argued that tourists actively overcome entrenched Western 'complicity' (Kapoor, 2005) in developing world underdevelopment and poverty by participating in NGO study tours. In direct contrast to most Western touristic pursuits in the developing world, participation in an NGO study tour might be viewed as benevolent and lending to a more active form of solidarity with Cuba (post tour).

If it can be argued that this is a form of tourism that attempts to overcome Western complicity in developing world poverty through an educational tour programme and subsequent development of networks, then we can take this argument one step further; participants in development study tours are, through their solidarity efforts, agents of a rights-based form of development. The tours have the power to affect participants in positive ways that encourage them to be more active in a growing social movement of support for Cuba. Tourists become agents of development by supporting NGO development projects and participating in Cuban solidarity. Thus, both Cuban organizations and international NGOs are meeting their objectives in conducting these tours. What is produced here is rights-based tourism.

Rights-based tourism is not just about material and financial exchanges but also about intellectual and affective elements that are exchanged and developed.

This fits within a rights-based development framework where the notion of well-being is achieved by broadly conceived notions of political and moral support that is not just about money. Tours contribute (on different scales) to the development of dignity and well-being of local people through a sense of connection and the commitment to support development in Cuba. Local Cuban people and international NGO tourists play an important role in teaching the world about Cuban social development – triumphs and tribulations.

The sharing of ideas with local people, fellow tour members and with people back home can promote greater understanding of issues regarding systems of aid and thereby increase the contributions tourists make to development. It is this impact that leads to the 'transformation' from tourist to agent of development, because tour participants are engaged in more long-term intellectual and instrumental exchanges that transcend the tour itself. Notions of touristic transformation are multifaceted forms of identification, from refutation of mass tourism to refutation of neo-liberal globalization. NGO tourists demonstrate identification with certain interests (e.g. ecology and organic farming). It is often the 'peasant' who is valued within these tourist encounters as a way of learning from them. Transformation is qualified by the tourists' affirmation of values espoused in the West – such as social equity and collective community – but no longer considered valid with the collapse of the Soviet Empire. Cuba forms an example of a model that tourists are compelled to visit, study, support and promote.

What we can see taking place is a form of development that is more than just about structural adjustment leading to economic development that is so prevalent throughout Latin America. It is a form of rights-based tourism where local Cuban people who are actively engaged in the development process also create networks with international tourists through NGOs in an effort to foster solidarity. Creating solidarity through networks is linked to the capacity of tourism to bring about subjective changes in the conditions of Cuban people. Arguably, this form of tourism promotes increased self-respect and self-realization of local people and tourists alike through a programme of educational and affective exchanges that enhance notions of empowerment and independent agency.

Conclusion

What is clear is that NGO tours offer people a set of experiences that lead to critical perspectives about development. NGO study tours, which orchestrate forms of social interaction through exchanges of ideas and knowledge, facilitate the establishment of new networks and international links that in turn assist Cuban solidarity. Arguably, they foster a nascent but discernable form of rights-based development.

It is a moral imperative that drives an increasing connection between globalized social movements, development and tourist concern with social change. The educational exchanges taking place on tours are helping Cuba to find a voice and in this sense retrieve some sort of agency within a global network. Such exchanges allow Cuban people to become more of a presence within a wider geopolitical and social world in which they have been subject to a decade-long embargo excluding Cuba from world markets. The engagement of tourists and locals is an integral part of the development process as they share their knowledge and expertise with each other. Subjective micro-transformations of this kind lead to potential multiplier effects beyond the tours themselves in the form of new networks being built, role models being created and positive social change being promoted. Such experiences, combined with the goals of the NGOs and the intentions of the Cuban government, indicate several positive outcomes. First, aside from material support for local Cuban organizations, the positive outcomes consist of imparting knowledge about Cuban realities, thereby facilitating solidarity between countries and potentially empowering Cuban people. This can subsequently impact on future international relations for Cuba in potentially assisting in their future development (i.e. through tourists returning home to lobby their politicians about trade relations), which has been threatened by the US trade embargo. Second, for the NGOs who organize study tours to Cuba the positive outcomes consist of participants learning about development efforts and disseminating this knowledge on their return home and perhaps becoming more committed to supporting the NGO's development efforts. Third, for the participants the positive outcomes are partaking in a study tour that contributes money and possibly a sense of well-being to the local communities, gaining 'backstage' (McCannell, 1973) access not otherwise available to tourists, being educated while travelling and meeting like-minded people. But most importantly they become actively engaged in activities linked to social solidarity and change. While they are not new social movements per se, they lend themselves to particular outcomes associated with the power of new social movements. The level of impact on the tourists themselves through transformative learning leads to agency that in turn enhances social capital in Cuba.

This chapter provides a brief insight about the contributions of this form of tourism to a rights-based development. To what extent and how consistently such tours improve the social and cultural environment of local people by enhancing their sense of well-being and dignity remains unclear. However, the implication that international networks and solidarity are created through such tourism leads us to ask such questions. I have argued that development tours have the power to establish relationships that extend beyond the brief but intense tour experience itself. This chapter, more than anything else, demonstrates that if a development tour is found to encourage or intensify solidarity with Cuba or social movement participation in some form then the results could be used to promote rights-based tourism as a means of encouraging organized social action and rights-based development.

References

Appadurai, A. (1996) *Modernity at Large: Cultural Dimensions of Globalization*. University of Minnesota Press, Minneapolis, Minnesota.

Barkan, S., Cohn, S. and Whitaker, W. (1995) Beyond recruitment: predictors of differential participation in a national anti-hunger organization. *Sociological Forum* 10, 113–132.

Butcher, J. (2003) *The Moralization of Tourism: Sun, Sand...and Saving the World?* Routledge, London.

Deleuze, G. and Guattari, F. (1988) *A Thousand Plateaus: Capitalism and Schizophrenia.* Athlone Press, London.

Kapoor, I. (2005) Participatory development, complicity and desire. *Third World Quarterly* 26(8), 1203–1220.

Klandermans, B. and Oegema, D. (1987) Potentials, networks, motivations and barriers: steps towards participation in social movements. *American Sociological Review* 52, 519–531.

Klein, N. (2004) Reclaiming the commons. In: Mertes, T. (ed.) *A Movement of Movements: Is Another World Really Possible?* Verso, London.

Knoke, D. (1988) Incentives in collective action organizations. *American Sociological Review* 53, 311–329.

Lichterman, P. (1996) *The Search for Political Community: American Activists Reinventing Commitment.* Cambridge University Press, Cambridge.

Ljumgman, C. (2005) A rights-based approach to development. In: Mikkelsen, B. (ed.) *Methods for Development Work and Research – A New Guide for Practitioners.* Sage, New Delhi, pp. 199–215.

Marcus, G. (1995) Ethnography in/of the world system: the emergence of multi-sited ethnography. *Annual Review of Anthropology* 24, 95–117.

McAdam, D. and Rucht, D. (1993) The cross-national diffusion of movement ideas. *AAPSS Annals* 528, 56–74.

McCannell, D. (1973) Staged authenticity: arrangements of social space in tourist settings. *American Journal of Sociology* 79(3), 589–603.

McGehee, N. (2002) Alternative tourism and social movements. *Annals of Tourism Research* 29(1), 124–143.

Mowforth, M. and Munt, I. (2003) *Tourism and Sustainability: New Tourism in the Third World.* Routledge, London.

Pfaff, S. (1995) Collective identity, informal groups, and revolution mobilization. MSc thesis. University of North Carolina, Chapel Hill, North Carolina.

Poon, A. (1989) Competitive strategies for a new tourism. In: Cooper, C. (ed.) *Progress in Tourism, Recreation and Hospitality Management.* Belhaven, London.

Sarantakos, S. (1993) *Social Research.* Macmillan, South Melbourne, Australia.

Turner, V. (1977) *The Ritual Process: Structure and Anti-Structure.* Cornell University Press, New York.

5 'Make a Difference!': the Role of Sending Organizations in Volunteer Tourism

E. Raymond

Department of Tourism, University of Otago, New Zealand

Volunteer tourism is generally seen to provide a reciprocal form of travel from which both the volunteer and the host communities are able to benefit. It has been described as having the potential to 'elevate both the giver and the receiver' (Wearing, 2003, p. 3) and 'make a difference to the lives not only of those served but also of the servers as well' (Butcher, 2005, p. 110). It could be argued, therefore, that the recent increase in volunteer tourism programmes (VTPs) should be celebrated as providing a shift towards more responsible and sustainable forms of tourism. Indeed, it has been suggested that volunteer tourism may provide a model of 'best practice' in tourism (Wearing, 2004).

However, such enthusiasm for volunteer tourism is increasingly being challenged. The following quote is illustrative of the growing cynicism, particularly within the UK, regarding the actual benefits that young, enthusiastic, but essentially unqualified volunteer tourists bring to host communities:

> First they went climbing in Kathmandu. Then they stumbled into a local school and taught English to baffled Nepalese. Fifty spliffs and a thousand emails later, they returned home with a Hindu charm and tie-dye trousers. They had lots of great stories but the world remained thoroughly unsaved.
>
> (Barkham, 2006)

Recently, volunteer tourists have been criticized not only in the media (Brown, 2003; Barkham, 2006; Brodie, 2006; Frean, 2006) but also within academia (Griffin, 2004; Roberts, 2004; Simpson, 2004, 2005a,b; Callanan and Thomas, 2005; Lewis, 2005). It is increasingly being suggested that volunteer tourism does not always represent a *mutually* beneficial form of tourism and that while volunteer tourists may experience a range of benefits, in many cases, the organizations that host such volunteers gain far less.

Simpson (2004) argues that the lack of benefits gained by host organizations can, in part, be attributed to the dominant ideology 'that doing something is better than nothing and therefore, that doing anything is reasonable' (p. 685). While this argument relates specifically to UK sending organizations catering for the gap year market, it does highlight the inappropriate assumption that sending volunteers overseas will automatically benefit host communities.

Despite such criticism there has been little attempt to examine what can be done to ensure that volunteer tourism does benefit all those involved. There is now some important work relating to good practice in volunteer tourism (e.g. Year Out Group, 2005; Comlámh, 2007; IVPA, 2007; Simpson, 2007), but there is limited literature on this topic aimed at an academic audience. Existing academic literature has tended to take either a positive stance, pointing to the potential benefits of volunteer tourism (mainly for the volunteer) or a critical stance, discussing the problems surrounding volunteer tourism. Although authors have highlighted the need for more effective management of VTPs and have begun to make suggestions as to what this might entail (Wearing, 2001; Ellis, 2003; Griffin, 2004; Roberts, 2004; Callanan and Thomas, 2005; Jones, 2005), little academic research exists focusing specifically on how to achieve mutual benefit in volunteer tourism.

This research sought to begin addressing this gap, by investigating the role of 'sending organizations' in volunteer tourism. A sending organization is the organization which develops and organizes a VTP and can range from a locally based non-profit organization, to a multinational commercially run organization. While volunteer tourism also occurs without such organizations, the focus of this research was specifically on sending organizations. The decision to concentrate on the role of sending organizations was based on the fact that many of the criticisms faced by volunteer tourism have been directed towards the growing number of short-term programmes offered by such organizations. Furthermore, although the success of VTPs is not only influenced by the sending organization, it is suggested that many of the problems associated with VTPs can be reduced through careful planning and management by this organization.

Methodology

In order to research this topic, an exploratory approach was taken which involved case studies of ten different sending organizations. This chapter focuses on two of these, Foundation for Sustainable Development (FSD) and International Student Volunteers (ISV), and more specifically the FSD internship programme in La Plata, Argentina and the ISV programme run through Kuaka in New Zealand. As a result, the benefits and issues that will be discussed cannot be assumed to be representative of either sending organization's work as a whole.

These case studies were chosen because they highlight examples of two US-based sending organizations operating very different styles of VTPs. The FSD programme researched involved individual placements for a minimum of 9 weeks in a local non-governmental organization (NGO). In comparison, the ISV New Zealand programme involved a large group of approximately 40, volunteering on a variety of projects over a period of 2 weeks. It will be suggested that both were successful in benefiting the volunteers and their host organizations, albeit in different ways.

Despite the different styles of VTP offered by FSD and ISV, they are both seen to be illustrative of the concept of 'volunteer tourism' because the individuals involved were looking for 'a tourist experience that is mutually beneficial, that will contribute not only to their personal development but also positively and directly to the social, natural and/or economic environments in which they participate' (Wearing, 2001, p. 1). Nevertheless, the debate and ambiguity surrounding the term 'volunteer tourism' (Lyons, 2003; Uriely *et al.*, 2003) were taken into consideration during this research. It was recognized that individuals labelled as 'volunteer tourists' may not actually perceive themselves as such (Wearing, 2001) or may move between identities of 'volunteer' and 'tourist' (Simpson, 2005b). Moreover, sending organizations often wish to remain separate from mainstream tourism and the negative connotations associated with the term 'tourist' (Rowe and Hall, 2003; Simpson, 2005b). This was particularly apparent with FSD who refer to their participants as 'interns' and do not consider their programmes as 'holidays'. As a result, labels were used with discretion throughout fieldwork but the terms volunteer tourism and volunteer tourist are used in this chapter in order to provide consistency with the majority of previous work in this area.

Qualitative methods were selected for this study due to the lack of existing empirical research on this topic and the need to access a range of complex issues and personal opinions. Within the range of qualitative methods, Appreciative Inquiry (AI) was used.

> Appreciative Inquiry is the cooperative, coevolutionary search for the best in people, their organizations, and the world around them. It involves systematic discovery of what gives life to an organization or a community when it is most effective and most capable in economic, ecological, and human terms.
>
> (Cooperrider and Whitney, 2005, p. 8)

The decision to use AI was based on the study's objective to identify examples of good practice in sending organizations. Previous studies by Ludema *et al.* (2006) and Reed *et al.* (2005) showed that AI would be an appropriate and innovative methodological approach to achieve this.

The first two stages of AI involve appreciating 'the best of what is' and envisioning ideals of 'what might be' (Cooperrider and Srivastva, 1987). For this study, this was achieved through semi-structured interviews and/or focus groups conducted with volunteer tourists, representatives of host organizations and representatives of sending organizations. The decision to involve these three groups was based on the assumption that each group has different agendas and that a successful VTP should therefore simultaneously meet the needs of each group (Gazley, 2001).

Stage three involves co-constructing 'what should be' (Cooperrider and Srivastva, 1987) and was addressed through using an online 'blog' in which preliminary findings could be discussed between all those involved in the study. Stage four relates to experiencing 'what can be' and was thus beyond the scope of this study. The steps taken in each stage are summarized in Table 5.1.

Table 5.1. Stages in appreciative inquiry method.

Stage	Steps	Purpose
DISCOVERY (appreciating and valuing the best of 'what is') AND DREAM (envisioning 'what could be')	(i) Contact sending organizations and invite their participation (ii) Observe the positive aspects of volunteer tourism programmes by focusing on what they are visibly achieving and how they are doing this (Discovery) (iii) Conduct interviews with representatives of sending organizations and host organizations; explore what is effective and successful in current practices (Discovery) and discuss ideals and aspirations for the future (Dream). (iv) Conduct focus groups with volunteer tourists; explore what is effective and successful in current practices (Discovery) and discuss ideals and aspirations for the future (Dream).	• Reinforce existing positive imagery and develop positive visions by focusing on the benefits and successful management strategies of each organization • Bring together characteristics of successful management from each organization so that a preliminary framework of good practice for sending organizations can be developed
DESIGN (co-constructing 'what should be')	(v) Encourage comment and discussion between participants from the Discovery and Dream stages by placing the preliminary framework of good practice in an online forum (blog) (vi) Revise and adapt framework of good practice based on comments made in the forum	• Encourage dialogue between different sending organizations with similar goals. Allow them to find common ground by sharing ideals and empower them to adopt positive ideas from each other • Develop revised framework of good practice which represents shared ideas
DESTINY (sustaining 'what will be')	(vii) Essentially beyond the scope of this study although final results were sent to each sending organization	• Communicate stories and good practices to encourage organizations to adopt some of these ideas

Case Studies

Founded in 1995, FSD is a non-profit organization based in the USA. FSD's mission is to support the work of grass-roots development organizations, raise international awareness of the economic challenges facing developing countries and support communities in finding more effective solutions to development issues (FSD, 2007). FSD runs programmes in Latin America, East Africa and India which range from internships to study tours. This research focused on the FSD internship programme in La Plata, Argentina. This programme places volunteers in locally run NGOs for a minimum of 9 weeks.

ISV is also a non-profit organization based in the USA and they have been conducting educational volunteer work programmes for the last 5 years. Their mission is to 'create an environment that combines conservation, community development, education and recreation into the ultimate adventure travel programme for people who desire to make a difference by volunteering in communities abroad' (ISV, 2007). They work with grass-roots, government and national host organizations focused on community development and/or conservation in Australia, Costa Rica, the Dominican Republic, Ecuador, New Zealand, North America and Thailand. The main programme they offer is the 'standard ISV four-week programme', which involves 2 weeks on a group volunteer project, followed by a 2-week adventure tour.

The programme researched was the volunteering component of a standard ISV 4-week programme based in Tauranga, New Zealand. Although ISV provided their own team leaders, the programme was run in conjunction with ISV's partner organization, Kuaka. Kuaka is based in Tauranga and aims to provide students with 'an in depth and hands on experience of New Zealand culture and environment that reflects the interconnections between the people and the land' (Kuaka, 2007).

The Role of the Sending Organization

Both case studies suggest that volunteer tourism can benefit both the volunteer tourists and the host organizations. The FSD programme was perceived as mutually beneficial by all four host organizations involved with FSD as well as the programme coordinators and the volunteers: 'We are mutually enriched' (President of host organization A); 'We make sure that it's a relationship that both gives and receives' (Programme coordinator B); 'It's a very reciprocal relationship with the NGO. . . . It's a very two way street' (Volunteer A).

Similarly, despite the short duration of the ISV programme, quotes from all the key groups involved suggest that the programme benefits both the volunteers and the host organizations: 'There's a mutual benefit' (Representative of host organization B); 'It's just a real win-win' (ISV team leader); 'Not only was it a benefit to the country we came to, but it was a benefit to ourselves' (Volunteer E).

Volunteers in both VTPs highlighted benefits such as self-fulfilment, self-development, new friendships and new skills. In addition, participants claimed that they had gained a far more 'real' experience of the host country and deeper understanding of the local culture than they would have achieved as conventional 'tourists'. Host organizations also identified a range of benefits. Interestingly, the group of ISV volunteers were valued primarily for their combined manpower, whereas volunteers participating in the FSD individual placements were often appreciated for the personal influence they had on their organization and the particular experience and skills they had brought with them.

However, it is argued that the achievement of mutually beneficial programmes and the development of cross-cultural understanding are not an automatic result of sending volunteers overseas, but rather reflect careful planning and management on behalf of FSD, ISV and Kuaka. Through the Discovery, Dream and Design phases of the AI (see Table 5.1), the researcher therefore attempted to establish how the sending organizations were facilitating the achievement of such benefits. Through asking questions such as 'What are the key factors that make FSD/ISV a successful organization?' to volunteers, sending organizations and host organizations, three important issues were identified.

First, it is essential that sending organizations develop a strong relationship with the host organizations, based on mutual respect and trust. Initially, the sending organization should visit potential host organizations to explain their programme and discuss whether it is appropriate for them to host volunteers. It is important that sending organizations are honest from the very beginning with regard to what will be expected of the host organization and, in turn, what they can expect to gain from hosting volunteer tourists. This relationship should then be maintained through regular communication and, where possible, visits to the host organization. Regular evaluations of the project should also be conducted to ensure that the programme is working well and to make any necessary changes.

In the case of FSD the relationship with host organizations is developed and maintained through FSD's programme coordinators. They are based in Argentina and are therefore in a position to develop strong relationships with members of the host organizations:

> We spend time with them. We visit their organizations. We participate in their events, they participate in our events. It's a really interesting thing that builds over time. And with that comes a different element. ... They realise that you are there and you're going to continue to come and you're going to continue to provide them with a level of support.
>
> (Programme coordinator B)

In comparison, ISV work with a Tauranga-based partner organization, Kuaka, to achieve the development of such relationships. While ISV is an international organization running VTPs worldwide, Kuaka is locally based and owned, and is thus able to develop a high level of cooperation with the host organizations on behalf of ISV: 'There's a lot of trust, a lot of cooperation, a lot of respect both ways' (Director of Kuaka). This is facilitated through regular visits to the projects as well as continuous communication. In addition, Kuaka has recently been co-developing memoranda of agreement with the host organizations which outline the rights and requirements of each organization.

The importance of developing strong, honest and equal relationships with host organizations has also been identified by the Year Out Group (2005), Comlámh (2007) and Simpson (2007). It can also be linked to academic literature on volunteer tourism which repeatedly points to the historical roots of volunteer tourism in missionary movements (e.g. Lewis, 2005; Simpson, 2005b). Such literature implies that sending organizations could be exposed to some of the criticisms faced by missionaries such as paternalism and a lack of respect given to host communities. Host organizations should therefore be involved in decision-making processes, in order to ensure that sending organizations do not impose foreign and potentially inappropriate values and principles on host organizations.

Such issues are also relevant at a broader theoretical level. It has been argued that volunteer tourism has the potential to develop as a sustainable and alternative form of tourism that moves beyond the colonialist attitudes of mass tourism (Wearing, 2001). However, if those affected by the volunteer tourists are not actively involved in all the stages of developing VTPs, volunteer tourism could lead to many of the negative impacts associated with mass tourism. For example, a number of authors have pointed to the ways in which sending organizations often market their programmes using neocolonialist or imperialist representations of the host communities rather than incorporating the voices of these communities (Wearing, 2001; Griffin, 2004; Simpson, 2005b).

A second important theme relates to the concept of experiential learning. Simpson's work (2004, 2005a,b) suggests that many sending organizations that are orientated towards the gap year market do not encourage participants to engage critically with their experiences. There appears to be a belief that through contact with 'the other', volunteers will automatically experience a broadening of horizons and develop a deep understanding of the host communities. A number of authors have highlighted the inaccuracy of such assumptions and suggest the need for VTPs to include a stronger educational component and encourage reflection by the volunteers (Crabtree, 1998; Griffin, 2004; Jones, 2005; Simpson, 2005a; IVPA, 2007).

The present study, as well as previous research, suggests that volunteer tourism can lead to cross-cultural understanding (Brown and Lehto, 2005; Clifton and Benson, 2006; Zahra, 2006) and even a sense of global citizenship (McGehee and Santos, 2005). Yet it is argued that if volunteer tourism is to have a long-term influence on the lives of the volunteers and the ways in which they think about the world, it is important that sending organizations take an experiential learning approach to their programmes. This means providing volunteers with the opportunity not just to 'experience', but also to reflect upon their behaviours and think critically about the bigger issues surrounding their programme.

The case studies of FSD and ISV are informative here as they both have a strong focus on education. This may be linked to the fact that both organizations are based in the USA and offer their volunteers the option of gaining academic credit. In comparison to the more frequently criticized UK gap year VTPs, US programmes are often approached as 'service-learning' projects and therefore frequently recognize the importance of experiential education

(Crabtree, 1998; Simpson, 2005a). For example, FSD requires volunteers to write a grant proposal in order to apply for funding for a sustainable project to be implemented by the volunteer with their host organization. This encourages volunteers to develop their awareness of the issues surrounding sustainability and development. Volunteers are also required to write an evaluation of their experience and they are encouraged to keep journals. While one intern found such requirements rather bureaucratic, she did recognize their value: 'In a lot of ways it was kind of annoying to have to fill out forms all the time and have all these meetings and check in but then I think they want to make it a process rather than an experience' (Volunteer A).

ISV also emphasize the educational component of their programmes. They expect host organizations to provide an educational experience, and ISV project leaders are required to conduct three group discussions per week with the volunteers. In addition, volunteers gaining academic credit are expected to keep a daily field journal, lead one group discussion and write an essay regarding their experience. In general, the volunteers felt positive about the level of reflection which was required of them as it encouraged them to think on a deeper level about their experience and also helped them to realize the value of their work: 'There is a definite sense of accomplishment and reflection every day. I think that was really important because we sat around as a group and we talked about what we did, why it was important' (Volunteer C).

The third theme relates to the value of approaching VTPs as part of a process rather than simply as an isolated experience. The FSD case study highlights the need to select appropriate volunteers. Moreover, both case studies underline the need for pre-departure preparation and in-country orientation, as well as the importance of debriefing volunteers after the experience. Such ideas are also apparent in IVPA's (2007) principles and practices, which separate criteria into pre-programme, programme and post-programme. Similarly, Comlámh (2007) suggests that volunteering overseas should be viewed as a continuum.

Although both FSD and ISV ask their volunteers to go through an application process for their programmes, FSD seems to attach more significance to this. It can be argued that the placement-style programme requires volunteers to have certain skills so that they can make a genuine contribution to the host organization. In particular, language is an issue here. It is suggested that volunteer tourists' ability to communicate in the local language should not be underestimated as a factor that influences the potential benefits of volunteer tourism. Some FSD volunteers who go to Argentina have a very limited level of Spanish and this can considerably limit their capacity to contribute to the host organization: 'When we bring an intern without strong Spanish skills, it is unavoidably going to be a burden rather than an asset to the organization' (Programme coordinator A). FSD have become increasingly aware of this and they are moving towards a more stringent process for selecting appropriate volunteers.

In comparison, ISV did not have a strict selection process as, due to the nature of the work in which the volunteers were involved, this was not deemed necessary. This suggests that if sending organizations are not prepared to have a selection process for choosing appropriate volunteers, a programme involving work that can be easily taught will be more suitable. In particular, if volunteers do not speak the local language, there is a risk, especially with placement-style VTPs, that they may be more of a burden than a help to host organizations. In such a case, working in a group run by a bilingual team leader may provide a more mutually beneficial approach.

The importance of pre-departure preparation was also apparent in the FSD programme where volunteers sometimes had unrealistic expectations regarding what they could achieve:

> The other issue is ideological. Here wanting to do something isn't the same as being able to achieve it. . . . It was challenging for her (the volunteer) to adapt to the realities of being here. . . . She had the belief that she could change the social situation but I explained to her 'you will not change it. The State cannot change it, the country cannot change it, how are you going to change it in two months?'
>
> (Representative of host organization C)

Clearly, if volunteers have idealistic assumptions about their potential level of contribution to a host organization, or even to a country as a whole, this can lead to disappointment on behalf of the volunteer and subsequent implications for the host organization. Pre-departure preparation is therefore important in order to provide volunteers with realistic information regarding what they can feasibly achieve during their programme.

Preparation should also contribute to developing an appropriate attitude within the volunteers so that when they arrive in the host country, they come with an open mind and a willingness to learn. This was apparent from these two case studies and has also been identified in previous work (Wearing, 2001; Butcher, 2005; Simpson, 2007). It has been suggested that volunteers should assume the role of learner and guest so that volunteer tourism could be based on mutual learning and exchange. This will then encourage volunteers to take on the approach of 'collaborator' and it will help promote an environment of shared power and purpose (Crabtree, 1998). In fact, Simpson (2007) claims that 'the best volunteers are those who feel they have as much if not more to learn as they have to give'. It can be argued that this is especially import-ant when volunteers from developed countries work in developing countries. Previous research suggests that volunteers can sometimes inappropriately take on the role of 'expert' and this can be perceived as maintaining and reinforc-ing power inequalities between developed and developing countries (Wearing, 2001, 2004; Griffin, 2004).

Detailed background information on the host country should also be pro-vided for the volunteers, including important details regarding cultural norms. This information can then be expanded upon through orientation and/or brief-ings once volunteers arrive in the host country. Both case studies show that volunteer tourists appreciate such support as it allows them to feel better pre-pared and to know what they are responsible for. This also supports previous research by McGehee and Santos (2005) which states that many volunteer tourists involved in their research, prior to their trip, 'craved support from the organization in which they had placed their faith and resources' (p. 773).

Support may also be needed after the experience of volunteering. Indeed, the FSD case study suggests that volunteers involved in such programmes may require debriefing once they have returned home. In an interview with an intern who had returned to the USA after a 6-month programme, this was particularly apparent: 'You sort of feel like a part of your soul stays behind in this other part of the world. . . . It's a strange disorienting kind of feeling' (FSD volunteer B). Similarly, research undertaken by Broad (2003) and McGehee and Santos (2005) claims that some volunteer tourists may find it difficult to readjust to a 'normal lifestyle' when they return. This relates to the concept of reverse culture shock: 'the process of readjusting, reacculturating, and reassimilating into one's own home culture after living in a different culture for a significant period of time' (Gaw, 2000, p. 83).

While reverse culture shock may not be as strong for participants in the 2-week ISV project, one volunteer did anticipate that returning home could present some difficulties: 'No-one at home is going to understand what you actually did. It would be like "oh my gosh we spent five hours clearing this fence" but no-one is going to understand' (ISV Volunteer A). As a result, sending organizations may choose to play a role in facilitating this transition home through debriefing and/or developing alumni networks through which volunteers can stay in touch, such as the ISV Campus Clubs. ISV propose that such clubs can also help to encourage volunteers to continue 'making a difference' when they return home through sharing their experiences with others or through volunteering in their own community. Interestingly, Comlámh (2007) argues that volunteers' *main* contribution will be when they return home and are in a position to share their knowledge and experiences with others.

Conclusion

This study sought to further our understanding of volunteer tourism by exploring the role that sending organizations play in developing and maintaining VTPs that benefit both the volunteer tourists and the host organizations. An 'appreciative' approach was deliberately employed in order to identify examples of good practice within sending organizations. While it was not assumed that achieving mutually beneficial VTPs was the sole responsibility of sending organizations, this research focused specifically on their role due to the recent increase in such organizations.

Two case studies have been discussed in this chapter to illustrate that volunteer tourism has the potential to bring important benefits, both to the volunteer tourists and the host organizations. The case studies were selected to represent two very different styles of VTP: individual placements and group projects.

The key conclusion that can be drawn from these discussions is that neither placements nor projects should be assumed as automatically benefiting both the volunteer and the hosts. While this research was exploratory and therefore only touched the surface of some of the issues relating to volunteer tourism, it highlights the need for sending organizations to develop and manage their programmes both deliberately and carefully. This chapter has argued that in order to create mutually beneficial programmes, sending organizations need to be aware of the importance of their relationship with host organizations. It has also built on previous work by Simpson (2005b), highlighting the value of including an element of education alongside the 'experience'. In addition, it has been suggested that sending organizations need to recognize that VTPs involve a process rather than an isolated experience and that volunteer selection, pre-departure preparation, orientation and debriefing are important components of this process.

While these three issues have been shown to be significant for FSD and ISV, it is argued that sending organizations should also consider a number of other factors. Sending organizations need to be aware of issues ranging from broader ethical considerations such as the type of work which volunteer tourists should be involved in, to more practical decisions such as the way in which the demands of the volunteers are matched with the needs of the host countries. Furthermore, it is recognized that the way in which volunteers are involved and managed should also depend on the country in which they are working (Meijs *et al.*, 2003).

Although this chapter has taken an optimistic view of volunteer tourism, suggesting that through proactive management on behalf of sending organizations, mutually beneficial VTPs can be achieved, it is necessary to recognize that the 'appreciative' approach taken throughout data collection and analysis may have influenced this. In addition, it is important to note that both ISV and FSD are non-profit organizations and are therefore not representative of the many for-profit sending organizations operating VTPs. It is argued that with organizations that are fundamentally acting as tour agents and where financial gain is a central objective, further challenges may arise if the VTPs they offer are to be mutually beneficial.

In summary, this research points to the vital role that sending organizations can play in order to ensure that VTPs 'make a difference' to both the volunteers and the host organizations. Through looking at two examples of good practice, this research has begun to raise some important issues which sending organizations should, at least, consider. It has also highlighted the importance and value of including the voices of those affected by the work of volunteer tourists. Clearly, if volunteer tourism is to genuinely benefit the volunteers and their hosts, both groups should be involved in future research. It is hoped that through continued research in this area, it will be possible to expand our knowledge regarding how to ensure that volunteer tourism provides an alternative and mutually beneficial form of tourism.

References

Barkham, P. (2006) Are these the new colonialists? *The Guardian*, 18 August. Available at: http://www.guardian.co.uk/g2/story/0,,1852717,00.html

Broad, S. (2003) Living the Thai life – A case study of volunteer tourism at the Gibbon Rehabilitation Project Thailand. *Tourism Recreation Research* 28(3), 63–72.

Brodie, J. (2006) Are gappers really the new colonialists? *The Guardian*, August 26. Available at: http://www.guardian.co.uk/travel/2006/aug/26/gapyeartravel.guardiansaturdaytravel section

Brown, P. (2003) Mind the gap: why student year out may do more harm than good. *The Guardian*, 6 September. Available at: http://education.guardian.co.uk/students/gapyear/ story/0,,1037642,00.html

Brown, S. and Lehto, X. (2005) Travelling with a purpose: understanding the motives and bene- fits of volunteer vacationers. *Current Issues in Tourism* 8(6), 479–496.

Butcher, J. (2005) The impact of international service on host communities in Mexico. *Voluntary Action* 7(2), 101–113.

Callanan, M. and Thomas, S. (2005) Volunteer tourism – Deconstructing volunteer activities within a dynamic environment. In: Novelli, M. (ed.) *Niche Tourism Contemporary Issues, Trends and Cases*. Butterworth-Heinemann, Oxford, UK, pp. 183–201.

Clifton, J. and Benson, A. (2006) Planning for sustainable ecotourism: the case for research ecotourism in developing country destinations. *Journal of Sustainable Tourism* 14(3), 238–254.

Comlámh (2007) Code of good practice/volunteer charter. Available at: http://www. volunteeringoptions.org/index.php/plain/volunteer_charter

Cooperrider, D.L. and Srivastva, S. (1987) Appreciative inquiry in organizational life. In: Woodman, R. and Pasmore, W. (eds) *Research in Organizational Change and Development*. JAI Press, Greenwich, Connecticut, pp. 129–169.

Cooperrider, D.L. and Whitney, W. (2005) *Appreciative Inquiry: A Positive Revolution in Change*. Berrett-Koehler, San Francisco, California.

Crabtree, R.D. (1998) Mutual empowerment in cross-cultural participatory development and service learning: lessons in communication and social justice from projects in El Salvador and Nicaragua. *Journal of Applied Communication Research* May, 182–209.

Ellis, C. (2003) Participatory environmental research in tourism: a global view. *Tourism Recreation Research* 28(3), 45–55.

Frean, A. (2006) Gap years create 'new colonialists'. *Times Online*, 15 August. Available at: http://travel.timesonline.co.uk/tol/life_and_style/travel/holiday_type/gap_travel/ article609259.ece

FSD (2007) Foundation for Sustainable Development. Homepage. Available at: http://www. fsdinternational.org

Gaw, K.F. (2000) Reverse culture shock in students returning from overseas. *International Journal of Intercultural Relations* 24, 83–104.

Gazley, B. (2001) Volunteer vacationers and what research can tell us about them. *E Volunteerism: The Electronic Journal of the Volunteer Community* 1(2). Available at: www.e-volunteerism.com

Griffin, T. (2004) A discourse analysis of UK sourced gap year overseas projects. MA thesis. University of the West of England, UK.

ISV (2007) International Student Volunteers New Zealand. Available at: http://www.isvonline. com/newzealand.html

IVPA (2007) IVPA principles and practices. Available at: http://www.volunteerinternational.org/ index-principles2.htm

Jones, A. (2005) Assessing international youth service programmes in two low-income countries. *Voluntary Action* 7(2), 87–99.

Kuaka (2007) Kuaka New Zealand. Homepage. Available at: http://www.kuaka.co.nz/

Lewis, D. (2005) Globalisation and international service: a development perspective. *Voluntary Action* 7(2), 13–25.

Ludema, J.D., Cooperrider, D.L. and Barrett, F.J. (2006) Appreciative inquiry: the power of the unconditional positive question. In: Reason, P. and Bradbury, H. (eds) *Handbook of Action Research*. Sage, London, pp. 155–166.

Lyons, K.D. (2003) Ambiguities in volunteer tourism: a case study of Australians participating in a J-1 visitor exchange programme. *Tourism Recreation Research* 28(3), 5–13.

McGehee, N.G. and Santos, C.A. (2005) Social change, discourse and volunteer tourism. *Annals of Tourism Research* 32(3), 760–779.

Meijs, L.C.P.M., Hnady, F., Cnaan, R., Brudney, L., Asocli, U., Ranade, S., Hustinx, L., Weber, S. and Weiss, I. (2003) All in the eyes of the beholder? Perceptions of volunteering across eight countries. In: Dekker, P. and Halman, L. (eds) *The Values of Volunteering: Cross Cultural Perspectives*. Kluwer, New York, pp. 19–35.

Reed, J., Jones, D. and Irvine, J. (2005) Appreciating impact: evaluating small voluntary organizations in the United Kingdom. *Voluntas: International Journal of Voluntary and Nonprofit Organizations* 16(2), 123–141.

Roberts, T. (2004) Are western volunteers reproducing and reconstructing the legacy of colonialism in Ghana? An analysis of the experiences of returned volunteers. MA thesis. Institute for Development Policy and Management, Manchester, UK.

Rowe, T. and Hall, C.M. (2003) Generation Y: building a future through volunteer tourism? In: Ranga, M. and Chandra, A. (eds) *Tourism and Hospitality*. Discovery Publishing House, New Delhi, pp. 170–191.

Simpson, K. (2004) 'Doing development': the gap year, volunteer-tourists and a popular practice of development. *Journal of International Development* 16, 681–692.

Simpson, K. (2005a) Dropping out or signing up? The professionalisation of youth travel. *Antipode* 447–469.

Simpson, K. (2005b) Broad horizons? Geographies and pedagogies of the gap year. PhD thesis. Newcastle University, UK.

Simpson, K. (2007) Ethical volunteering. Homepage. Available at: http://www.ethicalvolunteering.org/index.html

Uriely, N., Reichel, A. and Amos, R. (2003) Volunteering in tourism: additional thinking. *Tourism Recreation Research* 28(3), 57–62.

Year Out Group (2005) Operating guidelines for the volunteering sector. Available at: http://www.yearoutgroup.org/code-volunteering.htm

Wearing, S. (2001) *Volunteer Tourism: Experiences that Make a Difference*. CAB International, Wallingford, UK.

Wearing, S. (2003) Editorial. *Tourism Recreation Research* 28(3), 3–4.

Wearing, S. (2004) Examining best practice in volunteer tourism. In: Stebbins, R.A. and Graham, M. (eds) *Volunteering as Leisure, Leisure as Volunteering: an International Assessment*. CAB International, Wallingford, UK, pp. 209–225.

Zahra, A. (2006) The unexpected road to spirituality via volunteer tourism. *Tourism Review* 54(2), 173–185.

II Inward Journeys: Motivations, Needs and the Self

6 The Volunteer's Journey Through Leisure into the Self

S. Wearing,[1] A. Deville[1] and K. Lyons[2]

[1]School of Leisure Sport and Tourism, University of Technology Sydney, Lindfield, Australia; [2]School of Economics, Politics and Tourism, University of Newcastle, Callaghan, Australia

Volunteer tourism is in essence a form of leisure behaviour. Perceived freedom and choice (Neulinger, 1974), intrinsic motivation (Iso-Ahola, 1982), satisfaction and enjoyment (Kaplan, 1975), and identity and selfhood (Kelly, 1983) are central tenets of leisure that are clearly evident in emerging definitions of volunteer tourism (e.g. Wearing, 2001; McGehee and Santos, 2005). However, it is the relationship between volunteer tourism as leisure and the conceptualization of 'the self' that is the focus of this chapter.

Volunteer tourists engage in a range of self-challenging and self-complexifying activities that leisure scholars have long theorized and studied. However, the concern with the project of the self that has occupied the theoretical and conceptual debates among a number of leisure studies researchers over the past few decades, apart from some notable exceptions such as Cohen (1979) and Kottler (1997), is largely missing in tourism studies. Given that volunteer tourism has emerged primarily as an area of scholarly inquiry within tourism studies, there is a risk that analyses of the self in volunteer tourism may also be overlooked. This is particularly of concern when one considers how volunteer tourism is as much a journey of the self as it is a journey to help others. In some instances, it is possible that volunteering can be life-changing and life-fulfilling, but it can also cut one adrift from self-knowing to the sometimes unnerving worlds of self-discovery and self-doubt (Lyons, 2003).

The purpose of this chapter is to provide some insights into the way the self has been examined in the context of leisure studies and to a lesser degree in tourism studies. It reviews the trajectory of the self in conceptualizations of leisure and concludes by considering its implications for volunteer tourism. Partly, this is an attempt to avoid the reinvention of wheels that can occur when one fails to take note of developments in cognate fields. In addition, volunteer tourism is a relatively new form of leisure behaviour and presents an array of issues and challenges not previously considered in examinations of the relationship between leisure and the self and so presents opportunities to expand understandings of

this relationship. This chapter also provides a conceptual and theoretical starting point for this section of the book. In the chapters that follow, there are a
number of cases presented that each build upon and illustrate the importance
volunteer tourism plays in the self-development of volunteers as they embark,
sometimes unwittingly, on existential and ontological journeys into themselves.

Leisure and the Self

Early definitions of leisure focused upon activities that were specifically and
voluntarily chosen by an individual (Goodale and Godbey, 1988). Many of
these definitions recognized that such choice took place within the context
of a period of time in which individuals were free from everyday responsibilities associated with work and family life. Leisure time was essentially time for
oneself (Rojek, 1995). There was also acknowledgement that what constituted
leisure varied from one person to another, dependent upon personal tastes and
preferences and was therefore subjective. Finally, a significant characteristic of
leisure in most of these definitions is an affective–experiential one: a feeling of
satisfaction and enjoyment associated with experiencing something worthwhile
(Kleiber, 1999). The key issues in these earlier views of leisure are captured in
Kaplan's (1975) definition, which describes leisure as a

> relatively self-determined activity-experience that falls into one's economically
> free-time roles that is seen as leisure by participants, that is psychologically
> pleasant in anticipation and recollection, that potentially covers the whole range of
> commitment and intensity, that contains characteristic norms and constraints, and
> that provides opportunities for recreation, personal growth and service to others.
>
> (p. 26)

However, the path towards understanding leisure has had many facets (Kleiber,
1999). Dumezadier (1974) claimed that leisure in contemporary society grew
out of changes associated with the industrial revolution. According to this perspective, leisure is the recuperative essence that provides an opportunity to
enhance and develop a sense of self – something that modern society fails
to offer through work or other social institutions (Dumazedier, 1974). Early
work by John Neulinger (1974) conceptualized leisure as a subjective condition characterized by perceptions of freedom and intrinsic motivation. This led
a number of leisure scholars particularly in North America to recognize that
leisure creates contexts in which individuals not only choose what they want to
do but also who they want to be, and to answer the question of who they are.
What followed were several decades of research into the relationships between
leisure and self-development, self-expression and identity.

A key theorist in the study of self in leisure is John Kelly. Kelly proposed
that leisure provides a much needed environment for experimenting with
self-representation – a process where we 'continue to become' (Kelly, 1983,
p. 73). Kelly (1983) suggested that contemporary life has forced individuals
into having to conform with social expectations and roles. These roles provide
little opportunity to get in touch with one's self. Kelly proposed that in leisure

we can create and try on identities. Haggard and Williams (1991) extended this idea, suggesting that leisure opportunities provide discrete attributes that can be selected by participants as representative of oneself. In addition, they proposed that once a person participates in activities that promote a certain image, these images become affirmed. Central to this experimentation is the need for a social audience with whom the individual symbolically engages. This work on the self drew from work developed by Mead (1972) who provided a conceptual foundation not only for leisure studies, but also more broadly for sociological theories of the self. Mead traced how social interaction, language and role-taking create the human mind and the 'self'. Given the central role Mead's work has played in providing a theoretical foundation for much of the research on the self and leisure, it warrants a brief review.

Mead sought to explain how society 'gets into' the individual, determines behaviour and becomes part of 'self', suggesting that the mind is a process through which individuals adapt to their environment, using language and symbols in communication with others. Through language, growing individuals take on and internalize attitudes of significant others, towards both the environment and self. They learn to relate to significant reference groups and to a generalized other, that is, the community as a whole and its values. However, Mead also suggests that individuals have an autonomous part of the self that acts on and influences this social (or socialization) process. Mead referred to the perception by the individual of himself/herself as a whole person, as the 'I' or the self-conception. The 'me' is an entity that is formed socially, depending on different situations and contexts. But it is the thinking person (the 'I') that actively constructs and integrates society into the individual identity (Cuff and Payne, 1984), still allowing for individuals to respond differently in different situations.

Mead's pragmatist philosophy underpins the sociological school of thought known as symbolic interactionism, which developed to better account for rapid social change than the more static functionalist sociological thinking of the time was able to accommodate (Macey, 2000). Stryker (1980) argued for the utility of a symbolic interactionist perspective in understanding observed patterns of human behaviour, observing that the meaning of an experience to an individual is strongly affected by social processes, particularly social interaction, which in turn affects behaviour:

> Behaviour is largely governed by the individual's social definition of the situation, interaction with others in the social milieu, and the self concept [which is] governed to a large extent by others in a social process.
>
> (p. 27)

Through the theoretical lens of symbolic interactionism, the status and significance of others in a social group are recognized as a dominant construct and force. Individuals are engaged in a never-ending search for meaning and identification (Denzin, 1992) in an attempt to contextualize one's sense of self within his/her environment. This perspective emphasizes the micro-social context, particularly compared with research based in psychology, which tends to regard the influence of others as more peripheral in relation to individual decision making and behaviour.

Destabilizing the Self and Leisure

The symbolic interactionist perspectives that drew from Mead and underpinned work by Kelly (1983) and later influential work by Samdahl (1988) are premised on the social institutions in which interactionism is housed, such as family, class and especially work and leisure. These contexts provided stable and unquestioned environments for an ordered process of self-development and self-discovery where experimentation is followed by selection and commitment (Haggard and Williams, 1991). But significant interconnected sociocultural and economic shifts at a global level have occurred since these earlier characterizations of the self in leisure that largely revolved around a work–leisure dichotomy.

While the march of modernization has transformed the nature, amount and availability of leisure time (albeit unevenly and less than perhaps had been imagined by modernist utopians), postmodernism has sought to demonstrate the existence of a break from the modernist thinking of the recent past. Rojek (1995) describes the latter phase of the modern era as being made up of contradictory forces that 'simultaneously pull in the direction of greater unity and greater disunity, more standardisation and more diversity, further centralisation and further de-centralisation' (p. 101). Postmodernism embraces the 'feelings' of this latter stage of modernism wherein individuals are able to question the previously unquestionable powers of authority, particularly by adopting new or 'alternative stances' in relation to them. A postmodernist perspective has encouraged the examination of accepted 'norms' of the past, and from the perspective of such standpoints, people have been empowered to ask 'why?'

The notion of self that implies a rational and stable 'I' as a component of the self is among the key domains being questioned. This is evident in post-structuralist critiques of the self in leisure as essentialist and problematic (see Wearing and Wearing, 2001). There has been a general move towards seeing the self as more of a political construct, accounting for the existence of many subjectivities and many 'I's. For example, Butler (1990) argued that subjectivity is a process of 'becoming', through repeated performative acts. Thus, the postmodern era has seen a re-evaluation of the importance of leisure and its definition as well. The traditionally dichotomous relationship between work and leisure has been somewhat redefined to take into consideration the new attitude of postmodernism, such that leisure has become 'part of the representational and symbolic machinery that we use in order to negotiate daily life' (Rojek, 1995, p. 131). This broadening of the definition of leisure was in part a necessary response to the emergence of a growing leisure consumption phenomenon.

In addition to leisure being re-evaluated as a necessary part of (post)modern life, there has been a global shift in the axis of the construction of personal identity from production (i.e. one's productive role in modern society) to consumption (Lynch and Veal, 2006). Leisure-experience consumption has become a means to express our 'desired' selves and how we present the way we live our lives within an increasingly narcissistic culture.

This review of leisure studies' accountings for the self has important implications for volunteer tourism which we address later in this chapter. For now, we turn our attention to how tourism research has explored the concept of self.

This literature is clearly less developed than the work we have considered that has emerged from leisure studies. Nevertheless, it provides important insights into the unique characteristics of volunteer tourism that may further our understandings of the self.

Tourism and the Self

Tourism as a specific form of leisure creates a context 'where individuals have certain autonomy over their lives, free from the disciplines of work and the responsibilities of home' (Wearing, 1998, p. 47). The act of travel and the physical and emotional removal from one's home world essentially creates a circumstance in which it becomes important that 'the human agent ... focus on adapting the self rather than the environment' (Wearing, 1998, p. 201). The contemplation, interpretation of and interaction with, the surrounding environments (inclusive of the people, customs and landscape) provide the opportunity for tourists to learn new forms of behaviour and develop appropriate coping mechanisms, sometimes as a matter of survival. While we can consider tourism to be a type of leisure experience, it is useful to consider different types of tourism experiences to contextualize volunteer tourism and to better define how such a form of tourism might impact on the different selves involved in a tourism experience.

Acknowledging that people vary and evolve, Cohen (1979) distinguished five main 'modes' of the tourist experience on the basis of where and how people currently locate themselves in relation to their own culture. Beginning with those most strongly adherent to the 'spiritual centre' of their own culture, the five modes are recreational, diversionary, experiential, experimental and existential. With these modes, Cohen sought to give structure to a 'phenomenology of tourism experiences', mirroring the initial motivations of different people in seeking the tourism experiences they do.

Tourists travelling in the recreational mode are primarily seeking enjoyment, rest and relaxation, with a rational belief in the value of leisure as restorative, while tourists travelling in the diversionary mode are seeking distraction and escape from their boredom with routinized daily lives and various degrees of alienation. In both modes, Cohen and Taylor (1976) argue, the tourist or holiday maker is primarily concerned with using all aspects of the holiday for the manipulation of well-being. Recreational and diversionary tourists are often trapped and become estranged and alienated from the people and surroundings they visit. The vast bulk of conventional mass 'tourism' activity–experience is designed and structured in a way that visitors never have to engage the local population where they are holidaying. In these first two modes, tourists may gaze, albeit fleetingly (Urry, 1990), at local sites and people encountered. Host cultures are expected primarily to host relaxation and recreational enjoyment and provide curious 'diversions' for the tourist from their own dominant culture. Some critics of conventional mass tourism forms adopt a post-colonialist position (such as Wearing and Wearing, 2006), suggesting that the recreational and diversionary tourist understands the local population and culture as 'other' and (already or later) comes to view them as inferior to their own dominant and advanced culture. Kottler (1997, p. 103) reaffirms that these two mainstream tourism modes 'do not lead to substantial change'. Their purpose 'is primarily for entertainment, business, or a well-deserved rest from the stresses of daily life'. He continues: 'If you are really after personal growth, you will want to adopt a particular attitude and select a special perceptual filter that will allow you to see things, and yourself, a bit differently. This will only happen if you immerse yourself in the world you are visiting, not as a tourist but as an adventurer.'

The experiential tourist mode described by Cohen (1979) is one in which there is a renewed quest for meaning outside the confines of one's own society through the search for 'experiences'. This mode is engaged in by those with 'lost centres' who are unable to lead an 'authentic life' at home. Meaning for them is sought or (re)captured vicariously by experiencing the seemingly authentic life of others. Leaving aside the problematic questions here of defining and distinguishing authenticity and the issue of 'acceptance' of simulacra and the virtual (Boorstin, 1964), Cohen (1979) notes that it is 'otherness' that forms the basis of attraction for experiential tourists, who nevertheless remain a 'stranger' as their vicarious experience does not provide new meaning or real guidance to their life.

The experimental tourist is more predisposed to try out alternative life ways in their quest for meaning away from home cultures. They 'sample' life in a trial-and-error process to discover that 'form of life which elicits a resonance' (Cohen, 1979, p. 189). Although they might immerse themselves in the authentic life of others, they are unable to fully commit to it and their search through tourism (or 'travelling') may become a way of life itself, without permanent commitment to anything.

Finally, the existential mode of tourist experience is that of travellers who become fully committed to an elective spiritual centre external to their native society and culture and who switch worlds, attaching themselves and submitting completely rather than remain permanently in exile from their elected spiritual centre. Their frequent visits nourish them, and the travel between given and chosen worlds is analogous to pilgrimage (Cohen, 1979, p. 190).

While there are many types of tourism to consider and all can be considered a form of leisure, Cohen's typology reinforces our understanding that many or most types of tourism do not lead to fundamental personal change. Yet these five overlapping modes of tourist experience offer a way of focusing on the sliding scale of opportunity that exists through travel to 'other' places, to position oneself in a context that challenges and changes one's notion of self in a much enlarged world. Cohen's work implies that differences in the motivation of tourists and changes to the self that result from the tourist experience rely on the tourist being able to see beyond the staged space of tourism. These changes are the product of being able to access and observe the realities of other people's lives (Wearing and Wearing, 2001). The initial motivation for individual tourist choices is important, as is the degree of adherence or otherwise to the 'spiritual centre' of their own culture resulting from the tourism experience choices they make. Yet, the actual experience that the tourists have may well be authentic for them and can expand and reaffirm a sense of their enculturated selves (Wearing and Wearing, 2001).

Conclusions: Transformations of the Self Through Volunteer Tourism

Wearing (2001) has described a volunteer tourist as one who chooses to use their free time to engage in meaningful experiences, such as helping others in need, restoring the environment, immersing themselves in another culture and then stepping back into their own world a changed person. The key character-istics of leisure defined by several notable leisure scholars as a transformative experience (Kaplan, 1975; Kelly, 1983; Samdahl, 1988; Kleiber, 1999) are clearly captured in this description.

We argue here that it is the capacity of leisure to invoke change in indi-viduals that has most relevance to understanding volunteer tourism. For some individuals, being a volunteer tourist provides opportunity to undergo a 'rite of passage' and display independence from others while seeking new experiences possibly unavailable to them at home. Being in the context of 'otherness' and removed from the influence of traditional reference groups may encourage the individual to think more for himsef/herself and assume a proactive role in decision making. In doing so, the individual must assume responsibility for his/ her actions – right or wrong (Heller, 1970) – and, in the process, learn to be independent and cope. Fussell (cited in Craik, 1986) points out that the experi-ence of travel is interconnected with self-discovery, therein illustrating that the effects of volunteer tourism on one's development of self may indeed be quite profound and carried on into all other aspects of one's life.

The theoretical framing of leisure through symbolic interactionism described earlier in this chapter is relevant to explaining this transformative potential of volunteer tourism. Interactions that volunteer tourists have with new surround-ings including people, places and activities are often profound and not only can provide opportunities to experiment with representations of the 'me' but also may lead to long-lasting reworkings of the 'I'. These experiences can involve the development of intimate relationships among group members (where groups are involved) and sociable contact with representatives of host communities and elements of their local natural environment. Wearing and Neil (1999) have examined such experiences in particular volunteer tourism settings and found that there was a clear expectation by group participants that these types of social interactions were a key component of the 'volunteer tourism experience'.

Indeed in a postmodern world an increasing proportion of the economy is now generated by the business of producing and consuming a range of these leis-ure 'experiences' which can be seen as part of the larger 'experience economy' (Pine and Gilmore, 1999). These experiences are selected by savvy volunteer tourism consumers who are able to identify and select specific experience attri-butes and use them to negotiate the fast-changing world by being masters of multiple and fragmented subjectivities of the self. Change and transformation of individuals through volunteer tourism is inevitable from a postmodern perspec-tive because the world itself in which volunteer tourism is located is destabilized.

From a more modernist perspective such as that taken by Cohen (1979), only specific tourism contexts evoke short-term or long-term changes in the individual while some do not. Of course, Cohen's characterizations of tourism were developed at a time prior to the emergence of a number of new forms of tourist behaviour including volunteer tourism. However, Cohen's experimental and existential modes of tourist experience are relevant to our consideration of a journey into self through volunteer tourism experiences. They characterize the type of experience which makes possible a journey of self-discovery and self-understanding through the search for, and experience of, life alternatives. It is the adoption of different contexts of 'other' places and people and the relative freedom offered to individuals in volunteer tourism that 'makes possible the investment of self that leads to the fullest development of ourselves, the richest expression of who we want to become, and the deepest experience of fulfillment' (Kelly, 1996, p. 45). Throughout the case studies presented in this book, particularly in the chapters that follow in this section, the insights and comments and motives of volunteer tourists further illustrate how the leisure experience of volunteer tourism is inextricably linked to the project of the self.

References

Boorstin, D. (1964) *The Image: A Guide to Pseudo Events in America*. Harper, New York.
Butler, J. (1990) *Gender Trouble: Feminism and the Subversion of Identity*. Routledge, London.
Cohen, E. (1979) A phenomenology of tourist experiences. *Sociology* 13, 179–201.
Cohen, S. and Taylor, L. (1976) *Escape Attempts*. Penguin, Hannondsworth, UK.
Craik, J. (1986) *Resorting to Tourism: Cultural Policies for Tourist Development in Australia*. Allen & Unwin, Sydney, Australia.
Cuff, E.C. and Payne, C.C.R. (1984) *Perspectives in Sociology*. Allen & Unwin, London.
Denzin, N.K. (1992) *Symbolic Interactionism and Cultural Studies: The Politics of Interpretation*. Blackwell, Malden, Massachusetts.
Dumazedier, J. (1974) *Sociology of Leisure*. Elsevier, Amsterdam.
Goodale, T. and Godbey, G. (1988) *The Evolution of Leisure: Historical and Philosophical Perspectives*. Venture, State College, Pennsylvania.
Haggard, L.M. and Williams, D.R. (1991) Self-identity benefits of leisure activities. In: Driver, B.L., Brown, P.J. and Peterson, G.L. (eds) *Benefits of Leisure*. Venture, State College, Pennsylvania.
Heller, A. (1970) *Everyday Life*. Routledge & Kegan Paul, London.
Iso-Ahola, S. (1982) Towards a social psychology of tourist motivation – a rejoinder. *Annals of Tourism Research* 9, 256–261.
Kaplan, M. (1975) *Leisure: Theory and Practice*. Wiley, New York.
Kelly, J. (1983) *Leisure Identities and Interactions*. Allen & Unwin, London.
Kelly, J.R. (1996) *Leisure*. Allyn & Bacon, Needham Heights, Massachusetts.
Kleiber, D.A. (1999) *Leisure Experience and Human Development: A Dialectical Approach*. Basic Books, New York.
Kottler, J.A. (1997) *Travel That Can Change Your Life: How to Create a Transformative Experience*. Jossey-Bass, San Francisco, California.
Lynch, R. and Veal, A. (2006) *Australian Leisure*. Longman, Melbourne, Australia.
Lyons, K.D. (2003) Ambiguities in volunteer tourism: a case study of Australians participating in a J-1 Visitor Exchange Program. *Tourism Recreation Research* 28(3), 5–13.
Macey, D. (2000) *The Penguin Dictionary of Critical Theory*. Penguin Books, London.
McGehee, N.G. and Santos, C.A. (2005) Social change, discourse and volunteer tourism. *Annals of Tourism Research* 32, 760–779.
Mead, G.H. (1972) *Mind, Self and Society*. University of Chicago Press, Chicago, Illinois.

Neulinger, J. (1974) *The Psychology of Leisure*. C. Thomas Charles, Springfield, Illinois.

Pine, J. and Gilmore, J. (1999) *The Experience Economy*. Harvard Business School Press, Boston, Massachusetts.

Rojek, C. (1995) *Decentring Leisure: Rethinking Leisure Theory*. Sage, London.

Samdahl, D. (1988) A symbolic interactionist model of leisure: theory and empirical support. *Leisure Sciences* 10, 27–39.

Stryker, S. (1980) *Symbolic Interactionism: A Social Structural Version*. Benjamin/Cummings, Menlo Park, California.

Urry, J. (1990) *The Tourist Gaze*. Sage, London.

Wearing, S. (1998) The nature of ecotourism: the place of self, identity and communities as interacting elements of alternative tourism experiences. PhD thesis, Charles Sturt University, Albury, Australia.

Wearing, S. (2001) *Volunteer Tourism: Experiences That Make a Difference*. CAB International, Wallingford, UK.

Wearing, S. and Neil, J. (1999) *Ecotourism: Impacts, Potentials and Possibilities*. Butterworth Heinemann, Oxford.

Wearing, S.L. and Wearing, B. (2001) Conceptualising the selves of tourism. *Leisure Studies* 20, 143–159.

Wearing, S.L. and Wearing, M. (2006) Rereading the subjugating tourist in neoliberalism: postcolonial otherness and the tourist experience. *Tourism Analysis* 11(2), 145–162.

7

Gibbons in Their Midst? Conservation Volunteers' Motivations at the Gibbon Rehabilitation Project, Phuket, Thailand

S. Broad[1] and J. Jenkins[2]

[1]*ACHIEVE Life Transformations, Brisbane, Australia;* [2]*School of Tourism and Hospitality Management, Southern Cross University, Lismore, Australia*

Wildlife conservation holidays are a specific type of volunteer vacation, where paying volunteers are a source of labour and funding for projects ranging from 1 week's duration to several months. Volunteer vacation opportunities exist in the fields of education, archaeology and community development, but conservation projects appear to offer greater opportunities for volunteering in animal care, rehabilitation and research. Many people seek out opportunities to interact with wildlife in a range of captive and non-captive settings, and demand for these experiences is growing (Reynolds and Braithwaite, 2001). For many people, travel also involves a search for authentic and/or meaningful experiences (MacCannell, 1976). Volunteering on a wildlife conservation holiday is an intense type of experience, during which people can interact with wildlife in a manner that is authentic and meaningful.

This chapter presents a case study of volunteer tourists' motivations for 'holidaying' at the Gibbon Rehabilitation Project (GRP) in Phuket, Thailand. The chapter describes the case study setting and the methods for gathering data, profiles volunteers at the GRP and explores the place of volunteering in GRP participants' lives generally and their motivations for volunteering at the GRP specifically. Understanding volunteers' motivations is vital to the design and operation of successful conservation programmes that rely on volunteers as their primary labour source. It is particularly so when a project such as the case study herein requires a long-term commitment from volunteers. These volunteers seek to make a contribution to conservation principles and practices and often require considerable commitment of resources on the part of organizations as they need to educate and train volunteers during their stay. Furthermore, volunteers travel long distances and invest much time and money. They often pay for the privilege of volunteering. If their motivations are not carefully considered, programmes will struggle to recruit and retain 'holiday workers'.

The Case Study Setting: Thailand and Phuket

Thailand covers an area of more than $514,000\,km^2$. Mass international tourism tends to be restricted to urban areas such as Bangkok and coastal resorts such as Pattaya and Phuket. *Thailand, a Lonely Planet Travel Survival Kit* (Cummings, 1997), a popular travel guide, projects Thailand as an easy country in which to travel, with Thai people described as being well known for their friendliness and hospitality. Phuket is the largest island in Thailand covering an area of $540\,km^2$ and has a permanent population of 230,000 people (Cummings, 1997). It is connected to the mainland by a bridge, and therefore is easily accessed. A range of wild flora and fauna still exists in and around Phuket. For instance, dolphins, whales, whale sharks, turtles and a variety of coral and fish species are found in surrounding waters. Mammals (e.g. bears, macaques and deer), snakes (e.g. the king cobra) and many bird species inhabit the protected forest areas, especially Khao Phra Thaew Wildlife and Forest Reserve (Stewart-Cox, 1995). This reserve is Phuket's last remnant of primary rainforest and is a popular destination for ecotourists. It is the site of the country's first GRP (Stewart-Cox, 1995). Gibbons are small apes exclusive to South-east Asia, and all 11 species are endangered. In Thailand, gibbons are poached from forests to be kept as pets or used as tourist attractions.

The Gibbon Rehabilitation Project (GRP)

The GRP's operations are conducted from three principal locations in or close to Phuket, Thailand. The main project headquarters, consisting of an office, volunteer accommodation and quarantine housing for gibbons, is located in Bang Rong, a small, predominantly Muslim village about 45 min from Phuket Town. Located in Phang Nga Bay Marine National Park are three islands used in the gibbon release programme. Ko Thong and Ko Daeng are uninhabited islands, used for supported release of the gibbons; Ko Boi is where volunteers stay when visiting the release islands.

The GRP is a research division of the Wild Animal Rescue Foundation of Thailand (known as WAR) – a non-profit charitable organization in Phuket. The GRP offers volunteers the chance to take an active part in environmental conservation and wildlife rehabilitation. Volunteers are given opportunities to work closely with the project's white-handed gibbons (*Hylobates lar*), to learn about gibbons, to take part in decision-making processes concerning the GRP and to meet volunteers from around the world, many of whom share similar interests. Volunteers work 6 days a week, building and maintaining cages, feeding and observing the project's caged gibbons and educating visitors about gibbons and the project's objectives.

Volunteers live in shared accommodation at the project headquarters in the village of Bang Rong. Volunteers' free time is spent engaging in common daily village activities (e.g. shopping at village markets, travelling by public transport, hitchhiking with local villagers), socializing, sightseeing and participating in recreational outings and festivals with other volunteers and local Thais.

Methodology

This research took the form of an ethnographic case study of the GRP, aimed at understanding the everyday lives, experiences and world of the volunteers (Taylor and Bogdan, 1998). Through this approach, ethnographers 'become intimately involved with the people [they] study' (Bourgois, 1995, p. 13). The study examined volunteer participants at the GRP in Thailand over a 10-month research period in 1999–2000. Sue Broad, the participant observer and primary author of this chapter, spent a total of 36 weeks between 1 April 1999 and 15 January 2000 in Thailand collecting data and volunteering. However, data collection extended beyond the period Sue was in Thailand, to include post-trip e-mail questionnaires. The following briefly explains the instruments used for collecting data.

OBSERVATIONS. Participant observations were undertaken during the 24-week volunteering period at the GRP. During that time, Sue was actively involved in all of the volunteering duties at the GRP and immersed herself in the volunteering experience. Apart from volunteering and recording observation data, 'free' time was spent sightseeing and socializing with other volunteers and a number of local Thais, thus also becoming immersed in the Thai culture like many other volunteers. The researcher was familiar with the issues and as committed to the concept of wildlife conservation as most other volunteers at the GRP.

Prior to arriving at the GRP, correspondence had primarily been with a representative of WAR, who received a copy of the research proposal. On arrival at the GRP, the Director was aware of the primary author's research intentions, but WAR's head office had not given him any details. The researcher's initial status as an 'observer' was, therefore, overt to the project management but covert to volunteers. When volunteers and other staff were first encountered they were advised of the nature of the research and the use of diaries and interviews to collect data. However, volunteers were not informed that observations would be made of the setting and activities that were taking place at the project.

Additional observation data were also collected throughout the 9 weeks that Sue was based in Phuket Town. These data came from observations and informal conversations with volunteers and staff, both during visits to the project and meetings in Phuket Town. Observation data were thus recorded throughout the data collection period, on the entire population of staff and volunteers. Observed behaviour, overheard comments or conversations and informal conversations with volunteers were also recorded using the language and ideas as expressed by the volunteers, so their stories could be told in their own words. Data were recorded by making entries in a notebook or by talking into a dictaphone at the first appropriate opportunity.

RESEARCH JOURNAL. Before and during the volunteering period, a research journal was used to record and describe the researcher's (i.e. first author) feelings, experiences and daily routines. Diary entries were made because it has been argued that participant observers should be reflective and record their own feelings (Taylor and Bogdan, 1998). The research journal was also used to make comments about methodological or ethical issues, to keep track of ideas, document links to the literature and to record themes and tentative analytical categories as they were identified in the data.

INTERVIEWS. Face-to-face, open-ended, semi-structured interviews were undertaken to secure comparable data, while also obtaining in-depth data where the volunteer participants could use their own words and, where relevant, determine the subject matter to be discussed. A convenience sample (Taylor and Bogdan, 1998) of 19 volunteers was interviewed shortly before their departure from the project.

QUESTIONNAIRES. Questioning of volunteers during the post-travel phase of their experience was carried out using e-mail. The e-mails included questions on the consequence of the volunteering experience, and on volunteers' memories and feelings towards the project. Questionnaires were sent to the 23 volunteers who provided valid e-mail addresses, 14 of whom responded.

Who Were the Volunteers?

Using data from formal interviews, informal conversations and secondary data, such as the volunteer application forms, volunteer participants were profiled in order to identify similarities and differences in their characteristics.

The volunteers at the GRP had travelled to a project in a foreign country to give their time and money to volunteer for periods of 3 weeks to more than 12 months. The volunteers were an average age of 25, with an age range of 18–48. There were 25 females and 15 males. While there was no time when there were no males at the project, it did range from there being 1 or 2 males out of 9 or 10 volunteers for several weeks prior to the peak volunteering time, to 8 males out of 17 volunteers during some of that peak time.

Most volunteers took part to some extent in all of the different types of work undertaken at the project. However, the males undertook more of the heavy cage-building and land-clearing work. This meant that it was when both the overall volunteer and male numbers were high that more of this physically demanding work was carried out.

None of the volunteers had children, and the majority of volunteers (33) classified themselves as single when they joined the project.

Ten nationalities were represented: England (16), the Netherlands (11), USA (3), Belgium (3), Japan (2) and one from each of Germany, Finland, France, Switzerland and New Zealand. This nationality 'breakdown' fluctuated during the volunteering period.

Volunteers had attained the following qualifications:

- High school – seven (one still studying, two about to start a Bachelor's degree);
- Diploma – three (one still studying);
- Bachelors degree – 25 (eight still studying);
- Postgraduate – five (four still studying).

Only seven of the volunteers were employed prior to joining the project and were returning to an existing job after volunteering. The majority of volunteers (33) were not in paid employment, as they:

- Were returning home after volunteering to commence or continue study (16);
- Had recently finished studying (6);
- Had left employment for a long-term holiday (5);
- Had left employment to volunteer (5);
- Had retired early (1).

English was a requirement of participation, and all volunteers indicated they could speak this language. Nine volunteers spoke only English, with two languages spoken by 14 volunteers, three languages spoken by 12 volunteers and four languages spoken by five volunteers. Collectively, the volunteers could speak ten other languages: French, German and Dutch were the most commonly identified, with the other seven being Japanese, Spanish, Russian, Swedish, Welsh, Swiss-German and Finnish.

The minimum length of time a volunteer stayed at the GRP was 3 weeks, the maximum stay was 17 months and the average stay was around 4 months. A further analysis of the results showed that 27 volunteers stayed for 3 months or less, seven stayed for between 3.25 and 6 months, one stayed for 6.25 months, two stayed for between 9.25 and 12 months and three stayed for more than a year. However, six of the population of volunteers were still at the project at the end of the research period.

The cost of a volunteer holiday influences a person's ability to volunteer at a given project and how long they can stay. Although limits are placed on a person's length of stay at the project, frequent turnover of staff can place great strain on resources directed to training staff and staff developing an understanding of the project and their work. Information was gathered on how volunteers funded their stay at the project, and responses were received from 23 volunteers. Ten of the volunteers were still dependent or partly dependent on their families.

Of the 13 independent volunteers, two had their travel and volunteering expenses fully funded by their universities. The income level of the remaining 11 independent volunteers varied, and appeared to be associated with lifestyle choice, but all financed their trips through savings.

When comparing the GRP volunteer profile with findings from previous studies into wildlife tourism, ecotourism and volunteer vacations a number of differences can be identified. First, the average length of volunteering at the GRP, at around 4 months, is significantly longer than previously reported ecotourism and volunteer vacation experiences. For instance, Obua and Harding (1996) found that 85% of ecotourists stayed less than 1 day in Kibale National Park. In her study of North American ecotourists, Wight (1996) found that ecotourists preferred an 8- to 14-day trip duration. In relation to volunteer vacations, while Gazley (2001) suggested they may range from 'a few days to several months', most of the projects she discussed were only of several weeks' duration. Likewise, the organizations discussed by Turner *et al.* (2001) also generally run projects of only several weeks' duration. Furthermore, it has been suggested that most Earthwatch Expeditions, one of the most popular volunteer vacations, are of a 2-week duration (Weiler and Richins, 1995), which was the case with Russell's (1995) study of Earthwatch participants on an Orangutan Project.

Second, the employment status of volunteers at the GRP, with 55% being students, or having finished studying immediately prior to volunteering, was substantially different to previous studies. For instance, students were found to make up only 8% of wildlife tourists in Muloin's (1998) study, 14% of volunteers in Russell's (1995) study and 15% of ecotourists in Obua and Harding's (1996) study. Likewise, it has been found that a high proportion of wildlife tourists, eco-tourists and volunteers are employed as 'professionals/managers', with results of 23% (Muloin, 1998), 32% (Davis *et al.*, 1997), 61% (Weiler and Richins, 1995), 70% (Obua and Harding, 1996) and 81% (Russell, 1995). However, at the GRP only 17.5% of volunteers were employed in any capacity.

Third, the average age of volunteers at the GRP (25) is lower than the average reported in previous studies. For instance, wildlife tourists have been found to have average ages of 33 years (Davis *et al.*, 1997) and 42 years (Muloin, 1998). Similarly, in relation to Earthwatch volunteers, Russell (1995) has suggested they have a median age in the mid-forties, while Weiler and Richins' (1995) results indicated 86% were aged 26 or over.

Eco-based and nature-based tours are often associated with experiences that require a high expenditure and with tourists who have higher than average incomes (Weiler and Richins, 1995; Milne, 1998). Of the 23 volunteers who provided information on themselves and/or their family's income levels, the highest proportion (39%) classed themselves or their families as having just a middle-range income, with the remaining volunteers split evenly between a low–low/middle and middle/high–high income. Furthermore, it should be noted that 43% of the 23 volunteers were students or had recently completed their studies and classified themselves as dependent on their families.

One similarity was found between the GRP volunteer profiles and profiles from other studies. The high level of education of volunteers at the GRP, with 75% studying for, or having completed, at least a Bachelor's degree, was consistent with other studies. For instance, it has been found that ecotourists/volunteer vacationers had college or university education rates of 64% (Weiler and Richins, 1995), 82% (Wight, 1996) and 87% (Obua and Harding, 1996).

GRP Conservation Volunteers' Motivations

Volunteer vacation providers appeal to the motivations of volunteers, by promoting their experiences as having the following specific characteristics:

- Foci – they are able to meet a tourist's special interest, such as animals/wildlife.
- Experiences – they are authentic and participatory in nature and provide opportunities to meet and work with like-minded people.
- Values – they involve purposeful travel.
- Impacts and outcomes – they contribute resources, such as labour and funding, to aid the host organization's activities in areas such as conservation, while new friendships, learning and skill development are examples of outcomes the tourist may experience.

In addition, articles on volunteer vacations in the popular press highlight benefits to participants, such as learning new skills, meeting like-minded people,
experiencing a new destination or culture and providing a worthwhile experience (Hutchings, 1996; Mihaly, 1996).

In order to determine if the GRP volunteers had been motivated to
participate by such characteristics or perceived benefits, data from the volunteers' application forms, interviews and informal conversations related to
their motivations for volunteering were analysed. A set of categories of motivation was then determined, which was grounded in the data and which fit all
responses. Each volunteer was motivated by more than one type of the four
motivation categories: 'altruism', 'travel', 'career development' and 'personal
interest/development'. A fifth category, 'GRP factors', was also identified
which could overlap with the other four categories. It related to why volunteers chose to volunteer at the GRP specifically, as opposed to an alternative
project. The following discussion describes each category further, and provides
examples of volunteers' responses.

Altruism

Just under two-thirds of volunteers were motivated by an altruistic desire to
help wildlife/conservation as demonstrated by the following responses:

> We humans have an obligation to protect the natural world for all of us animals.
> The Gibbon Rehabilitation Project offers me the chance to do something against
> the prevailing trend of destruction and indifference to nonhuman life.
>
> (Dianne)

> I really felt like the world is in a bad condition. ... We [Anita and her boyfriend,
> Max, who also volunteered] read that [the GRP] created a center to free gibbons
> that were once captured and we thought it was what we were looking for. We
> believe that in helping [the GRP] we will make a little step to improve the world.
>
> (Anita)

> The project seemed a very positive thing to do, and would directly help these
> animals; they're an endangered species so they need a hand. ... Conservation is
> very important to me; through my interest in biology I have learnt a great deal
> about it and am anxious to help the situation in an effectual way as possible.
>
> (Stephanie)

The volunteers' willingness to volunteer for altruistic reasons is consistent with
the findings of research in other countries and environments. People's support for a cause and feelings of being useful or needed can be motivators
for ongoing volunteering (McSweeney and Alexander, 1996; Gazley, 2001).
Volunteer vacations appeal to tourists who support the protection of wildlife habitats and ecosystems (Turner et al., 2001), and in fact an increasing
number of tourists are prepared to volunteer to help wildlife (Orams, 1996)
and take part more generally in environmental activities that benefit society
(Lerner, 1994).

For several of those volunteers who had not described an altruistic motive (e.g. Jodi, Jesse, Stephen), their responses indicated that they were more motivated by a desire for an alternative tourism experience, rather than an experience working with or for animals/wildlife. However, several other volunteers, who had also not described an altruistic motive, had discussed their intention to follow a career path working in the field of wildlife conservation or animal welfare (e.g. Jonas, Sally, Andrea, Ross, Brant). It appears, therefore, that rather than seeing volunteering as a short-term opportunity to help animals/wildlife, they considered volunteering as an initial step towards their longer-term goal for a career working with and helping animals/wildlife.

Travel

Two-thirds of the volunteers indicated that volunteering at the GRP was at least partly motivated by a desire to travel and a variety of volunteers' responses are given below. This supports Gazley's (2001) view that both traditional volunteering and tourism motivations may apply to the volunteer vacationer.

> It was a cheap way to travel and to experience a different culture.
>
> (Sasha)

> I decided it might be better if I went working on a project; this kind of scenario where you're with people all the time so you get to know people. It's much more enjoyable than just travelling, backpacking. ... The project being in Thailand is a bonus as I am very keen to experience as many different cultures as possible.
>
> (Dean)

> I wanted a way-out exotic experience.
>
> (Michelle)

> Several years ago I spent two weeks in Thailand as a normal tourist. Now I would like to see this country with all its beauty and problems from a different point of view. I hope that I can make friends with some Thai people and learn something about the country, the Thai culture and lifestyle.
>
> (Lyle)

Some volunteers had a particular desire to visit Asia or Thailand, while others were looking for opportunities they did not associate with more common tourism experiences, such as a chance to be settled or to immerse oneself in a different culture. In addition, several volunteers were searching for a placement for their studies, and indicated that they were very keen to travel as part of that placement (e.g. see Kate's responses below).

It was acknowledged earlier that there has been debate with regard to what extent a search for authenticity motivates tourists. An analysis of the responses given by volunteers such as Heidi, Stacey and Lyle indicates that they did associate volunteering with the chance to experience the 'real' or authentic Thailand. Indeed, MacCannell (1976) argued that tourists do seek to experience the life of the places they visit.

Furthermore, tourism has frequently been seen as providing opportunities for tourists to escape their everyday environment and lifestyle (Pearce, 1995).

Examining the volunteers' above responses, such as those by Dean and Michelle, suggests that some volunteers did see volunteering as a chance to escape.

For several of the younger and wealthier volunteers who had not demonstrated a travel-orientated motivation (e.g. Sally, Kristy, Stephen), volunteering was just one part of a more extensive tourist itinerary. Several others who had not indicated a travel motivation demonstrated in their responses that it was a particular desire to volunteer at a primate rehabilitation project, rather than where that project was located, or any opportunity it provided for travel that motivated their participation (e.g. Ross, Winona, Heather, Amanda, Hokira, Luis).

Career development

About half of the volunteers indicated that they hoped to gain experience relevant to their studies and future career plans. All but two of these volunteers were already studying, or had completed a degree in a field highly relevant to the GRP, such as veterinary science, zoology, animal management, environmental science and ecotourism. In fact, for Kate, Andrea, Monika and Brant, volunteering was a placement component of their studies. The other two volunteers both had plans prior to volunteering to establish a future career working with animals/wildlife. Allan was intending to commence relevant studies subsequent to volunteering; Winona was hoping to use the practical experience she gained from volunteering as a way to enter the field.

> I knew it would be a great experience for my career. ... I am pursuing a future career in wildlife rehabilitation and know from prior experience that international conservation projects can offer great experiences in field research, observational techniques and an understanding of social and political aspects of conservation.
>
> (Sally)

> I had to do a practical experience for my education, and I wanted a wildlife management practical.
>
> (Andrea)

> Personally, it would be an experience that could only enrich me and teach me new skills and further develop the ones I have; allowing me to carry on and pursue further work in the field of wildlife rehabilitation. ... I also want to get primate experience so I can work in the future with the Jane Goodall Foundation.
>
> (Amanda)

> I would be interested in following a career, which involves work with animals. When I return from Thailand I intend to begin a degree in zoology. I hope that the experience of working with animals for a prolonged period of time will prove a good basis for my university study.
>
> (Allan)

The volunteers' motivations to use volunteering, at least in part, as a means of gaining new skills and enhancing their career prospects are consistent with the literature. For instance, it has been argued that a desire for work experience can motivate volunteers (McSweeney and Alexander, 1996; Gazley, 2001); learning and skill development can be motivators for engaging in leisure and travel activities (Roggenbuck *et al.*, 1990; Weiler, 1991); and volunteer vacations appeal to tourists who value educational travel (Turner *et al.*, 2001).

Personal interest/personal development

More than half of the volunteers expressed a motivation that could be related to a personal interest or a desire to develop personally as a result of volunteering. The following are a number of such responses.

> An extended stay at the GRP would be an invaluable experience in itself.
>
> (Dean)

> More selfishly, I am fascinated by animals and especially primates and relish the chance to learn more about them.
>
> (Dianne)

> To get to know other people, and to extend my horizons.
>
> (Heidi)

> I really wanted to do something that I would probably never do the rest of my life ... working with animals that you're not very familiar with, it's so interesting ... and doing it on my own/taking that first step.
>
> (Hannah)

> I wanted to learn more about our ancestors [primates]; to learn more about their habitat and idiosyncrasies and to meet like-minded people.
>
> (Michelle)

> Because it's an interesting experience [to] work with scientists and learn something about gibbons. ... Volunteering can be a very good way to get to know the people from other countries; by working together people really learn from each other.
>
> (Max)

> I thought it would be a great experience for me personally.
>
> (Sally)

The opportunity to work with primates or gibbons more specifically and to meet and work with like-minded people were particularly valued by volunteers (also see Orams, 1996; Davis *et al.*, 1997; Reynolds and Braithwaite, 2001). Achieving personal benefits such as developing friendships, a sense of belonging and personal growth, and experiencing social interaction and camaraderie with like-minded people can motivate participation by tourists (Krippendorf, 1987; Muloin, 1998) and volunteers (Lerner, 1994; McSweeney and Alexander, 1996; Gazley, 2001).

GRP factors

The final motivation category, that of 'GRP factors', overlapped many of the above categories. It relates to why volunteers chose to volunteer at the GRP specifically, as opposed to an alternative project. The following are a range of their responses.

> The GRP's willingness to have me and the chance to work directly with gibbons.
>
> (Dianne)

Because I'm fascinated by primates.

(Angela)

The reason that I'd like to work at [the GRP] is because I'm very fond of apes and in the future I hope to find work with apes or other animals in the tropics.

(Brant)

It would be a great chance to learn about the Thai culture … and being able to work with primates 'hands-on'. It was the cheapest, and with primates.

(Sasha)

I decided to go to the GRP after speaking to a former volunteer in Holland who told me that he thought it to be a lot of fun and a good project.

(Heidi)

It being in Thailand, and being relatively cheap and very closely working with animals.

(Hannah)

I came here because it was the cheapest, and I wanted to work in an Asian country.

(Stacey)

I chose the GRP because it was the cheapest and it was far away.

(Jesse)

I chose the gibbon project because of the possibility to do my own inquiry there. I looked for a combination of tourism and nature protection and this is one.

(Monika)

It's 'hands on' conservation and it allowed me to stay for a relatively short time.

(Ross)

The volunteers' responses regarding why they chose the GRP specifically further support the preceding discussion and the claims that volunteers are particularly motivated by opportunities to work for and with animals/wildlife. Many volunteers were also motivated by the cheap cost of volunteering at the project and the project's location in Thailand. Thailand is a popular and relatively cheap tourist destination (Cummings, 1997), which affords great cultural, nature-based and ecotourism opportunities (Cummings, 1997; Li and Zhang, 1997; Weaver and Oppermann, 2000).

To further demonstrate how volunteers were influenced by more than one category of motivation, Table 7.1 focuses on one volunteer, Kate, illustrating how her participation at the GRP was in some way motivated by each of the five categories.

Conclusion

Too few studies have undertaken a detailed, long-term examination of volunteer vacations or wildlife tourism generally. Despite past criticisms that qualitative research case studies are generally descriptive and lack explanatory power, the participatory nature of ethnographic research, with fieldwork being undertaken for an extended period, can give great insights into wildlife tourism and volunteer tourism.

Table 7.1. The categories of motivation that influenced Kate.

Type of motivation	Volunteer (Kate's) response
Altruism	I wanted to help to conserve animals ... with a view to ultimately aiding their conservation and ensuring their long-term survival.
Travel	I really didn't want to spend my year out in England. I wanted to experience a new culture as well. I wanted to go somewhere totally different. ... Working at the project would allow me to experience a whole new culture and to see a beautiful country, so different to the one I live in.
Career development	My decision to volunteer was as part of an [optional] work placement year from uni. I thought that volunteering at any project was a great opportunity to learn more about conservation projects, their problems and strengths. I thought that by going abroad I would see how the project fitted into the community. ... I have a long-standing interest in conservation and animals, and intend to pursue this path as my career. ... I wanted a chance to work on another project before the end of my degree, in order to fully integrate practice with theory, therefore, the university work placement scheme is an ideal chance for me.
Personal interest/development	The project would also give me the opportunity to work and live closely with new people. I greatly look forward to meeting new people, sharing and learning from their experiences and outlooks.
GRP factors	Gibbons had always rated in my top five animals. I am also very interested in rehabilitation as a means of conservation, so the project just seemed like the ideal place to spend my work placement year. ... I hadn't expected to get an ideal project and here was an ideal project, it was with gibbons, it was rehab, and it was in Asia. I was like 'wow', it was an ideal project so I couldn't believe my luck.

At the GRP, volunteers have substantial opportunities to make positive contributions to wildlife conservation activities but a lengthy commitment is needed. The profile of volunteers at the GRP differs in many respects when compared to profiles presented in previous studies into wildlife tourism, ecotourism and volunteer vacations. The profile of volunteers at the GRP demonstrated a younger than average age of volunteers (25 years), a longer than average length of volunteering (around 4 months), a higher percentage of students and recent graduates among volunteers (55%) and a lower percentage of volunteers engaged in employment (17.5%).

At 4 months, the long length of the average volunteering stay may be a factor in explaining the differences between the profile of the GRP volunteers and participants on other wildlife tourism, ecotourism and volunteer vacation programmes. For instance, perhaps fewer employed or older people volunteered at the GRP because they had family and/or career or financial commitments, which they may not have been able or prepared to disrupt. In contrast, volunteering may have been easier to incorporate within the lifestyles of volunteers who were students, recent graduates or others not in employment. Perhaps, too, volunteering may have been undertaken at a time of transition in volunteers' lives, such as after leaving education, or on retirement. Furthermore, volunteers may have anticipated that the volunteering experience would be beneficial to their career plans.

The five GRP motivation categories were grounded in the data, and they were very similar to categories of motivation discussed in previous studies regarding volunteering of both an ongoing and episodic nature. For instance, in his theoretical examination of volunteer motivations, Parker (1997) identified four different types, being 'altruistic volunteering', 'market volunteering', 'cause serving volunteering' and 'leisure volunteering'. However, Parker did not classify these typologies as pure types, with overlap possible. Similarly, Wearing (1998) identified seven types of motivation in his analysis of participants undertaking a Youth Challenge International project, categorized as 'altruism', 'travel/adventure', 'personal growth', 'cultural exchange/learning', 'professional development', 'the YCI program' and 'right time/right place'. Finally, Gazley (2001) suggested that volunteer vacationers are likely to be motivated by altruism, personal development and the benefits associated with recreational travel.

It may well be that the people, situations and course of events described in this chapter are specific, perhaps unique to the GRP. However, other conservation projects relying heavily on volunteers might experience similarities in volunteers' profiles and motivations, particularly in contexts where volunteers bring Western values and interests to a host organization and community in a developing country. There is a tremendous opportunity for people to pursue research in an arena which on the surface promotes conservation principles in developing countries. Of course, the success of such projects must be the subject of future work.

Acknowledgements

The authors wish to acknowledge the support provided by a grant from the Winifred Violet Scott Trust, and the comments of anonymous reviewers of this chapter.

References

Bourgois, P.I. (1995) *In Search of Respect: Selling Crack in El Barrio*. Cambridge University Press, Cambridge.
Cummings, J. (1997) *Thailand: A Lonely Planet Travel Survival Kit*. Lonely Planet, Hawthorn, Australia.

Davis, D., Banks, S., Birtles, A., Valentine, P. and Cuthill, M. (1997) Whale sharks in Ningaloo Marine Park: managing tourism in an Australian marine protected area. *Tourism Management* 18(5), 259–271.

Gazley, B. (2001) Volunteer vacationers and what research can tell us about them. *E Volunteerism: The Electronic Journal of the Volunteerism Community* 1(2). Available at: www.e-volunteerism.com

Hutchings, C. (1996) In Patagonia. *Geographical Magazine* 68(4), 28–31.

Krippendorf, J. (1987) *The Holiday Makers: Understanding the Impact of Leisure and Travel*. Butterworth-Heinemann, Oxford, UK.

Lerner, S. (1994) Local stewardship: training ground for an environmental vanguard. *Alternatives* 20(2), 14–19.

Li, Z. and Zhang, W. (1997). Thailand: the dynamic growth of Thai tourism. In: Go, F. and Jenkins, C. (eds) *Tourism and Economic Development in Asia and Australia*. Cassell, London, pp. 286–303.

MacCannell, D. (1976) *The Tourist: A New Theory of the Leisure Class*. Macmillan, London.

McSweeney, P. and Alexander, D. (1996) *Managing Volunteers Effectively*. Ashgate, Aldershot, UK.

Mihaly, M. (1996) Volunteer vacations. *Industry Week* 6 May, 38–40.

Milne, S. (1998) Tourism and sustainable development: exploring the global-local nexus. In: Hall, C.M. and Lew, A. (eds) *Sustainable Tourism: A Geographical Perspective*. Longman, Harlow, UK, pp. 35–48.

Muloin, S. (1998) Wildlife tourism: the psychological benefits of whale watching. *Pacific Tourism Review* 2, 199–213.

Obua, J. and Harding, D. (1996) Visitor characteristics and attitudes towards Kibale National Park, Uganda. *Tourism Management* 17(7), 495–505.

Orams, M. (1996) A conceptual model of tourist–wildlife interactions: the case for education as a management strategy. *Australian Geographer* 27(1), 39–51.

Parker, S. (1997) Volunteering: altruism, markets, causes and leisure. *World Leisure and Recreation* 3, 4–5.

Pearce, D. (1995) *Tourism Today: A Geographical Analysis*. Longman, Harlow, UK.

Reynolds, P. and Braithwaite, D. (2001) Towards a conceptual framework for wildlife tourism. *Tourism Management* 22, 31–42.

Roggenbuck, J., Loomis, R. and Dagostino, J. (1990) The learning benefits of leisure. *Journal of Leisure Research* 22(2), 112–124.

Russell, C. (1995) The social construction of orangutans: an ecotourist experience. *Society and Animals* 3(2), 151–169.

Stewart-Cox, B. (1995) *Wild Thailand*. New Holland, London.

Taylor, S. and Bogdan, R. (1998) *Introduction to Qualitative Research Methods: A Guidebook and Resource*. Wiley, New York.

Turner, R., Miller, G., and Gilbert, D. (2001) The role of UK charities and the tourism industry. *Tourism Management* 22, 463–472.

Wearing, S. (1998) The nature of ecotourism: the place of self, identity and communities as interacting elements of alternative tourism experiences. PhD thesis, Charles Sturt University, Albury, Australia.

Weaver, D. and Oppermann, M. (2000) *Tourism Management*. Jacaranda Wiley, Milton, Australia.

Weiler, B. (1991) Learning or leisure? The growth of travel-study opportunities in Australia. *Australian Journal of Leisure and Recreation* 1(1), 19–22.

Weiler, B. and Richins, H. (1995) Extreme, extravagant and elite: a profile of ecotourists on earthwatch expeditions. *Tourism Recreation Research* 20(1), 29–36.

Wight, P. (1996) North American ecotourists: market profile and trip characteristics. *Journal of Travel Research* 34(4), 2–10.

8 Discovering Self and Discovering Others Through the Taita Discovery Centre Volunteer Tourism Programme, Kenya

A. LEPP

Recreation, Park and Tourism Management, Kent State University, Kent, Ohio, USA

Volunteer tourism has been described as bilateral in nature in that it aims to benefit both the host and the guest (Wearing, 2001). Certainly the obvious aim of volunteer tourism is to improve the condition of a particular society or natural environment through the deliberate and organized efforts of volunteer tourists. What is less obvious, however, is that well-managed volunteer tourism aims to benefit the volunteer as well. Volunteer tourism has been shown to provide a range of benefits to volunteers including enjoyment, satisfaction, self-confidence, cross-cultural exchange, the development of new skills, social networking and an increased interest in social and environmental justice (McGehee, 2002; Stoddart and Rogerson, 2004; McGehee and Santos, 2005). Studying volunteer tourists in Costa Rica, Wearing (2001) noted three important and interrelated benefits: increased awareness of self; increased awareness of others; and, ultimately, personal growth and development. In the study, Wearing noted that the intense interactions that volunteer tourists have with a destination's host community and natural environment contribute to the production of these benefits. In this way, volunteer tourism is unique and provides opportunities for growth and development not available in a typical packaged tour.

Personal growth and development has long been recognized as an expected benefit of tourism (Pearce, 1985). However, the exact conditions which produce that growth and development are not as easily understood. Recently, Pearce and Lee (2005) found that the most experienced of travellers identified 'host-site involvement and nature seeking' as the tourism contexts best suited for personal growth and development (p. 235). Importantly, these two activities are central to volunteer tourism. Indeed, Wearing (2001) identified two distinct types of volunteer tourists: community volunteers and wildlife volunteers. As he described them, community volunteers 'volunteer in an organized way to undertake holidays that might involve aiding or alleviating the material poverty of some groups in society... or research into aspects of society' and wildlife volunteers 'volunteer in an organized way to undertake holidays that might involve the restoration of certain environments or research into aspects of the environment' (p. 1). Certainly both types of volunteer tourists undertake challenges ripe with opportunities for the production of personal benefits. Yet on the surface, these two types of volunteer tourists appear to be quite different. If differences exist, might these two types of volunteer tourists benefit from the experience in different ways?

To date, the distinction between community volunteers and wildlife volunteers has been based primarily upon the activities in which the volunteers participate. Therefore, there is a need for a greater description of these two types of volunteer tourists. For example, they may be distinguishable by previous travel experience, previous volunteer experience, motivations and perceived benefits. Certainly previous tourist typologies such as Cohen's (1972) typology of international tourists have provided a wealth of sociological and psychological insights as well as significant management implications. Therefore, in consideration of the above, research into volunteer tourism was conducted at Kenya's Taita Discovery Centre (TDC) during June and July 2006. TDC has been facilitating community volunteers and wildlife volunteers for over a decade. The purpose of the case study was threefold: first, to describe TDC's programme and its contribution to community development and wildlife conservation; second, to describe TDC's community volunteers and wildlife volunteers and to identify similarities and differences which might exist between them; and third, to identify any benefits the volunteers received as well as the conditions which produced them.

Setting

The TDC is located in south-east Kenya in the heart of the arid yet wildly animate Tsavo ecosystem. At the turn of the 20th century, the Tsavo's international reputation was inauspiciously born as its lions terrorized workers and slowed construction of the Kenya–Uganda railway. The Tsavo is still famous for its lions, although ironically these dangerous predators are what attract so many tourists to the area today. The 43,000 km² Tsavo ecosystem is relatively untrammelled and provides critical habitat for large mammals, which need vast open spaces for their survival. Wildlife is abundant in the Tsavo and there are important environmental, cultural and economic (tourism) reasons to protect it. As a result, nearly half of this ecosystem is preserved in two national parks, Tsavo East and Tsavo West. However, these two parks, and thus the Tsavo ecosystem, are divided by the Nairobi–Mombassa highway and large tracts of private and communal land to the south of the highway. This private and communal land rests upon a natural migration route for wildlife which moves from one park to the next following the seasonal patterns of rain and drought. TDC is located along the wildlife migration route amidst the matrix of communal and private land. By working closely with the varied landowners, TDC aspires to create the largest non-governmental nature conservancy in East Africa – a protected wildlife corridor spanning over 16,000 km² and connecting Tsavo East and West National Parks.

TDC's research indicates that nearly 1000 elephants use this corridor annually in addition to lions, cheetah, hyena, giraffe, buffalo, zebra, various antelope and a host of less charismatic but equally important species of wildlife. This illustrates the importance of protecting the corridor. Yet more importantly, the corridor is home to a growing human population. In the six villages where TDC has projects, there are approximately 12,000 people, most of whom are subsistence farmers or cattle keepers. Although strong and proud, these people are among the world's poorest. Their poverty stems from a variety of sources. For more than 100 years, Kenyans were disempowered as colonial subjects of England. After independence in 1963, economic development has been hampered by a corrupt and ineffective central government. Also perhaps more directly, the harshness of the arid Tsavo ecosystem, with its periodic droughts and sandy soils, makes it difficult to earn a living from the land. Resources are scarce, and to compound the problem, humans and wildlife are competing with each other for what is available. Crop raiding by elephants and livestock predation by lions are common occurrences with devastating results. For example, a primary school teacher from the area explained to the researcher with certain bitterness how elephants destroyed his entire mango plantation and maize crop in a single night. Understandably, such incidents create negative attitudes about wildlife among local people. Thus, wildlife conservation is a tremendous challenge.

It is this challenge that TDC is confronting and hopes to overcome. Importantly, TDC recognizes that conservation is as much a social process as it is an ecological process. Therefore, in addition to employing the biological sciences as conservation tools, TDC strives to involve local people in conservation, particularly in the receipt of conservation's benefits. This two-pronged approach to conservation is made possible largely by the efforts of volunteer tourists. They are attracted to TDC by the opportunity to contribute labour, ideas and money to wildlife conservation and related causes. As the manager of TDC's wildlife conservation programme explained, 'this is a new type of tourist, they are selfless, they really want to make a direct contribution and they are apart from the conventional tourist'. For these volunteer tourists, TDC offers two distinct opportunities: a science-based wildlife conservation programme and a community development programme. In a given year, TDC facilitates roughly 40 wildlife volunteers and 15 community volunteers. Most tourists volunteer from 1 to 3 months.

The wildlife conservation programme is the most popular. It offers volunteers the opportunity to live at TDC's headquarters and work on a daily basis with TDC's well-trained naturalists towards long-term wildlife conservation goals. The primary task of the wildlife volunteers is to collect scientific data in order to understand how wildlife uses the proposed conservation area. Special attention is given to understanding the movements of lions and elephants, an ongoing census of the proposed conservation area's wildlife, and monitoring human and wildlife use at critical watering holes. In addition, research into vegetation, soil ecology and invertebrates is also being conducted. As a result, wildlife volunteers spend their days using radio telemetry to track collared lions, photographing and identifying individual elephants and mapping their movements, learning and using wildlife sampling techniques and, of course, recording and entering all data into computers for analysis. A unique but important part of the experience is the interaction that volunteers have with TDC's all Kenyan staff. Volunteers and staff live and dine together 'family style' at TDC's headquarters. Thus, opportunities for cross-cultural exchange are abundant.

TDC's community development programme is for volunteers interested in social causes who want a deep cross-cultural experience. Community volunteers stay in the villages, not TDC headquarters. They shop in local markets, prepare their own food and integrate themselves as best they can into village life. This is possible thanks to a partnership between TDC and six local communities whose populations are critical for the long-term success of conservation in the area. In each community, a cooperative of local people was formed and then provided with assistance from the African Wildlife Foundation (AWF) to construct simple tourist accommodations. The community contributed 40% to the project and AWF contributed 60%. The accommodations were constructed using local materials, methods and labour. TDC then books these accommodations for the entire year and uses them to house their community volunteers. Each cooperative grosses US$6000 per year from the project. Some of this money goes to the maintenance, repair and improvement of the facilities; however, there are annual dividends for the cooperatives' members. More importantly, the volunteers who stay in these accommodations immerse themselves in community life and lend their expertise and labour to a variety of development projects. TDC's community volunteers have rebuilt local schools, trained local teachers, built a library and vocational training centre, made improvements at local health clinics such as installing biomedical waste incinerators, organized youth football leagues and launched educational campaigns targeting themes as diverse as AIDS and garbage collection. While there are a few ongoing projects volunteers may contribute to, they are free to develop and implement their own projects based on their abilities, interests and the needs of the community.

Methods

The researcher was a guest at TDC for 2½ weeks during the months of June and July 2006. The researcher divided his time equally between studying the experience of wildlife volunteers and the experience of community volunteers. In studying wildlife volunteers, he actively participated with them in conservation duties, shared meals with them at TDC and engaged in many informal conversations. In studying community volunteers, the researcher travelled to the villages to observe their various projects and interactions with local people. The researcher shared meals with the community volunteers in the homes of local people and engaged in many informal conversations. Throughout the research, informal conversations were dutifully recorded in a field notebook and elaborated upon in a journal later that same day. Formal interviews were an important means of data collection as well. All volunteers present during the time of the study were interviewed. This amounted to three wildlife and four community volunteers. All volunteers were young adults. Three were university students, one was a recent university graduate and three were working professionals. Five were female and two were male. The interviews targeted the volunteer experience and were conversational in style, yet a list of predetermined questions was used to guide each conversation through areas of interest. Questions included: Do you consider yourself a tourist in your role here? How would you describe your experience at TDC? What makes this experience possible? How have you benefited from this experience? All interviews were tape recorded and transcribed. Interviews lasted from 45 to 90 min. In addition, 63 programme evaluation forms from the previous year were analysed. Evaluation forms contained several meaningful open-ended questions such as 'what was the best aspect of your experience?' Furthermore, three managers and two local informants were interviewed about various aspects of TDC. Lastly, each volunteer was e-mailed six open-ended questions approximately 3 months after completing their tour. Questions targeted the impact of the experience. Six volunteers responded to the e-mail in detail. All data were analysed with qualitative methods allowing for the emergence of central themes. The purpose of the following sections is to describe TDC's wildlife and community volunteer tourists, their perception of benefits and the conditions which produced them. Thus, it is to a description of these volunteer tourists that the chapter now turns.

The Volunteer Tourists

Adhering to the maxim that conservation is a social as well as ecological process, TDC relies heavily on both community volunteers and wildlife volunteers to accomplish its goal of creating the largest non-governmental nature conservancy in East Africa. Thus, TDC provides fertile ground for comparing the two. This comparison suggests that while similarities exist, there is a significant difference that makes each type unique.

One similarity among the wildlife and community volunteers at TDC is that neither type wanted to do anything 'touristy'. In fact, there was an anti-tourism theme evident in every interview. As Phoebe, a wildlife volunteer explained, 'I don't like touristic things so I didn't want to do a safari – just driving around in a car taking pictures and then going back home'. Similarly, William, also a wildlife volunteer, said: 'I always wanted to go to Kenya and see animals but not like a tourist. I wanted to have a part in the work of the guides.' Interestingly, William travelled to Greece to relax on the beach after finishing his work at TDC because, as he put it, he 'deserved a holiday'. Echoing those sentiments, Thomas, a community volunteer, explained that he came to TDC because he 'did not want to go on a real holiday'. Marilyn, also a community volunteer, explained that she wanted 'an experience that no tourist could get'. She added:

> For the people here I am not a tourist. And it is so obvious. Last week when the Americans came to [the village] it was so strange, I had the feeling that I was a local and they were the tourists.

Thus, both types of volunteer tourists seem motivated to have an experience outside the realm of traditional tourism. TDC management recognizes this characteristic and in response avoids the word 'tourism' or 'tourist' in communications with the volunteers. As one manager clearly stated, 'we try to do nothing touristy'.

Despite their common interest in alternative tourism, a clear distinction separates the community and wildlife volunteers interviewed at TDC. While each had substantial international experience, community volunteers were more accomplished travellers. As a result, they were looking for greater challenges and more novel experiences. Marilyn indicated the importance of a challenging community development project stating:

> One challenge of travelling is staying in a new community but I have already done that, I have done it so much. I don't have to prove to myself that I can do that. I need the bigger challenge of a project.

Kimberly, also a community volunteer, hinted at the importance of novelty, saying:

> I have already been to Kenya and have seen all the animals here. I wanted to do something different. I think working with people is more interesting. If I was a wildlife volunteer I would get bored just driving around looking at animals every day.

In contrast, each of the wildlife volunteers interviewed indicated that the novelty of the community programme might be overwhelming. William made this point by saying:

> If I went to the community it would be very different. There I would be trying to survive in a place so different than home that I would have to think about how to survive. Here I go to lunch, then I do computer work, monitor the animals, it's leisure, I have no worries.

For William, the novelty of the community was a deterrent while the structure of the wildlife programme was an attraction. The perception of security was also important for the wildlife volunteers. Grace contrasted TDC's base camp where the wildlife volunteers stay with the nearby communities by saying: 'Here it is secure and I am not for staying in the community yet so I thought the wildlife programme would be good enough for the first experience.' Interestingly, Grace left open the possibility of someday volunteering in the community once she acquired more experience.

Management has recognized these differences as well. TDC's director observed that 'a lot of people who go on the community programme have travelled around a lot already. Many have already visited Kenya and seen the animals and now they want to get to know the people'. Concerning the wildlife programme, he stated:

> I think it is easier to come out and do a wildlife program because there is no having to worry about living with other people or having to get to know people in the village. [wildlife volunteers] are instructed what to do. So, it is much easier.

In fact, the wildlife programme, in order to be scientifically rigorous, must be very structured. This structure seems to be an attraction for less experienced or less adventurous tourists.

Thus, interviews as well as management's observations indicate a difference between wildlife and community volunteers at TDC. Community volunteers tend to be more experienced travellers in search of greater challenges. Among the small sample interviewed at TDC, three of the four community volunteers had previously travelled to sub-Saharan Africa while none of the wildlife volunteers had. Likewise, two of the four community volunteers had previous volunteer tourism experience while none of the wildlife volunteers had any. In addition, novelty seems to be a greater motivator for the community volunteers and therefore they may be able to rationalize higher levels of perceived risk in the form of cultural differences. This relationship between a tourist's preference for novelty and tolerance of certain perceived risks has been identified in previous research (Lepp and Gibson, 2003). At TDC, management has reacted to these differences by allowing the community volunteers greater freedom and independence. For example, community volunteers choose which of the six communities they will live in as well as the particular project they will contribute to. If their interests are not represented in any of the existing projects, they are free to develop their own unique project. In contrast, the wildlife volunteers' programme is very structured. Each day is planned in advance by TDC staff in order to assure a comfortable stay while achieving the scientific objectives of the project.

The Intrapersonal Benefits of Volunteering at TDC

Despite this difference, TDC's community and wildlife volunteers benefited from their experiences in remarkably similar ways. All volunteers mentioned discovering self and discovering others as benefits. The purpose of this section is to describe these benefits in detail as well as the conditions which produced them. Referencing Pearce's (1985) travel career ladder, which posits that less experienced travellers focus on satisfying lower-level needs like food and safety while more experienced travellers focus on satisfying higher-level needs like personal growth and development, Wearing (2004) suggested that volunteer tourists would also be likely to focus on satisfying higher-level needs. This was the case with both TDC's community and wildlife volunteers. For example, Phoebe explained her motivation for travel saying, 'I took these three months to change. My life [at home] is a good life so I was not obliged to do this but I wanted to do something different and to see if it will change my life'. Certainly the satisfaction of higher-level needs like personal growth and development results from engaging in activities that are challenging, test an individual's skills and require prolonged effort (Csikszentmihalyi, 1990). Such are the characteristics of TDC's volunteer programmes. Despite differences in the 'nuts and bolts' of the community and wildlife programmes, all volunteers mentioned similar challenges related to adapting to life in rural Kenya and working with Kenyan counterparts. It was this cross-cultural context that enabled volunteers to discover much about themselves and others as they worked together towards TDC's conservation and community development goals.

Discovering Self

All volunteers interviewed were struck by the setting of their experience and their interactions with the people in it. Community volunteers lived in villages with no electricity or running water. Village houses were made of earthen bricks and surrounded by small gardens struggling against the heat. Shops contained essentials, the only luxury items being a few varieties of soda or beer. The streets were unpaved, rutted and filled with barefoot, playing children. Schools had dirt floors, some classrooms had no walls and where there were walls they were sometimes unpainted. Also the villagers, from whom counterparts would be recruited, were likely to be focused first on securing basic needs. This stark contrast between the village and the volunteers' home towns grabbed their attention and forced a reflection on the experience. Thomas was immediately struck by the differences. He reported feeling:

> Not ok by the thought that we were going up there with our new backpacks full of new clothes, a cell phone, a charger; and people see us with that stuff coming to live in their village and it must be very frustrating for them because they have nothing.

As a result, he reflected intensely on issues related to rural African development. Importantly, his reflections were not in isolation but informed by numerous conversations with a villager Thomas eventually described as 'a real close friend'. For every volunteer, confronting and pondering these inequalities was a significant challenge, and the process of doing so yielded important new understandings of themselves and others. Marilyn saw the value in this when she said 'living in rural Kenya is a great experience, understanding how poor people live and how they struggle to get through the day is healthy'.

The wildlife volunteers, who spent much of their time surveying the Tsavo ecosystem, were also struck by contrasts – the contrast between wild and primitive nature and their developed homeland. For Phoebe, this forced a reflection on the hubris of humanity. She stated:

> In our country we control nature. We control all things, the weather, the water. We have air conditioning. But here nature has control. That's different. When I see the wildlife, I feel very little. So I feel this nature must be conserved. It is very important. We forget these things in our countries.

To which the researcher asked: 'Why is it important to feel little?' She replied: 'Because humans think we are superheroes but when you see an elephant you see more clearly. People think that they are clever; instead, we must be always modest. It is important to realize that we are little.' Wildlife volunteers were also forced into reflection through their occasional visits to local villages. For example, in casual conversation, the researcher asked Grace if she intended to visit the neighbouring villages. She replied: 'Yes, because you have to know how lucky you are to be born on the other side of the world.' Most significantly, wildlife volunteers learned about the difficulties of rural Kenyan life through regular conversations with TDC staff. Grace stated that because of these conversations she 'learned how people live here and how hard they work and how long they spend without seeing their family; and all that just tells me that I have to rethink all my life and try to fix it better'. Thus, the community setting, the wilderness setting and interactions with local people forced volunteers into rethinking their own lives and the values they had previously accepted. This was the first step towards growth and development.

Throughout the research, Grace continually referred to herself as 'a work in progress'. Clearly, growth and development were priorities of hers. To catalyse the process, she placed herself in an environment that forced reflection. She explained it this way: 'I came to Kenya to lose my reference. I wanted to feel unbalanced. Europe doesn't do the trick, you can't lose your reference there.' Striking a similar note, Marilyn said: 'I do believe you grow every time you put yourself in such a strange situation.' While these quotes emphasize the importance of a novel setting, it is the reflection which the setting triggers that results in new discoveries. A common discovery was that many of the problems that volunteers wrestle with in their daily lives were trivial compared to the problems confronted by rural Kenyans. Phoebe explained it this way:

> When I have a problem and see the life of others in Kenya and these people are happy, I say I do not have a problem. So at home people have more things but are not always happy. There is a good lesson there.

Likewise, Heather, a community volunteer, took a life lesson away from her interactions with Kenyans, saying:

> I am very impressed with African women, they are too strong. They are so tough. The women are very strong and even though they have difficulties and struggle, they are just smiling. Even though [my home country] is now highly developed, it has the highest suicide rate. Many people commit suicide. Like on the train, so many times the train stops because people jump in front. So we are suffering even though we are so rich economically. We are not happy. [My] people are not happy. But women here are just laughing and smiling even with so much difficulty. But in my country many people have a mental disease. That is a lesson to take home.

It seems that confronting global inequality and witnessing the resiliency of Kenyans in the face of it enabled volunteers to put their own problems in perspective. This is a benefit of TDC's programme which transfers readily into volunteers' ordinary lives. In an e-mail, sent months after returning home, Kimberly explained:

> Now when something goes wrong, I can put it in perspective, I can see it as small compared to what I encountered in Kenya, I am a little more realistic now. And all these changes are caused by the contact I had with the local people.

Importantly, Kimberly's comments emphasize the people and the setting as the source of change. By volunteering in rural Kenya, individuals are forced to think about themselves in relation to a world vastly different than the one they had grown comfortable with at home. As Grace mentioned, this led her to 'rethink' her life. Similarly, Phoebe said: 'I have a lot of questions about Africa and my own life.' Often, this reflection led volunteers to discover that their current life direction lacked meaning. By building on their TDC experience, some volunteers began plotting a more meaningful course. For example, William, in casual conversation asked the researcher: 'Do you think you could do your job forever?' This question led to a discussion of his chosen profession – law. He confessed he no longer believed he could do that forever. He explained he had been thinking a lot about it since volunteering at TDC. When the researcher asked why he chose law originally, he explained: '[T]he profession provides money and prestige but now I don't think that will keep me happy.' Later, in the formal interview, William readdressed the issue saying: 'Here I think about lots of things that I don't normally think about, here I think about my future. I think about how I can contribute to the world.' He then added: 'All the things I have been thinking about here will be interesting to continue in my life. For example, I would like to continue working for wildlife [conservation].' Similarly, Grace reflected:

> I have a great job. But now I know I don't like it. ... I don't like the company. I like the people. I like what I do, but I don't agree with the culture of the company and now I know. It is all money. Money is the first thing, so now I know it is not good.

Kimberly, a recent college graduate with a new job waiting at home, realized that she would 'like to work and live in Kenya one day if that would be possible'. And writing in an e-mail, Heather described an actual change she enacted as a result of her experience volunteering:

> I came to think that it's better for the poor to take risks, to borrow money and to take the responsibility to pay it back. The poor can be more independent and self-sufficient that way. After realizing this, I made a new goal – I decided to write my thesis about microfinance and I'm also interested in pro-poor markets. If I didn't go to Kenya this summer, I would not be interested in this topic.

As a final example, Phoebe discovered this about herself: 'I know that I am now ready to have children. I would like to transmit all my experiences to them, to travel with them and to teach them about the importance of respecting others.' Indeed, many volunteers felt their personal discoveries were valuable, life-changing and worth sharing. This was particularly evident in what volunteers discovered about the rural Kenyans they interacted with on a daily basis.

Discovering Others

In addition to discovering self, volunteers discovered much about Kenyans and Africans in general. These discoveries resulted from the intense cross-cultural interactions which are at the heart of the volunteer tourism experience. TDC's director explained it like this:

> The purpose of [volunteer tourism] is to get a lot out of the experience and really to just benefit from it. I mean, it isn't all about seeing a project completed. A lot of it is about that meeting of minds which occurs when people come together and share an experience. It is really important that when these people go back to their home countries that they become a little expert, in a small way, about Africa. About what Africa is really like. Not about what they are seeing on television, nor read in newspapers. Here they get to know some Kenyan people for a month,

to experience their warmth and everything and they see that everybody here
is struggling, but they are still smiling. Then they go back to the UK or where
ever it is and when they hear people say 'oh the Africans are such and such,'
bringing them down, they can turn around and say, 'well actually it isn't like that,
I have been there'. So that is worth more than painting a school building. But
it was while they were painting the school building and working along side the
locals that they came to know this. The project is the vehicle that provides [the
volunteer tourists] with the opportunity to get to know Kenyan people.

A wildlife volunteer unknowingly echoed the director's final point in response to
the question 'Do you feel like you are working here?'. The volunteer responded:
'No. I feel there is an exchange taking place. I am from France, I speak about my
country. Kenyans speak about their country. It is not work.' Thus, the project, by
deeply embedding the volunteer tourist in a unique setting with unique people,
encourages the cross-cultural exchange and reflection from which benefits flow.

TDC's director identified three benefits related to discovering others: an
increased understanding and respect for Kenyans and Africans; the correc-
tion of common misconceptions about Africans; and an inspiration to correct
misconceptions about Africans after returning home. In fact, these benefits
emerged naturally from the analysis of this study's data. In interviews and casual
conversation, every volunteer expressed an increased understanding of Kenyans
and Africans. Kimberly wrote in an e-mail that 'travelling to Kenya was an
unforgettable experience that made me a person with a lot more knowledge
about another rich culture'. Heather discovered that 'Kenyans are very creative.
They showed me how to make a toothbrush and medicine from plants. They
can make whatever they need from nature'. Likewise, Grace said: 'I realize that
there are a lot of educated people in Kenya. The TDC guides are just like ency-
clopedias!' William noted: 'I better understand the Africans and the problems we
can meet here together.' In an e-mail about what she learned at TDC, Phoebe
wrote: 'I learned that we are all the same. The only difference is that we are
not all born in the same place!' Considering these comments, perhaps Marilyn
expressed a fundamental truth of volunteer tourism when she said: '[T]ravelling
as a volunteer gives you the opportunity to get more knowledge about the country and the people – a knowledge you will not get if you are just a tourist.'

Misconceptions about Africa are abundant in Western culture (Keim,
1999). Therefore, some volunteers were surprised when their initial experience of Africa did not conform to preconceived notions. For example, Phoebe
professed: 'In Kenya, I did not see only problems. There is humanity. People
there have a lot of respect and take time to live.' This suggests that before
the TDC experience, Phoebe had reason to believe that she would encounter
mostly problems in Kenya and humanity would be suppressed by the weight
of them. This is certainly a message put forward by the Western media (Hawk,
1992) and it is most likely reinforced by volunteers' friends and family. This was
pointed out by Kimberly who explained:

People who haven't been to Africa can not imagine what it is like. People just
think everyone is in a mud hut with no electricity. It is different ... it is more
developed than what people think. And most people have a wrong idea about
the African people. They think they are not friendly. Every time you hear watch

your back, be careful. I don't think people in this village will steal from us. Maybe in a big city but that is in every culture. I think people at home have the wrong perception.

Another misconception was that Africans are lazy and this is the cause of their poverty. Thomas said:

I used to think that people in Africa couldn't live. All I knew was that they were poor with no money and I didn't think they had the luxury to have a life. I didn't think they did work or ever tried to make things better. But already I see that many do work and try to make things better.

No doubt, such misconceptions contribute to the unfavourable opinions many Western people still have of Africans. There is evidence to suggest that by correcting these misconceptions, the TDC experience improves volunteers' opinions of Africans and reduces prejudice. Grace came to this conclusion while reflecting on her experience during the interview. As she put it:

I've learned a lot, more than I thought I would, and not only about animals and wildlife but about people. I had a subconscious prejudice about black people. And I don't have any friends who are black people. And now that is all gone. I'm not saying I didn't like black people but I just didn't know any and didn't feel like meeting any, now here I don't see the difference between black and white people. So that tells me I have grown up a lot!

Lastly, as TDC's director suggested, these benefits gained from 'discovering others' can transfer to volunteers' everyday lives. For example, volunteers may be more likely to correct misconceptions of Africa when encountering them. Phoebe expressed this desire saying:

If I can understand this way of life in this part of Kenya, then I could explain what I understand to my friends and then maybe others will begin to understand what I see. ... I think it is important to transmit my experience.

Or, volunteers may try harder to understand people of different backgrounds. As Grace mentioned: 'At home I just didn't feel like going to [people of African descent]. Now maybe I'll do it, if only to understand them better.' And, finally, as Marilyn said, cross-cultural exchange develops skills helpful for discovering others wherever you are:

When you travel as a volunteer you really get to know people and their culture. This is a foundation for understanding others and why they do things in a certain way. It is something that you cannot learn just by reading. ... When you have greater understanding of others' culture, it makes it easier to understand and meet new people – not only people from other cultures, but also people in your everyday life.

Conclusion

TDC's purpose is to create the largest non-governmental nature conservancy in East Africa – a wildlife corridor spanning over 16,000 km² and connecting Tsavo East and West National Parks. While the proposed corridor is used by an abundance of wildlife, it is also home to more than 12,000 people. TDC recognizes that protection of the corridor is not possible without the interest and support of these people. Therefore, scientific wildlife conservation techniques are used in conjunction with socially just community development strategies. TDC accomplishes its conservation and development objectives with the use of volunteer tourists. To date, the work of the volunteer tourists has provided tremendous benefits for the region including the identification of seasonal patterns of wildlife usage of the corridor. Such information will be valuable for the scientific management of the proposed conservancy and may actually help reduce crop-raiding and livestock predation. Direct community benefits include income generation, the improvement of school buildings, educational curriculum and health clinics. Yet, the relationship is bilateral, for the volunteer tourists benefit in tremendous ways as well. The purpose of this case study has been to describe TDC's community and wildlife volunteers, their perception of benefits and the conditions which produced them. Much of what was learned conforms to the previous, albeit limited, studies of volunteer tourism.

Previous research has identified two primary types of volunteer tourists, wildlife conservation and community development (Wearing, 2001). Both types are active at TDC. This case study suggests that both types are similar in that they are seeking an alternative tourism experience. Furthermore, volunteer tourists are sometimes reluctant to identify themselves with traditional tourists. This has been previously reported (Wearing, 2001; Stoddart and Rogerson, 2004). However, this case study suggests that community volunteers may be more accomplished and adventurous travellers than their wildlife counterparts. TDC's management accommodates these differences by providing wildlife volunteers with a secure environment complete with familiar indicators of home such as western-style food. In addition, the wildlife programme is very structured. In contrast, community volunteers are immersed in a village setting where they have complete freedom in choosing a project and organizing their daily routine. They only return to TDC headquarters on weekends.

Despite differences in the wildlife and community programmes and the volunteer tourists who participate in them, this case study found that all participants benefited from the experience in similar ways. Wearing's (2001) analysis of volunteer tourists in Costa Rica found that an intense interaction between the volunteer tourist, the host community and the natural environment was central to the production of benefits. The study at hand confirmed this to be true of both wildlife and community volunteers. Volunteers indicated that intense and regular interaction with the setting and the people in it forced reflection. In both leisure and adventure contexts research suggests that reflection is the key to benefiting from novel experiences (Lee *et al.*, 1994; Priest and Glass, 1997). Through reflection, volunteers were able to realize several benefits from the experience. Benefits related to a discovery of self and others were the most common. Specifically, volunteers discovered that their daily struggles were often trivial compared to the daily struggles of a rural Kenyan. They discovered that much less was required for happiness. As a result, they developed a new perspective on life at home. They discovered an intrinsic need for meaning and purpose in their lives. This discovery motivated some volunteers to make positive changes in their lives. As a result of the experience, volunteers developed a greater understanding of Kenyans and Africans in general. For most volunteers, previous misconceptions about Africa were proven incorrect. This led to a greater respect for Africans and an increased tolerance for people of different cultural and ethnic backgrounds. Similarly, volunteers reported an increased awareness of issues related to development and global inequality. As a result of these discoveries, volunteers became more complex individuals. Awareness of this added complexity was cathartic and explains the 'tears of joy' that TDC's managers described often witnessing at the conclusion of a volunteer's tour. Finally, there was evidence that these benefits transferred to the volunteers' daily lives after returning home. These results support and expand upon the findings of previous research into the benefits of volunteer tourism (Wearing, 2001; McGehee, 2002; McGehee and Santos, 2005).

Considering the benefits received by the tourists, the environment and the local people, the essence of TDC's volunteer tourism experience is summarized nicely by William, a wildlife volunteer, who said: 'When you do for others and you do for yourself you make a good experience.'

Acknowledgements

The author would like to thank, first, Kent State University's Center for International and Intercultural Education for generously funding this study and, second, the volunteers who participated.

References

Cohen, E. (1972) Toward a sociology of international tourism. *Social Research* 39, 164–182.
Csikszentmihalyi, M. (1990) *Flow: The Psychology of Optimal Experience.* HarperCollins, New York.
Hawk, B. (ed.) (1992) *Africa's Media Image.* Praeger, New York.
Keim, C. (1999) *Mistaking Africa: Curiosities and Inventions of the American Mind.* Westview Press, Boulder, Colorado.
Lee, Y., Dattilo, J. and Howard, D. (1994) The complex and dynamic nature of leisure experience. *Journal of Leisure Research* 26, 195–211.
Lepp, A. and Gibson, H. (2003) Tourist roles, perceived risk and international tourism. *Annals of Tourism Research* 30, 606–624.
McGehee, N.G. (2002) Alternative tourism and social movements. *Annals of Tourism Research* 29, 124–143.
McGehee, N.G. and Santos, C.A. (2005) Social change, discourse and volunteer tourism. *Annals of Tourism Research* 32, 760–779.
Pearce, P.L. (1985) A systematic comparison of travel related roles. *Human Relations* 38, 1001–1011.
Pearce, P.L. and Lee, U.I. (2005) Developing the travel career approach to tourist motivation. *Journal of Travel Research* 43, 226–237.
Priest, S. and Glass, M. (1997) *Effective Leadership in Adventure Programming.* Human Kinetics, Champaign, Illinois.

Stoddart, H. and Rogerson, C.M. (2004) Volunteer tourism: the case of Habitat for Humanity South Africa. *GeoJournal* 60, 311–318.

Wearing, S. (2001) *Volunteer Tourism: Experiences that Make a Difference*. CAB International, Wallingford, UK.

Wearing, S. (2004) Examining best practice in volunteer tourism. In: Stebbins, R.A. and Graham, M. (eds) *Volunteering as Leisure, Leisure as Volunteering: An International Assessment*. CAB International, Wallingford, UK, pp. 209–224.

9 Negotiated Selves: Exploring the Impact of Local–Global Interactions on Young Volunteer Travellers

A. MATTHEWS

School of Humanities and Social Sciences, University of Newcastle, Callaghan, Australia

What else does travelling mean? For me, it is the notion of venturing into a new world...seeing things you wouldn't see in Australia....What I love is those moments that show a culture for what it really is...don't get me wrong, I still marvel at great scenery such as the stunning splendour of the Italian Alps...or the raw energy of Katherine Gorge. It is, however, also those personal moments like playing football with local Fijians using a coconut; these are the moments that stay with you well after the tan disappears. It is the awe-inspiring gift of travel that I have fallen in love with, offering up insight into people and cultures.

(Richardson, 2006, pp. 38–39)

This excerpt from an article featured in a recent edition of the Youth Hostels Association (YHA) Australia members' magazine, *Backpacker Essentials*, clearly invokes the idea that during one's travels, interactions with others (and, in particular, interactions with locals) may inspire greater appreciation of the world, its people and cultures. Further, according to the writer it seems that when such understanding or knowledge is attained in a personally meaningful manner, it has lasting impact for the individuals involved, rendering them in some way changed or transformed. These ideas actually echo the stated aims of the YHA, which are – in part – to encourage intercultural understanding and education through travel (Hostelling International, 2006a). They also resonate strongly (albeit in a less schematic way) within the broader backpacking community and are made manifest in a variety of travel media and industries, including the independent and alternative tourism markets, which cater to volunteer travellers (O'Reilly, 2006).

Here, then, the old adage that 'life is about the journey, not the destination' rules paramount and (clichés aside) associated notions of 'stopping to smell the roses', of 'taking pleasure in the finer details' and 'making the most of one's freedom' are also deemed significant. In short, it seems that the 'awe-inspiring gift of travel' that Richardson pays homage to in this article, is that of self-discovery. It is a 'gift' well-recognized by travellers, industry organizations and academics alike, one that has long association with notions of journeying, pilgrimage, rite of passage, identity formation, 'otherness' and authenticity (see Cary, 2004; Noy, 2004). In turn, it is the latter three themes that inform much of this chapter, which is concerned with exploring the impacts of local–global interactions on young volunteer travellers, their self-perceptions and understandings of the world around them.

More specifically, by examining travellers' desires for authenticity and otherness, the chapter will demonstrate that it is the personal transformation promised in these experiences of alterity which prompts individuals to engage in the sort of local–global interactions that are common to volunteer travel. Subsequently, it will be suggested that the oppositions encountered in these exchanges, whether physical or discursive, also house a regenerative and evolutionary potential, instigating change at both individual and sociocultural levels. For instance, it appears that physical and social engagements between localized 'others' and globalized travellers, who of course perform 'otherness' for locals, their relationship being founded in relativity (see Doron, 2005; Maoz, 2006), may give rise to contradictions between expectation and experience, fantasy and reality. Many of these inconsistencies oscillate around romanticization and stereotype, and yet as a number of recent studies into independent travel have found, these idealized visions, once overcome, clear the way for more fruitful, reflexive and realistic depictions of self and other (Doron, 2005; Lyons, 2005; West, 2005; Young, 2005; O'Reilly, 2006). Likewise, where there may be implicit difficulties in importing macro-discourses into micro-spaces (and in the context of volunteering, I am here thinking of things like environmentalism, peacemaking and multiculturalism), attempts to resolve such difficulties seemingly give rise to new levels of intercultural dialogue.

On this basis, this chapter is offered as an alternative to what Regina Scheyvens (2002, p. 150) describes as 'accounts [that] may suggest that contemporary backpackers are engaging in a self-centred form of poverty tourism'. Correspondingly, the chapter also challenges arguments that backpackers and independent travellers are concerned with otherness and authenticity only in so far as they assure increased status or cultural capital (Elsrud, 2001; Sørenson, 2003). Rather, giving credence to the 'humanistic' narratives often employed by travellers, I would propose that a number of backpackers take part in volunteering and other alternative tourism projects as a result of a genuine interest in engaging with locals. These travellers are, to borrow from Cohen (2003, p. 98), more 'outwardly' than 'inwardly' focused, and motivated by concerns with personal transformation, desires for experiential knowledge, altruistic impulses and a need or desire to reconcile self and other through the creation of common bonds. This is not to say, of course, that motivations are in any case singular, that touristic or authentic behaviours and practices are mutually exclusive, or that local–global interactions are entirely unproblematic, but to argue that even the tensions that emerge between the local and the global may provide important opportunities for 'working the hyphens' between self and other (Fine, 1994) or, as Camille O'Reilly (2006, p. 1011) has noted, 'the chance to question, explore and confront' identity.

A Note on Methodology

With these theoretical contextualizations in place, it should be noted that the chapter, which is situated within a larger research project exploring the role of extended international travel in the lives of young Australian backpackers, is informed by a cross-disciplinary, triangulated or 'crystallized' (Richardson, 2000, p. 934) multimethod approach, involving ethnography, participant observation, semi-structured in-depth interviewing and textual analysis. Each of these methods, particularly ethnography, interview and participant observation, are inextricably linked and for the most part they were employed in an exploratory and reflexive fashion.

Serving both academic and pragmatic goals, textual and content analysis of key travel media and backpacking advertisements was conducted both prior to, and during, ethnographic fieldwork. For instance, in an attempt to gauge which global destinations would be most conducive to my research aims, prior to embarking on fieldwork I consulted various publications (such as the Lonely Planet guidebooks and *Backpacker Essentials* magazines referred to in this chapter), travel web sites and online forums, as well as advertisements from major travel operators in the youth travel and backpacking markets. Such texts, as well as those encountered during fieldwork (such as the infamous *TNT Magazine* and Gumtree web sites popular among antipodean travellers in the UK), were not only useful in identifying backpacker 'hot spots' but when subjected to image and discourse analysis also gave some indication as to how young independent travellers were both imagining themselves, and being imagined. Major themes (such as authenticity and freedom) and sub-themes (such as escape, fun, spontaneity, experience of the unknown and accumulation of knowledge) were identified in these materials. In turn, these discourses assisted in the development of interview questions or topic guides, and provided an initial framework for the analysis of primary research data.

Given the broader objectives of the research, 32 interviews were conducted with 34 young Australians (two interviews were conducted in pairs) aged 18–30, who self-identified and affiliated as backpackers or independent travellers, and who had been travelling overseas for a period of at least 3 months. Although somewhat arbitrary, this time frame was chosen as a means of delineating between individuals taking short breaks or holidays and those embarking on a more extensive trip, one that involved a significant departure from home commitments. Although some interviewees were recruited opportunistically or ethnographically (Flick, 2006) for the most part, interviews were secured through more indirect means – the posting of recruitment notices in places frequented by backpackers (such as youth hostels, bars, cafes, tour buses, staff/volunteer housing areas, employment recruitment centres and public libraries) and by advertising on Internet travel forums and web sites such as The Gumtree (www.gumtree.co.uk), TNT Online (www.tntmagazine.co.uk), Lonely Planet Thorntree (http://thorntree.lonelyplanet.com), Geckos (www.geckos.com.au) and India Mike (www.indiamike.com). Given the increased numbers of backpackers utilizing Internet facilities while travelling (Sørenson, 2003), it is not surprising that recruitment via cyberspace was more productive than recruitment in 'real' space. In hindsight, this also goes some way towards accounting for the fact that of the 32 interviews conducted, 14 took place face to face and 18 were conducted via e-mail.

The face-to-face interviews consisted of approximately 30 questions or topic guides and e-mail interviews in the first instance contained 35 questions, with the possibility of further communication to expand on or clarify responses as needed. Such follow-up communication was decided on an individual basis but ultimately it assisted in overcoming any major discrepancies between the richness of data elucidated in face-to-face interviews and that secured through e-mail communication, which is typically more concise. Interview questions were designed to gather information about participants' travel choices, motivations, expectations, experiences, perceptions of the travel community and broader life plans. While there was generally little difficulty in extracting responses from participants (most were interested in the study, enjoyed having a captive audience and seemingly appreciated my 'insider' status), both indirect and direct lines of questioning were employed and all of the questions were open-ended. Additionally, as much as possible, face-to-face interviews, which took anywhere from 45 min to 2 h, were conducted in a flexible and conversational manner, the aim being to provide participants with an opportunity to give expression to their travel narratives in a relatively relaxed environment. To help facilitate this, interviews were usually conducted in public places common to travellers such as hostel lounges, cafes and bars, and to avoid the disruptions of note-taking each were digitally recorded and later transcribed verbatim, before being subjected to thematic and discursive coding.

Finally, it should be noted that interview questions and recruitment techniques were reflexively monitored throughout the research project. Given the exploratory nature of the research, this was a necessary component, which also assisted in the implementation of saturated sampling. That is, once interview responses became increasingly repetitive and the emergence of new material declined, recruitment efforts were gradually decreased and interviewing ended (for further discussion see Flick, 2006). By and large, the cessation of all interviews corresponded with the completion of fieldwork, although there were a few e-mail interviewees who sent me their responses after I had returned home.

Fieldwork was conducted from April 2005 until March 2006 in a variety of international locations, which included Guatemala, Costa Rica, Cuba, the USA, Canada, Spain, England, Scotland, India and Thailand. During this time I kept a series of fieldwork journals, wherein experiences shared with me by others, as well as my own storied endeavours and observations as backpacker and/or researcher, were recorded. I attempted to make these notes as extensive and objective as possible but without a doubt they are the product of my emotions, actions and preoccupations at given points in time; there is no escaping the fact that ethnography is subjective and that fieldwork is a lived, embodied experience (Tedlock, 2000). In this regard, influenced by auto-ethnography, that is, an approach to research and writing 'that displays multiple layers of consciousness, connecting the personal to the cultural' and that results in the production of texts where 'concrete action, dialogue, emotion, embodiment, spirituality, and self-consciousness are featured, appearing as relational and institutional stories affected by history, social structure, and culture' (Ellis and Bochner, 2003, p. 209), I have attempted to make a few apologies for my presence in this research. Unlike the writers that Michelle Fine (1994, p. 74) cautions against who often 'self consciously carry no voice, body, race, class, or gender and no interests into their texts', I am invested both personally and professionally in this project and purposefully acknowledge the 'centrality' of my 'own experience...tellings, livings, relivings and retellings' (Clandinin and Connelly, 1994, p. 418). It is for this very reason that I have also drawn on e-mail correspondence with friends and family (at home and abroad) and photos taken during fieldwork as data worthy of analysis.

Although some in-country travel arrangements were made prior to departure, as much as possible I kept my fieldwork itinerary flexible, allowing for the all important 'word of mouth' recommendations and spontaneous moments that define the practice of backpacking (Murphy, 2001) to occur. For similar reasons, in an attempt to capture the heterogeneous nature of the backpacking culture (Cohen, 2003; Lyons, 2005), I made a conscious effort to engage in a broad spectrum of travel pursuits and activities while 'in the field'. To this end, alongside largely independent travels utilizing public transport, I took short backpacker tours in Canada, a package tour in Cuba, travelled with a globally established responsible small-tour company in India and enrolled in a Spanish language course and homestay programme in Guatemala. I spent time living and working in backpacker hostels, occasionally stayed in hotels and resorts, and occupied friends' spare bedrooms and living room floors whenever possible. Additionally and most importantly for present purposes, I also volunteered for 3 weeks on a wildlife conservation project in Costa Rica, took part in cultural education programmes run by Hostelling International, Chicago (where I resided for 2 months as a volunteer), and, finally, spent 2 weeks with a friend in the south of Thailand, where we worked with local primary and high school students as part of a volunteer English-teaching project.

Therefore, volunteer tourism is studied here as one of the many experiences that young backpackers or independent travellers undertake in an attempt to engage with 'others' and learn more about self. Although interviewees were not sought on the basis of volunteer experience, many had some knowledge of, or interest in, volunteering abroad and a number had actually incorporated volunteering stints into larger multidestination trips. To this end, before moving into an in-depth analysis of volunteer experiences it is necessary to examine more generally travellers' desires for localism and alterity, and the slippage that occurs between these desires and discourses of mutual benefit as they are encountered in alternative tourism endeavours.

The Enticement of Localism: Understanding Travellers' Desires for Alterity

I do like to meet some locals while travelling – in fact often I make a point of getting to some out of the way towns or villages just to take advantage of that opportunity....I expect nothing and accept everything, otherwise you cut yourself

off from amazing experiences and people to learn from and share with. And I
have therefore met sooooooo [sic] many different types of people of all various
ages, religions, nationalities and personalities. But they have all been so beautiful
in their own special way.

(Michelle, age 29)

As a portal to the unexpected and a gateway to the unknown, travel is frequently embraced as a means of satiating curiosity and accumulating experiential knowledge of the 'other'. As Luke Desforges (1998, pp. 180–181)
argues, travel is about 'checking out the planet', 'collecting places' and
'building up systematic knowledge about the world' or in Michelle's terms,
sharing knowledge about the world. Indeed, as society becomes increasingly fragmented, disembedded and globalized, and identity and other social
facts more and more contingent or ambivalent (Bauman 2001a,b), unme-
diated and experiential knowledge, the 'authentic' knowledge provided by
travel, becomes an evermore important and sought after commodity (Wang,
2000). Such preoccupations are exemplified in the following comments
from Filip, age 25:

I think [travel is] especially central now because what I find out when I actually
go and travel is that the world is a lot different from what we hear. . . . And I think
especially in these days, when y'know the whole world is coming together . . . we
have to be able to be objective I think. We can't just remain in our own belief
systems in our countries. . . . We have to go y'know to the other countries or
be involved with people from the other countries to find out what their actual
opinion is, what the opinion of the general masses are. . . . What's the true story,
y'know? Not what we're just being told.

These observations indicate that in late or 'liquid' modernity (Bauman, 2000)
many travellers are increasingly aware of the fact that 'truth' and authenticity
are rather elusive qualities, restricted perhaps to a distant past where travel was
edgier and less institutionalized (O'Reilly, 2006) and now only obtained with
substantial and considered effort. To this end, the following comments, again
from Filip, are significant:

That's part of . . . the best thing about travelling. You meet the local people, you
ask them how they grow their food, y'know, how many harvests they have – let's
say they're farmers. Or ah, how life is. . . . I'm usually always thinking that I'll be
meeting a lot more locals than travellers . . . even I'd say sometimes we shy away
from other travellers. . . . Just because we want, we want the experience of the
country [original emphasis]. . . . Y'know not sitting around in cafés drinking and
kind of just gossiping all day.

Here, locals are constructed as the anchor points of an experience; they remind
travellers of their location and ensure that they are not simply set loose in, as
some would argue, an increasingly homogenized world. What is also acknowledged in this statement is that, without locals – who often embody or signify
a specific place and/or time (MacCannell, 1989) – one's trip will be made
meaningless. For, at the end of the day, thanks to globalization, travellers can
be found in almost any destination sipping lattes or drinking pints of beer and
talking about a world a million (or a mere one or two – distance now being

rendered irrelevant) miles away. There is, in a sense, this idea that without the presence of 'real' locals, one could be anywhere or, worse still, one could just as easily be in Australia, negating the very reason for travel in the first place.

Local encounters then are experiences valued for their memoried significance, as well as the (symbolic) freedom they provide from everyday and 'known' worlds and the insight they offer into a place and its culture. Further, it stands to reason that in embracing the transformative potential that travel wields and in seeking experiential knowledge, individuals will aspire to existentially and serendipitously authentic moments, moments which are unlike any other (Steiner and Reisinger, 2006). After all, if objective authenticity cannot be guaranteed, personal moments of 'truth', which are not necessarily subjected to the same checks and balances but are invariably 'unique' and transitory, are seemingly better options for the savvy postmodern or liquid-modern traveller concerned with self-development. As Chaim Noy (2004, p. 91) writes: '[E]xperiencing adventures and encounters with authenticity are *means*, rather than ends, in the narratives, substantiating a claim made on a different level – not on that of undertakings but of identity – that the individuals underwent a change.' Significantly, he goes on to comment (2004, pp. 91–92):

> [R]emarkable personal changes are constructed and communicated as a
> natural consequence of a remarkable experience. . . . Rhetorically, the claim
> for this change is thus validated by the claim for the uniqueness of the
> experience . . . which, in turn, is founded on the uniqueness of the destinations.

Seemingly, these claims to uniqueness are encouraged by various travel media. Take for example, the following excerpt from the introduction to Lonely Planet's *Central America on a Shoestring* (Reid *et al.*, 2004, p. 9), where clear connections are made between adventure, authenticity, difference, uniqueness, challenging and fun experiences, and local interactions:

> Tiny on a map, Central America packs in more diversity than any comparably
> sized area on the planet. No matter when or how long you visit, daily adventures
> are for the taking, and they come in all types – fun, easy, bumpy, challenging,
> surprising, fulfilling – the sort you'll be talking about for decades. . . . Witness
> colorful Mayan life, not much changed over the centuries. . . . Stay with a family
> throughout, while studying Spanish, to open up more insights into daily life.
> Central America . . . is distinctly apart from its bigger, more well-known American
> neighbors. That it remains a mystery to so many, makes the trip all the more
> rewarding.

Not surprisingly, such sentiments are even more apparent in 'responsible tourism guides'. For example, Tourism Concern's *The Good Alternative Travel Guide: Exciting Holidays for Responsible Travellers* (Mann and Ibrahim, 2002, pp. xiii–xiv) reads:

> This guide contains two of the best holidays I've ever been on. The first was
> in the Australian Outback, about 300 kilometres from Uluru (or Ayer's Rock,
> as it used to be called). . . . The second was in the middle of the Ecuadorean
> Amazon, deep inside the world's greatest rainforest. . . . Two dramatic, and
> dramatically different, settings. What links them is that both holidays were run by
> the local aboriginal/indigenous communities: people who still live in remarkable

natural places and who still feel and understand the rhythms of nature…these community-run tours were a great way to get closer to the people and cultures I was visiting. A chance to step off the tired tourist treadmill for a few days.

Finally, Lonely Planet's *Code Green: Experiences of a Lifetime* (Lorimer, 2006, p. 8) also encourages travellers to make connections with local places and people, rather than simply passing through in a blur of superficial encounters:

> [I]f you think about your best travel experiences – the ones you'll never forget – they're almost always those where you made a *connection* [original emphasis]. Where you were blown away by a landscape so magnificent in its scale and purity that you were at once humbled – and exquisitely aware of your own integral place in the natural order. Or when you felt you really made a personal connection – and felt an equality of give and take – with someone from a world utterly different to your own.

With these texts in mind, I would argue that when backpackers choose local transport over tourist buses, local guides over global companies, responsible and ecotourism ventures and/or volunteering over package holidays, it is not simply a matter of practicality; nor, however, is it just a case of ideology. Rather, such complex decisions are multifaceted: made emotionally, discursively *and* pragmatically. Seemingly, language immersion programmes, homestay visits, cultural exchanges, community tourism and volunteer projects provide viable alternatives (or in many cases supplements) to some of the more 'touristic' activities offered to those travellers engaged in extended international journeys. These pursuits are valued, not on the basis of status or cultural capital (although in some instances this may be an added bonus) but on the assumption that deeper engagements with alterity – deeper understandings of the 'other' – may give rise to the accumulation of authentic knowledge and ultimately a deeper or more finely honed sense of self.

To this end, alternative tourism pursuits – and more specifically volunteering – are often regarded as mutually beneficial activities, for they promote all of the above, but also reinstate a sense of (at least symbolic) equality between self and other. By 'giving something back' a one-way process of knowledge consumption becomes a two-way process of knowledge-sharing and production, a mutual dialogue rather than singular monologue.

Localism, Altruism and the Discourse of Mutual Benefit

This discourse of mutual benefit is evident in the following comments from Christina, who spoke of her desire to put her medical expertise as a doctor to use in majority world countries. Here knowledge is characterized as something to be given and received freely and, while expertise is offered, useful and interesting experiences are simultaneously accumulated:

> I wouldn't mind doing some volunteering with Medecins san Frontiers but I don't think my French is sufficient.…But some kind of medical voluntary work I think would be an interesting experience.…I'd like to do at least a month to appreciate sort of Western medicine and just to look at the way different [medical systems

operate], I don't think you can appreciate the poverty until you've done it....I think it would be a good experience to have....And y'know hopefully I would...help them out.

(Christina, age 26)

The same idea of reciprocation, of 'helping out' and receiving beneficial experiences in exchange for one's efforts, is also present in the following comment from Niome (age 25), who detailed her desire to work in a school or orphanage based in Africa:

A friend of mine, Sarah...she went to Africa for a couple of months. To help out in an orphanage, which was really good for her....I'd love to go to Africa and help out as well. Like, to work in an orphanage or one of these schools teaching English.

Even the following comments from Jeanette and Lisa (who were experienced volunteers) balanced notions of responsibility and 'giving something back' with desires for localism, authenticity and knowledge acquisition:

[Y]ou can't see a country as a tourist and understand it properly and volunteer work gives you that opportunity and it also gives you the opportunity to give back to the local community...it [volunteering] gives other people a lot better opportunity to get to know the local people and what it's really like. You're not looking through the...rose-coloured glasses that tourists often have on when they're travelling sort of thing....I think if you're going to go to another country and clearly in that country people aren't as well off as you, then I think there's some sort of responsibility for you to be able to contribute...something back to them in a positive way....What they deem positive, not what you deem positive....So that they benefit from tourism, rather than the money coming into the country and then out again and then resulting in environmental destruction or loss of culture or other negative impacts.

(Jeanette, age 25)

At home I have volunteered for several community and student groups over the years so the idea of volunteering wasn't a new one to me. I get a lot of joy out of helping others. I also know that I come from a very privileged position in the world and thought that as I was going to be travelling to disadvantaged areas I would like to help out if possible. I had also recently finished my Dip Ed so it made sense for me to volunteer in an educational capacity if at all possible. I had also done my honors on organic farming and had volunteered for some environmental groups so [I] was keen to experience WWOOFing [*Willing Workers on Organic Farms programme*].

(Lisa, age 25)

Interestingly, this discursive juggling act – between altruism, authenticity, experiential learning, self-development and freedom – is also performed by those organizations promoting volunteer and responsible tourism projects. Take, for example, the following descriptions and slogans from International Volunteers for Peace, Hostelling International and Conservation Volunteers Australia (all of which I was involved with during fieldwork):

Live, Give, Grow. Experience the real world and make a difference [with] International Volunteers for Peace. Want to get off the beaten track and really immerse yourself in the local culture? See the world from a completely

new perspective through volunteering. . . . IVP runs workcamps to encourage
understanding amongst different peoples, to promote discussion and appreciation
of the issues different communities face in their struggles for social justice
and sustainability, to break down barriers and prejudices between nations and
establish paths to peace.

(International Volunteers for Peace, 2005)

In HI Youth Hostels around the world, you are able to encounter people of
different cultures, backgrounds, and experiences. HI Youth Hostels are a rich
resource for learning and for building a better, more peaceful world.

(Hostelling International, 2006b)

Why be just another tourist when you can be a conservation
volunteer? . . . Volunteers gain many benefits from participating in a World
Conservation Program. In addition to contributing to valuable projects assisting
the world's environment, volunteers learn new skills, meet new friends and
experience international cultures. . . . World Conservation Programs are a unique
experience, giving you the opportunity to go off the beaten track, meet some
great locals and not only learn about a new environment but make a positive
difference as well.

(Conservation Volunteers Australia, 2004)

Each of these descriptions clearly invokes notions of authenticity, of making
the most of one's time and of gaining experiential knowledge – knowledge that
will ultimately contribute to the 'greater good' and to the development of self.
Curiously, many of the expressions used here also feature in advertisements
for more mainstream backpacking tours and activities. These same discourses
also pervaded interviewees' discussions of their independent volunteering
experiences. Whether WWOOFing (volunteering on organic farms), volunteer-
teaching English, helping out at festivals or working in a soup kitchen, each
interviewee who had spent some time in alternative tourism pursuits spoke of
the lasting impacts they had (some of which were quite incidental to the activity)
and the great diversity of people they allowed them to meet. For instance, of
WWOOFing, Catherine (age 26) wrote: 'I . . . had such a wonderful time, and
stayed with wonderful, enthusiastic, kind and interesting people.' Likewise, Lisa
commented that she 'enjoyed WWOOFing and would like to do that again',
that 'volunteer work teaching English was heaps of fun' and that 'helping out in
a soup kitchen in Brazil had a large impact' on her. She also commented that
as a result of some of these pursuits she had met 'people from all ages and all
walks of life and [with] all kind of attitudes'. While this was not a stated reason
for her decision to volunteer then, it seemed to be a definite bonus. Similarly,
Michelle's discussion of her decision to go WWOOFing and her experiences
volunteering in this manner highlights the prominence of the notion of personal and incidental (perhaps even serendipitous) gain:

When I completed my TEFL certificate I knew I was going to head to
Granada to try to find work. Again, I didn't really know anything about it –
but I knew I had to go there. I looked for work for a couple of weeks but had
no luck finding [anything] full time. . . . I couldn't find enough paid work to not
dip into my savings for living expenses, so therefore thought it better to have
expenses covered so I could spend more time in the area . . . plus at this time

I was [also] looking to spend some time in the mountains!...So [I] decided to call up a number a friend had given me where I could go WWOOF-ing...it was at this address that I came across a man who provided me with a lot of information to assist in my next level of healing [Michelle had previously revealed that prior to travelling she had suffered 'from mild depression due to severe back pain from a car accident']. The mountains out there also have such amazing energy and I believe between these two influences, it has had quite a dramatic effect on my healing.

Notable in these reports then is the idea that travel experiences – particularly travel experiences that involve authentic interactions with locals – should (and do) leave one 'changed'. It is clear that volunteering is not just about 'doing good' for others, but it is also about 'doing good' for self, about reciprocal benefit. While some may argue that this defeats the purpose, I would suggest that this is a rather inevitable joining of discourses and that the heightened global awareness experienced by volunteers or responsible travellers as a result of their activities is a benefit almost as important as those delivered to the communities they are engaged with. Notwithstanding, there are conflicts that can and do emerge in the volunteer travel space, and it seems likely that more often than not these conflicts emanate from discursive collisions or the disparities that may emerge between expectation and experience, fantasy and reality. Nowhere was this made more apparent than during the sea turtle conservation project I enrolled in as part of my fieldwork in Costa Rica.

Global Discourses and Local Spaces, When Fantasy and Reality Collide

Operated by a local NGO (Asociación ANAI), this project was accessed through Conservation Volunteers Australia's (CVA) World Conservation Program. Over a 3-week period from May to June 2005, I volunteered alongside men and women from Australia, England, Ireland, Germany and the USA, working with local and international staff in the protection and conservation of endangered sea turtle populations. The project was based within a National Park on the Caribbean coastline, a location that proved to be rather idyllic once one grew accustomed to the isolation and rudimentary facilities. The following excerpt from an e-mail sent to friends and family at home documents the initial tensions that emerged as the project became a corporeal reality.

From: Amie Matthews
Sent: Sunday, June 12, 2005 2:47 PM
Subject: Hi

I must say I was pretty daunted by the whole thing when I first arrived in Cahuita – knowing I had to walk it each night, the long, long beach looked pretty intimidating, and stories of poisonous snakes in beds, deadly spiders, scorpions, the thought of meeting poachers on the beach (not that we were ever expected to confront them) didn't help quell my fears....However...once I settled into the place and got past my first impressions I came to really love it! I mean waking first thing in the morning to howler monkeys, watching raccoons and vultures in the backyard, spider monkeys out the front, geckos everywhere...wandering down to the black sandy beach in the early hours for a spot of yoga and a swim – with no one else in sight – spotting stingrays on a morning patrol, and listening to the waves pound onto the sand while you sleep is all pretty special. And that's without even mentioning the turtles!!!

To give you a general idea of our duties...while on the project we would walk the beach either from 8 pm to 12 am or from 11 pm to 3 am each night, generally amassing 10–12 km unless we came across a nesting turtle in which case we would stop and wait for her to nest, collect the eggs and then relocate them.

The main reason for relocation is to deter poachers who pose a huge threat to a very (and I mean very! – wasn't aware of how much so until I started the program) endangered population....For the first few nights this was done under the light of a full moon but for the rest of the time it was in the dark with only a few stars or fireflies to guide us. ...

Second night into the job I met both a Carre (hawksbill) and Baula (leatherback) turtle who were laying...and I must say that first sighting is pretty amazing....Another night I took the role of egg collector, which basically meant leaning into the nest, my head very close to the turtles nether regions, with a big plastic bag held out waiting for the eggs to fall....Very up close and personal hearing this giant, prehistoric looking creature breathe and grunt, laying flipper to arm, with sand flying all around.

Such a privilege to be there and to take part in something so important...certainly won't forget it in a hurry!

Although the tensions reported here were relatively minor and are best understood, perhaps in terms of culture shock, this excerpt also demonstrates how self was reconciled to otherness (in this case, symbolized by an unknown and foreign landscape) through a process of acculturation. Such processes are consistent with Stephen Wearing's (2002, p. 252) claim that 'as people travel with themselves, they see the other as a world they are travelling through; yet at some stage, that other becomes a part of themselves'. It is a claim expanded upon considerably in the following comment from Jeanette, who reflected on her experiences as a cultural exchange participant in Indonesia and the sometimes complex process of reconciliation (between individuality and conformity, self and other) that this involved:

[T]he other thing [that can be frustrating] is the lack of individuality when you're travelling in a group....And also the fact that people look at you as a group....And that it's very hard to express your individuality and to travel as an individual when you're confined by host families...and having people tell you 'this is the way it is, don't question it' and [them] not accepting situations and not accepting suggestions...[sometimes] to the point where people don't recognize that as an Australian we do have our own culture. And cross-cultural understanding isn't just about us understanding the local culture, it's about whoever we're sharing our culture with, them also at least attempting to recognize that Australia has a different culture to them and that doesn't mean we're going to jump when they say, or it doesn't sort of mean we're going to say 'how high should we jump?' when they ask us to....It's going to be, it's about give and take....I think it's hard because we [as Australians] do have a more global understanding already, so we're more willing to be flexible. And it's not that I'm saying they're not flexible, but I just sometimes think that...there just has to be a *little* bit more communication or a *little* bit more understanding [from both sides] and you'd end up a bit more balanced.

Here, according to Jeanette, bringing one's own (global or otherwise) values, ontologies and beliefs into a local space can be a difficult matter, especially as individuals often have significant attachments to the discourses under which they operate. Nevertheless, she suggests that increased flexibility would allow for greater reconciliation between self and other, between identities and cultures, going on to comment that travel (ideally) teaches one to 'learn to question without being judgmental'. Certainly this relativist position is popular with many backpackers, particularly those who expressed, as a result of their travels, a growing awareness of the interconnectedness between people and places, or, as O'Reilly (2006, p. 999) observed, a 'feeling of common humanity'. However, it seems that in the case of global ethics – in the face of things like human rights, environmentalism, gender equality, peace and multiculturalism – the situation is increasingly complicated, for it is often harder to reach a compromise and also more difficult to ascertain which views are in fact 'authentic' and representative of the local populations in the first place.

Case in point were the discursive tensions that I became aware of during the sea turtle conservation project in Costa Rica, and the questions such tensions raised regarding authentic otherness. For what I came to realize was that as a volunteer engaged in conservation work I was operating under discourses of environmentalism and, in a sense, was also charged with bringing these global codes and values into local space. But what and where was the local space? For, on the one hand, I was situated in a wilderness area, connecting in a very real and corporeal way with the local environment, and yet, on the other, I spent more time speaking English than Spanish and the ethics we, as volunteers, were enacting on a daily basis had varying degrees of support outside of the project site. After all, poaching was illegal, but it was also a source of livelihood for a number of local people. Therefore, not everybody in the surrounding areas viewed our efforts kindly and we soon had to learn to be guarded when discussing our activities outside of the project. In fact, one of the instructions in our volunteer manual read as follows:

> Project participants should not pass on specific information to members of the public about where and when turtles are found, what processes are used for relocating the nests, or information regarding the hatcheries. Remember that poachers sometimes pose as tourists or locals to gain valuable information.

Casting back to the Conservation Volunteers Australia brochure quoted earlier, it seems then that the interactions with 'locals' and international cultural experiences promised in their advertising material are sometimes restricted by discursive conflicts. In my experience, most international interaction and cultural exchange actually occurred between volunteer travellers, and the locals we worked alongside (being mostly National Park rangers) were not necessarily representative of the wider community, least of all the market stallholders we came across in our travels. Due to the work being conducted on the conservation project it became commonplace to ask the stallholders and craftspeople whom we encountered what their goods were made from. However, where other tourists may have responded with relish when they were told 'es tortuga', we responded in a seemingly uncharacteristic way, showing signs of disgust and total disinterest. And so a conversation would ensue whereby local stallholders would try to convince us to buy the product they were proudly proffering and we would try to inform an often nonplussed and slightly bemused audience that it was illegal and that we would not buy the products on display, as turtles were an endangered and protected species.

Seemingly though, such messages did not register with stallholders, for we were, in a sense, ontologically opposed. Certainly the message we delivered was not new – almost everyone in the region was aware that trading in sea turtle products was prohibited – but what was apparently different was the role we played as 'tourists'. In exchanges such as these it became apparent that we were not only transgressing commonly established modes of interaction and conversation between stallholder and foreign consumer, but also that our values and the discourses we were enacting were representative of the sometimes irreconcilable differences between globalism and localism. Such differences either had to be accepted or questioned if self and other were to be reconciled, and yet each party was equally attached to their own point of view. For the local seller it was a question of livelihood and tradition, and for myself and the other volunteers it was a question of globally sanctioned ethics, ethics that had, for us, become localized as we engaged corporeally with the turtles and ocean landscape.

Present here, then, are a number of issues regarding localism and authenticity, cultural relativism and global ethics. For what these small interactions attest to is that not only are localism and authenticity relative matters that are experienced intersubjectively, but that sometimes despite travellers' desires to reconcile self and other, to experience connection, to belong, to engage in as Jeanette put it 'give and take', there may well be discursive interference, roadblocks to reconciliation. Nevertheless, it is the attempt that is key to the development of more globalized, cosmopolitan and holistic identities. For as Bauman (2001a, p. 79) observed:

> Not every difference has the same value, and some ways of life and forms of togetherness are ethically superior to others; but there is no way of finding out which is which unless one is given an equal opportunity to argue and prove its case.

Reconciling Local and Global, Self and Other

In a similar fashion, but with more obvious reference to tourism, Wearing (2002, p. 256) has argued:

> [T]he self/other of tourist and host interact with each other with possibilities for enlarging individual psychic space as well as the social and symbolic space of communities and cultures. However, for this situation to happen, the voice of the other must be heard, rather than falling back on mere sightseeing, curiosity, objectification, inferiorization and exploitation.

This chapter has examined volunteer travel for the opportunities it provides in opening up such 'psychic', 'social' and 'symbolic' spaces. In particular, I have argued that volunteer travel is a manifestation of young backpackers' desires for otherness and authenticity and expectations for the accumulation of experiential knowledge and personal transformation. I have also argued that these simultaneous expectations foster the discourse of mutual benefit common to alternative tourism and that this discourse may assist in reinstating a sense of equality between locals and travellers. More specifically, while I have acknowledged that volunteer travel is not the only form of tourism implicated in this process, I have also demonstrated that the increased engagement, dialogue and negotiation between self and other necessitated by volunteering may result in the development of more reflexive, hybridized or cosmopolitan identities (Wearing, 2002; Lyons, 2005; West, 2005). To this end, volunteer travel and some forms of backpacking or independent travel have been characterized here as housing a positive sociocultural potential, which is not to deny the problems associated with tourism, but to suggest they can be overcome. Indeed the potential recognized in volunteer and independent travel is in the 'overcoming'.

It is the multiplicities and complexities that emerge in the volunteer travel space, the challenges of living in a transmutable, varied and ever-changing realm, a world with multiple subjectivities and fluid identities that most contribute to individuals' self-development. It is through grappling with these varied states of belonging and disbelonging, with notions of self and other and the space in between that one may develop a more worldly standpoint and increasingly holistic sense of self. It is here that individuals may, to quote Bauman, 'rise to the level of *humanity as such*' (as interviewed in Franklin, 2003, pp. 214–215) or adopt more cosmopolitan identities. Take the following comment from Filip:

> It's hard [to define my nationality] because I'm both Czech and Australian. . . . [But] I guess what it's [travel is doing is], it's kind of changing my identity – I feel more like a citizen of the world now. . . . But saying that, Australia's my favourite place and I'll always go and live there. . . . But I feel that, yeah that, I'm kind of becoming just a person of the world, y'know, without attachments to certain countries and defending, y'know, certain things that my country does . . . or feeling like a strong defensive [stance] or some attachments in a negative way.

Seemingly, then, what travellers embark upon in their overseas adventures is not only a search for uniqueness and difference, for an alterity outside of oneself, but also for otherness within oneself. It is through travel and, more specifically, volunteer tourism that many young Australians discover not only the world, but also new relationships, opportunities, friendships, capabilities, strengths and weaknesses: in short, they discover aspects of themselves anew. With this conceptualization in mind, travel then is perhaps just as much about the return journey, about bringing the world home, as it is about venturing out into it. It is about opening up to serendipity, chance and possibility, and in so doing reconciling near and far, ordinary and extraordinary, and self and other. In essence, it is about negotiating identities.

References

Bauman, Z. (2000) *Liquid Modernity*. Polity Press, Cambridge.

Bauman, Z. (2001a) *Community: Seeking Safety in an Insecure World*. Polity Press, Cambridge.

Bauman, Z. (2001b) *The Individualized Society*. Polity Press, Cambridge.

Cary, S.H. (2004) The tourist moment. *Annals of Tourism Research* 31(1), 61–77.

Clandinin, D.J. and Connelly, F.M. (1994) Personal experience methods. In: Denzin, N.K. and Lincoln, Y.S. (eds) *Handbook of Qualitative Research*. Sage, Thousand Oaks, California, pp. 413–427.

Cohen, E. (2003) Backpacking: diversity and change. *Tourism and Cultural Change* 1(2), 95–110.

Conservation Volunteers Australia (2004) World Conservation Programs. Available at: http://www.conservationvolunteers.com.au

Desforges, L. (1998) Checking out the planet: global representations/local identities and youth travel. In: Skelton, T. and Valentine, G. (eds) *Cool Places: Geographies of Youth Culture*. Routledge, London, pp. 175–192.

Doron, A. (2005) Encountering the 'other': pilgrims, tourists and boatmen in the city of Varanasi. *The Australian Journal of Anthropology* 16(2), 157–178.

Ellis, C. and Bochner, A. (2003) Autoethnography, personal narrative, reflexivity: researcher as subject. In: Denzin, N. and Lincoln, Y. (eds) *Collecting and Interpreting Qualitative Materials*, 2nd edn. Sage, Thousand Oaks, California, pp. 199–258.

Elsrud, T. (2001) Risk creation in travelling: backpacker adventure narration. *Annals of Tourism Research* 28(3), 597–617.

Fine, M. (1994) Working the hyphens: reinventing self and other in qualitative research. In: Denzin, N.K. and Lincoln, Y.S. (eds) *Handbook of Qualitative Research*. Sage, Thousand Oaks, California, pp. 70–82.

Flick, U. (2006) *An Introduction to Qualitative Research*. Sage, London.

Franklin, A. (2003) The tourist syndrome: an interview with Zygmunt Bauman. *Tourist Studies* 3(2), 205–217.

Hostelling International (2006a) HI Story. Available at: http://www.hihostels.com/web/story.en.htm

Hostelling International (2006b) Youth Hostelling for Peace and International Understanding. Available at: http://www.hihostels.com/pdf/YouthHostelling4Peace.pdf

International Volunteers for Peace (2005) Workcamps. Available at: http://www.ivp.org.au/workcamps

Lorimer, K. (2006) *Code Green: Experiences of a Lifetime*. Lonely Planet, Footscray, Australia.

Lyons, K. (2005) Ambassador, worker and player: independent travellers working in American summer camps. In: West, B. (ed.) *Down the Road: Exploring Backpacker and Independent Travel*. API Network, Perth, Australia, pp. 93–108.

MacCannell, D. (1989) *The Tourist: A New Theory of the Leisure Class*, 2nd edn. Schocken Books, New York.

Mann, M. and Ibrahim, Z. (2002) *The Good Alternative Travel Guide: Exciting Holidays for Responsible Travellers*, 2nd edn. Earthscan, London.

Maoz, D. (2006) The mutual gaze. *Annals of Tourism Research* 33(1), 221–239.

Murphy, L. (2001) Exploring social interactions of backpackers. *Annals of Tourism Research* 28(1), 50–67.

Noy, C. (2004) This trip really changed me: backpackers' narratives of self-change. *Annals of Tourism Research* 31(1), 78–102.

O'Reilly, C.C. (2006) From drifter to gap year tourist: mainstreaming backpacker travel. *Annals of Tourism Research* 33(4), 998–1017.

Reid, R., Prado, G.C., Miranda, C.A., St Louis, R. and Vidgen, L. (2004) *Central America on a Shoestring*, 5th edn. Lonely Planet, Footscray, Australia.

Richardson, L. (2000) Writing: a method of inquiry. In: Denzin, N.K. and Lincoln, Y.S. (eds) *Handbook of Qualitative Research*, 2nd edn. Sage, Thousand Oaks, California, pp. 923–948.

Richardson, S. (2006) Beyond the landmarks. *Backpacker Essentials* 10, 38–39.

Scheyvens, R. (2002) Backpacker tourism and third world development. *Annals of Tourism Research* 29(1), 144–164.

Sørenson, A. (2003) Backpacker ethnography. *Annals of Tourism Research* 30(4), 847–867.

Steiner, C. and Reisinger, Y. (2006) Understanding existential authenticity. *Annals of Tourism Research* 33(2), 299–318.

Tedlock, B. (2000) Ethnography and ethnographic representation. In: Denzin, N.K. and Lincoln, Y.S. (eds) *Handbook of Qualitative Research*, 2nd edn. Sage, Thousand Oaks, California, pp. 455–486.

Wang, N. (2000) *Tourism and Modernity: A Sociological Analysis*. Pergamon, Oxford, UK.

Wearing, S. (2002) Re-centring the self in volunteer tourism. In: Dann, G.M.S. (ed.) *The Tourist as a Metaphor of the Social World*. CAB International, Wallingford, UK, pp. 237–262.

West, B. (2005) Independent travel and civil religious pilgrimage: backpackers at the Gallipoli battlefields. In: West, B. (ed.) *Down the Road: Exploring Backpacker and Independent Travel*. API Network, Perth, Australia, pp. 9–31.

Young, T. (2005) Between a rock and a hard place: backpackers at Uluru. In: West, B. (ed.) *Down the Road: Exploring Backpacker and Independent Travel*. API Network, Perth, Australia, pp. 33–53.

10 Opening the Gap: the Motivation of Gap Year Travellers to Volunteer in Latin America

N. SÖDERMAN[1] AND S.L. SNEAD[2]

[1]Centre for Tourism Policy Research, University of Brighton, Brighton, UK; [2]School of Economics Politics and Tourism, University of Newcastle, Callaghan, Australia

The time between secondary school and university or vocational training is often considered a critical stage in a young person's life. In Great Britain, young people traditionally take what is known as a gap year, a period of time in which they are encouraged to leave home to travel and work in the world before deciding on a vocation or discipline to follow in adulthood. In concert with the rise of volunteer tourism among travellers in general, more and more gap year travellers are likewise choosing to volunteer abroad. Despite what would seem a positive trend, critics purport that volunteer tourism is less about altruism than about self-fulfilment for the traveller (Callanan and Thomas, 2005). Thus, it is vital that a clearer understanding of the motivations of volunteer tourists, and particularly young gap year travellers, emerges to understand this trend.

One destination popular among British gap year travellers is Latin America. In this chapter, we will discuss motivations as expressed by gap year travellers to volunteer in Latin America. We focus on those particularly who have chosen to participate in structured travel experiences as arranged by UK-based organizations, building upon the work first conducted by Wearing (2001) and Simpson (2005).

The original research in this chapter is based on a study conducted by the first author at gap year volunteering sites in Latin America. The foundation of this work is found in the literature regarding both the motivation of young people to travel in general and the motivation to volunteer, at home and overseas.

Why Do Young People Travel?

Various life stages and adult responsibilities (or the lack thereof) may affect travel motivations and plans of young people. According to Clark (1992), younger male travellers tend to have fewer major life commitments, such as employment or financial obligations like mortgages, allowing for more impulsivity in travel, which can be illustrated by these travellers' choices of spontaneous cheap deal travel packages and traditional tourist resort destinations. Often the motivations for travel include expressing/exploring independence, maintaining existing friendships, developing new social relationships and hedonism. Older female travellers tend to also seek ventures to share with friends and to make new friends in the process, but often are more discerning in their choice of travel plans and destinations, seeking value for money and specific activities. Older male travellers tend to choose travel packages based upon a product, such as a sport focus holiday like skiing. Peer companionship and enjoyment are still high motivations, but again value for money is a greater factor than it is with younger travellers.

Hottola (1999) noted that young travellers, namely backpackers, tend to move from destination to destination, seeking a constant change of experience, referred to as situational flexibility. Franklin (2003) adds:

> As children of consumerism, we crave and need change, we don't want satisfaction, we want to live in a constant state of desire, for new things to consume, new technologies, new experiences.
>
> (p. 266)

Volunteer tourism is one potential way for young travellers to satiate this desire for novelty, particularly with structured placements which may offer a range of experiences within one excursion. Little (2000) noted that most gap year travellers 'want to buy a round-the-world-ticket and find themselves' while 'charities are crying out for able-bodied young people' (p. 5). This seems to create an opportunity in which both travellers and volunteer hosts can mutually assist each other in attaining their goals.

Why Do Young People Volunteer?

Volunteering is undertaken by young people for a variety of reasons. This may arise from young people wanting to feel satisfaction from using their time constructively (Anthoney, 1999), or it may stem from genuine altruistic intentions (Foster and Fernandes, 1996). Young volunteers may also wish to gain new skills and contacts useful for employment (Foster and Fernandes, 1996). Volunteering in order to help oneself is sometimes called 'reciprocal altruism' (Abrams, 1978, in Lapham, 1990, p. 69), and is common of the 'new generation' of volunteers, compared to 'classic volunteers' (Hustinx, 2001).

With the 'new generation of volunteers' having grown up in a climate of increasing freedom of choice, their search for volunteering opportunities resembles consumerism. Rommel *et al.* (1997, in Hustinx, 2001) suggest that new volunteers seek short-term volunteer commitments matching their personal interests, for which they analyse the costs and benefits of the activities offered. Often they use volunteering activities as a means of reducing risk factors, for instance by experiencing a profession prior to committing to it.

The above poses challenges for volunteering organizations (Hustinx, 2001), as

> new volunteers need to be offered individually tailored tasks that meet their
> wishes, this in turn requiring a flexible organizational setting that guarantees the
> widest possible variety of volunteer programmes and opportunities to experiment.
>
> (p. 85)

Simpson (2005) discusses 'a geography of experimentation', which commenced during the era of colonialization, as the colonies became a place where activities not tolerated at home could be practised or engaged in as 'experimentation' (p. 112). This experimentation can be seen as an element of volunteer tourism, particulary applicable to young people. As explained by Simpson, professions such as construction work and teaching cannot be 'practised' without a qualification in the UK, whereas many organizations offering the opportunity to voluneer overseas specifically offer construction projects (Callanan and Thomas, 2005) or teaching opportunities (Griffith, 2003; Potter, 2004).

Why Do Young People Become Volunteer Tourists?

> I am not here to help or educate. I am twenty years old and know so little. I am
> here to learn.

This was said by a female American volunteer in India (Collins *et al.*, 2002, p. 3), clear on her role as a volunteer. Not all volunteers are as clear about their motivation to volunteer, especially when volunteering abroad. Even for those who are, the motivation factors are complex and largely under-researched.

Wearing (2001) explains that some motivation factors are similar to those felt by people volunteering at home, wishing to try a challenge or to develop new skills. Others regard volunteer tourism as a worthwhile way of spending a different kind of holiday, gaining inspiration from a different culture or broadening their horizon in terms of global issues.

Collins *et al.* (2002) list 'top ten bad reasons' and 'top ten good reasons' for volunteering overseas. Bad reasons include volunteering because 'everyone is doing it' and to impress future employers, while good reasons include doing so to familiarize oneself with another culture, to gain experience in one's field of study and to learn another language.

There is a considerable lack of destination-specific studies into the motivation of young people to become volunteer tourists; the studies by Simpson (2005) and Wearing (2001) are notable exceptions in the case of Latin America. The following seven motivational categories emerged in Wearing's study: altruism, travel/adventure, personal growth, cultural exchange/learning, professional development, structure of the programme and right time/right place. Most frequently mentioned by the participants were altruism and travel/adventure as significant motivational influences. The majority of participants identified having had previous volunteer work as an influence (Wearing, 2001).

Motivational categories emerging in Simpson's study (2005) included the wish to travel to a 'different' destination, rather than to a destination typically chosen by the majority of gap year travellers. However, Simpson also mentioned gap year travellers' desire for a bit of 'normality' in an unfamiliar setting, by choosing to experience an unknown destination as part of a group of peers from a familiar background. The second motivation depended on the availability of volunteering opportunities, with the third one specifically being the desire to acquire language skills as a base for further studies. The fourth motivational category represented the wish to travel to locations in the developing world, which was assumed to be more accessible through a gap year travel company familiar with the region, whereas destinations such as Australia or South Africa were regarded as being easier to visit independently and therefore could be travelled to at any time.

Thomas (2001) states that the motivation of young people to volunteer overseas depends on the background of the individual as well as on the product offered by the organization, with Miller (2003) adding the importance of an experience being well organized, fun and educational. There are numerous types of organizations that offer volunteer tourism experiences. Three types that are commonly found among UK-based organizations and are profiled in this chapter are travel companies, registered charities and non-profit organizations.

Structured Travel Experiences Involving Volunteer Work

Gap year travellers interviewed for the research in this chapter were travelling with one of three UK-based organizations, each with different structured volunteer tourism packages and typical of the types of organizations that offer overseas volunteer tourism opportunities. These different structures are compared and contrasted in Table 10.1.

As seen in the table, all three organizations offer a phase of language tuition prior to the volunteering phase, suggesting that skills in the local language may be necessary or advantageous for engaging in, and committing to, the volunteer work. However, the phase of language tuition also forms the shortest of the three phases in every case.

In addition to the language tuition and volunteering phases, the travel company and the registered charity each have a 6-week expedition. The charity calls this the 'jungle phase', preceding the language learning and the volunteer work. For the travel company, the expedition includes several forms of adventure tourism. The non-profit organization does not include an expedition but rather has two volunteering phases, both of these have a duration of 1 month, encompassing different tasks and in different settings of the same country.

The nature of the volunteer work differs among each organization. According to the categorization by Collins *et al.* (2002), the volunteer work offered by each organization can be classified as being short-term

Table 10.1. Typical structured travel experiences in Latin America involving volunteer work. (Modified from Promotional Material of Organizations used in 1st Author's Primary Research conducted during 2005 and 2006.)

Type of organization	Location	Elements of experience outside other than volunteering	Duration of volunteer work	Type of volunteer work
1 Company	South America	• 3-week language course • 6-week expedition	1 month	• Community welfare/building projects/ teaching
2 Registered charity	Central America	• 6-week expedition/ projects in jungle • 1-month language course	2 months	• Teaching (building projects/ miscellaneous – depending on initiative of volunteers)
3 Non-profit-making organization	South America	• 2-week language course	1 month in Amazon 1 month in urban outskirts	• 1 month conservation work • 1 month building projects/ teaching

or medium-term when the duration is 2 months rather than 1 month. The nature of volunteer work has been categorized according to the types used by Callanan and Thomas (2005), such as community work, teaching, conservation work and building projects. Community work includes volunteers conducting and participating in sport and recreation activities with school children. Volunteers also conduct formal classes with the children. Given this contact with children, Callanan and Thomas (2005) express concern at the numerous short-term projects worldwide which make no requirements of the volunteers to have skills in the local language or teaching qualifications.

Given the fact that Spanish is a widely taught subject in British schools with increasing popularity (BBC News, 2006), it is feasible that young volunteers from Britain could be linguistically prepared for volunteering in Latin America. Callanan and Thomas (2005), however, argue that this question of linguistic ability, together with the short-term nature of the experience, makes the contribution of these volunteers to the host community unclear and challenges the perception of volunteer work being altruistic in nature. This brings us to examine the motivation of volunteers for a clearer understanding of why British gap year travellers choose to volunteer in Latin America.

Methodology

Data were collected from 50 volunteers from the three organizations, using in-depth interviews. These were tape-recorded on location at the volunteer work site, and subsequently transcribed. Interviewing as a method, used in previous studies covering motivation of young people for volunteering (Hustinx, 2001; Wearing, 2001; Simpson, 2005), was deemed suitable. Open-ended questions were used, which allowed for free-flowing conversation, similar to the style adopted by Simpson (2005).

The contents of the transcribed interviews allowed for a number of themes to emerge, helping to establish a framework for examining the data. Direct quotations were used in the analysis to elaborate on the findings. Despite the three structured experiences having some differences, the responses were similar across the sample of volunteers interviewed.

The emergent themes were divided into three motivational categories: motivation to volunteer overseas, motivation for choosing Latin America and motivation for the choice of organization.

Motivation to Volunteer Overseas

Ten motivational factors for volunteering overseas emerged from the data. In no particular order, they are:

- Fulfilling a dream;
- Assumed linguistic practice offered by the project;
- Broadening horizons;
- Altruism/reciprocal altruism;
- Gap year ideal time;
- Influence of family/peers;
- Supply of volunteering projects;
- Positive experience of similar tasks;
- Experience for future; and
- Didn't want to just travel.

As listed, the motivation of gap year travellers to volunteer overseas is multifaceted, and not attributable to simply one or two factors. Starting with comments illustrating the theme 'gap year ideal time', many saw a gap year as an ideal time for having experiences that one could not have at home.

> Most other things you do on your gap year, you can do any time in your life. But you're never going to work in a shanty town again.

> A lot of the things organized by gap years, that is pretty much all volunteer stuff.

The interest in volunteering overseas was often triggered by the fact that members of participants' families as well as peers were aware of these opportunities, some of them having had direct experience of them.

> I had three friends who had done this…and they said this was the most rewarding phase.

Some gappers had prior positive experiences of volunteering.

> I spent a few summers working at summer camps in America and I did a bit of voluntary work back in Ireland, so that's why I wanted to try it out here.

Altruism was often part of the motivation, although usually in combination with benefits for oneself, and thus more in line with 'reciprocal altruism' or motivation similar to those of the 'new volunteers'.

> It's also a fun experience for me. If you want to help other people, you can just give money to Oxfam or whatever! I'm sure that's more useful than me spending like five grand on this!

> It's wiser to work in England. Just to come out to a country like where they're less developed…it's quite like clear that these sort of places are quite under developed, and they appreciate help.

Volunteering overseas was in many cases seen as providing experience useful for future studies or careers, but the activity in itself was not always regarded as requiring skills or qualifications.

> If you want to get paid to do teaching abroad, you need to have qualifications… whereas if you're volunteering…it allows you to have a similar experience without need to have done as much in the past and have any qualifications.

Those especially who had plans to study Spanish at university tended to specifically choose a Spanish-speaking destination. Choosing a community-based volunteering project was presumed to provide more opportunities to help develop skills in the language due to the close interactions with native speakers.

> The other projects were reforestation or animal sanctuaries and this is the one where I get to practice most Spanish.
> (I'm) hoping to meet more Spanish people! It's what we came for!

Analysing costs and benefits of the different experiences offered by different organizations played a role in the choice.

> I thought it's only a little bit more money, and that two months was practicing Spanish.

The opportunity to practise the language is quite significant, even if only for a minority of the group. This, however, was only one of the factors that emerged as a motivational factor among the British gap year travellers for specifically choosing Latin America as a volunteering location.

Motivation for Choosing Latin America for the Experience

Ten motivational factors for choosing Latin America emerged from the data. Again, without rank, they are:

- The unknown;
- Danger;
- Diversity;
- Scenery;
- Linguistic;
- Influence of siblings;
- Popularity among peers;
- Preference over other destinations;
- The experience; and
- Time factor.

The motivation factors of young people for specifically choosing Latin America as a destination, given the opportunities worldwide, are as mosaic as the ones to volunteer overseas. In many cases, students of Spanish, especially those who had studied the language at school and/or who have applied to do so at university, chose Latin America for the opportunity to practise their Spanish while volunteering. This initially seems peculiar, given the geographical proximity of Britain to Spain. However, Spain as a destination was rejected or not considered in light of the other motivation factors and opportunities offered by Latin America, such as the preference for volunteer work rather than paid work and the association of volunteer work with continents other than Europe.

> My main reason, before choosing anywhere, was to practice speaking Spanish. So when I made my shortlist, it was to Spanish-speaking countries. …There aren't that many companies that go to Spain. …I could've gone to work, but I wanted to volunteer specifically.

> I want to learn Spanish.

> *Researcher: You can do that in Spain!*

> Yeah, kind of third world…much different culture to Spain's.

Siblings and peers who had visited Latin America as part of a gap year provided first-hand information about the experience for current participants.

> I've got an older brother who's doing Latin American studies and he went to South America on his gap year and seeing his photos and hearing his stories made me want to come here.

In addition, Latin America proved popular among those with prior experience of other long-haul destinations, who wished to see something different from that of their peers preferring traditional gap year destinations or who had the possibility to travel to other destinations easily at any time.

> I know quite a lot of people that have done Thailand and Australia. But I don't know anybody that's come here. I felt it would be quite unusual to come here and most of my friends thought I was going to Africa because they had no idea where Belize was.

> That's the other real hot spot for gap years and I've seen a lot of that.

> I've got friends in South Africa. So it's easier for me to say, in a uni holiday or whatever, to say I'm going to South Africa, I'm doing South Africa. It'll be easier than coming out here.

Typical pull factors of destinations, such as scenery and diversity, also played a role in the decision making. The second speaker in particular was attracted to being able to learn Spanish in multiple settings and communities.

> Because they offered to go to the jungle which was the main thing that attracted me.

> Because of the range of countries and I wanted to learn Spanish and couldn't really do that in many other places.

Furthermore, at times it is not so much the destination but the experience as a whole, as well as the time of the year that it occurs, which proves to be the determining factor in deciding an experience.

> I was actually going to Borneo...but the time fitted better. I could have started in September but I didn't have the money, so needed time to fundraise.

Finally, the extent to which Latin America is 'unknown' as a destination forms a pull factor.

> I've always been interested in South America because I never really had an idea of what the culture was like. Living in England, it's just something, somewhere you don't know anything about.

The uncertainty and unease of 'the unknown' can be mediated by experiencing it from inside the comfort zone of a structured travel experience arranged by an organization. What organizations offered and what gap year travellers perceived to get out of the packages formed a third thematic category.

Motivation for the Choice of Organization

Nine motivational factors emerged from the data. Without particular order, they are:

- Wish to do more than just travel;
- Lack of confidence travelling independently;
- Reputation;
- Safety;
- Influence of family/peers;
- Variety offered;
- Specific elements of experience;
- Type of organization; and
- Marketing efforts of organization.

A complex set of motivational factors are displayed, with the influence of peers once again being important.

> I wanted to learn Spanish and work with children and trek...no other ones combine...apart from VentureCo.

> *Researcher: Why did you choose this organization over them then?*

> Because more of my friends had done it and said it was quite good!

> I was introduced to them through a colleague when I was talking about my gap year and she said 'Oh my God, you have to go with them, they're amazing!'

An important motivating factor was the variety offered by the organizations. Some admitted to being attracted to the organization offering the most variety or the best combination of elements to suit their preferences.

> I could possibly do this for another month, but I've got friends who're doing another organization, and they're doing the same thing for three months. I would just get bored with it.

> First of all I wanted to go to South America. Then it was the package that I really liked. . . . The three events. You've got the project, the Spanish, and the teaching. I didn't want six months doing one thing.

> Because of the project. And the variety. I didn't want to be stuck on something for ten weeks if I didn't like it. At least you've got three stages on this one. If you don't like it, you know you've only got two or three weeks left to get through it.

However, it is often a specific element of the experience which explains its popularity.

> I think the main reason I chose it was the Spanish phase, because I knew I'd be studying it and then I had some vague idea that I could speak Spanish while teaching.

> I wanted to do a conservational project, as I'm a farmer and interested in agriculture.

Profit-making companies tend not to trigger an interest, while registered charities and other non-profit making organizations do carry an appeal.

> It's not a company, which is a big plus!

> To come out here to volunteer . . . you don't want someone making profit out of it! . . . I don't want to go with a company, because it has profits to think about!

The way in which organizations portray themselves and are known for providing a safe experience in a supposedly unknown destination provides assurance for gap year travellers and their parents. Older travellers in an unknown destination may also be attracted to the same assurances.

> My mum heard about it and said it sounds really safe.

> I would have been interested to go with them just to the jungle and then I could have just come here and done the language course myself. When I was back home, I didn't know how the systems worked. It could have worked out cheaper if I'd come here off my own back, but a lot more complicated.

As previously discussed, volunteering both at home and overseas may be driven by the motivation to acquire experience and make contacts for the future. In the following case, the choice of organization was based on the project and the contacts at the destination.

> I really wanted to do the [charity] thing, because at some point in the future I'd like to work with the [charity] directly, and it would be good to see how they work and possibly get some contacts.

Conclusion

From the research we illustrated that motivations of British gap year travellers volunteering in Latin America are multifaceted and interlaced. No one or two factors can be attributed as the sole underlying reasons for gappers choices, but rather a multitude of influences, past experiences, ambitions, perceptions and present circumstances combine to form a mosaic of motivations for a gap year experience that will potentially be unique, purposeful and memorable for each individual gap year traveller.

These motivations are not wholly unlike motivations of young travellers in general or of other volunteer tourists. Gap year travellers seem akin to travellers described by Clark (1992) for whom destination and activity or product choices are important choice factors. Gap year travellers in this study also seem to epitomize the 'new volunteers' in which gappers select structured experiences after a comparison of other experience products, seeking variety and best value (Hustinx, 2001).

Learning a language principally with practice through conversation with local native speakers has previously been cited as an important motivational factor for volunteer tourists and particularly for gap year travellers (Wearing, 2001; Simpson, 2005). Some gap year travellers in this study cited the language tuition and interaction opportunities with local Spanish speakers as appealing factors in their choice of volunteering organization. This suggests that one avenue for further research is the relationship between language skills and volunteer tourism, as the implications could impact the way volunteer tourism organizations arrange their excursions and select potential volunteers. Also, in light of the gap year being such a culturally entrenched rite of passage in Britain, research into the relationship of language learning and volunteer tourism, particularly in Latin America, could well also have implications for British secondary and tertiary institutions offering Spanish language tuition.

In response to Callanan and Thomas' (2005) criticism, altruism is seen by the gappers as a motivational factor, as they perceive communities in Latin America as needing and appreciating their assistance. This observation is further explored in Simpson's work (2005). However, the overall concern about the efficacy of young volunteers' efforts overseas remains a pertinent question, one which numerous authors in this book are attempting to address (see Chapters 2, 4, 5, 14 and 15, this volume). As clearer understandings of all types of volunteer tourists emerge – including gap year travellers – we hope more effective volunteer tourism programmes can be developed which mutually benefit both the travellers and the host destinations.

References

Anthoney, D. (1999) *Volunteering: User-friendly for Youth? A Study of Volunteering by Young People in Scotland.* Volunteer Development Scotland, Stirling, UK.

BBC News (2006) School Language Decline Continues. Available at: http://news.bbc.co.uk/1/hi/education/4404998.stm

Callanan, M. and Thomas, S. (2005) Volunteer tourism: deconstructing volunteer activities with a dynamic environment. In Novelli, M. (ed.) *Niche Tourism, Contemporary Issues, Trends and Cases*. Butterworth-Heinemann, Oxford, UK, pp. 183–200.

Clarke, J. (1992) A marketing spotlight on the youth 'four S's' consumer. *Tourism Management* September, 321–326.

Collins, J., DeZerega, S. and Hecksher, Z. (2002) *How to Live Your Dream of Volunteering Overseas*. Penguin Books, London.

Foster, J. and Fernandes, M. (1996) *Young People and Volunteering: Research, Public Policy & Practice*. The National Centre for Volunteering, London.

Franklin, A. (2003) *Tourism: An Introduction*. Sage, London.

Griffith, S. (2003) *Teaching English Abroad: Talk Your Way Around the World*, 6th edn. Vacation Work, Oxford, UK.

Hottola, P. (1999) *The Intercultural Body*. The University of Joensuu, Finland.

Hustinx, L. (2001) Individualisation and new styles of youth volunteering: an empirical exploration. *Voluntary Action* 3(2), 57–76.

Lapham, S.L. (1990) Volunteer motivation and attitudes: field and laboratory studies of intrinsic motivation. PhD thesis, University of Exeter, UK.

Little, M. (2000) Gap year students would rather travel than volunteer. *Third Sector*, 7 September, p. 5.

Miller, G. (2003) Working holidays organized by environmental charities. In: Ritchie, B. (ed.) *Managing Educational Tourism*. Channel View, Clevedon, UK.

Potter, R. (2004) *Worldwide Volunteering, Hundreds of Volunteer Opportunities for Gap Year, Holiday or Vacation Projects*, 4th edn. How to Books, Oxford, UK.

Simpson, K. (2005) Broad horizons? Geographies and pedagogies of the gap year. PhD thesis, Newcastle University, UK.

Thomas, G. (2001) *Human Traffic. Skills, Employers and International Volunteering*. Demos, London.

Wearing, S. (2001) *Volunteer Tourism: Experiences That Make a Difference*. CAB International, Wallingford, UK.

11 The Dynamics Behind Volunteer Tourism

P.L. Pearce[1] and A. Coghlan[2]

[1]Foundation Professor of Tourism, School of Business, James Cook University, Townsville, Queensland, Australia; [2]James Cook University, Townsville, Queensland, Australia

This chapter directs attention towards the antecedents of one emerging form of contemporary tourism; specifically it focuses on the roots of volunteer tourism. It is argued here that there are four useful levels of analysis in seeking an understanding of the drivers of alternative tourism and its immediate exemplar of volunteer tourism. The levels are initially broad and inclusive but as each layer of analysis is considered and the questions it addresses are discussed, the focus becomes more specific. The first level of analysis is historical and broadly anthropological and here the development of civilizations, environmental ethics and the quest for otherness will be explored as sources of understanding. Next, a macro-sociological view will be explored. While at times such a view is closely allied to the cultural historians' and anthropologists' perspectives, some additional insights will be generated by considering the characteristics attributed to generational differences. In particular, the contrasting travel attitudes and values of baby boomers, generation X and generation Y cohorts will be considered. The active, embodied responses of these cohorts to what is broadly referred to as postmodernity complete a third and dynamic micro-sociological level of explanation. The final level of explanation to be employed is psychological with the frameworks of social psychology (in terms of equity theory) and motivational analysis both making contributions to the discussion. It will be argued that, like tourism itself, the roots of volunteer tourism are based in different layers of human and social needs which act in concert to create the forms we witness. For the participating individuals, for the companies which manage the volunteer experiences and for the communities and settings the volunteers assist, the sharper understanding of the forces giving rise to volunteer tourism can be used to assess its likely longevity. At a less pragmatic level, an understanding of tourism's role in shaping issues of identity and human growth is a particular insight from the focus on the roots of volunteer tourism.

Levels of Explanation

The perspective that there are somewhat self-contained levels of explanation for human conduct has been around for a long time (Peirce, 1877). In essence, this view suggests that there are distinctive questions posed by different disciplines as researchers and scientists seek to account for patterns and changes in human societies and social life. It is a view consistent with the apparent tribalism of disciplines and their quests for power and prestige (Becher, 1989). One way of viewing these disciplinary approaches to the roots of volunteer tourism lies in distinguishing between proximate and ultimate causes (Mayr, 1982). Ultimate causes tend to look beyond the short-term impacts of events and influences and seek to identify the larger molar forces which generate the initial conditions in which the proximate causes work. For volunteer tourism such a focus is aligned with understanding the conditions of life in the tourists' generating and receiving environments as well as movements in public consciousness. By way of contrast, proximate causes are those which focus on the immediate and enabling conditions fostering an activity or movement. For volunteer tourism this might be the reported motivations of a specific tour group, declining budgets in science for field research or the promotional efforts of travel companies branching out into new tourism forms. Proximate causes are therefore likely to be given by disciplines which are heavily influenced by contextual considerations. In this chapter, each of the levels of explanation discussed to explore the roots of volunteer tourism contains some proximate and some ultimate causes. Predictably perhaps, the balance between these explanations shifts as we move from broad cultural and anthropological perspectives to more specific psychological inquiry with the accompanying movement being from ultimate to proximate causes.

The historical and anthropological level

In a wide-ranging account of the differences among contemporary societies Diamond (1997) identifies four forces which have been determining factors shaping the world of the 21st century. Basing his argument on the critical role of plant and animal domestication as the route providing early communities with economic surplus and hence the opportunities for specialized non-food-producing roles, he asserts that continental differences in the supply of suitable species for domestication were a key factor. Europe was initially advantaged by this factor and coupled with an easier transfer of technology across the continent as well as being more centrally located for links to Asia and Africa, this area of the world benefited most from trade and the exchange of technologies. As an additional factor, the population of Europe was sufficiently large to support more inventors and innovators and, in time, the skills to explore and exploit other societies. The Western societies of today are the direct beneficiaries of these biogeographical advantages which fostered the rise of Europe and the European-based settlements around the globe.

It can be noted quite readily that the source countries for volunteer tourists are these same European-based settlements. Mostly, volunteer tourists are from Western Europe and North America and to a lesser extent from Australia and New Zealand (Wearing, 2001; McGehee, 2002; Galley and Clifton, 2004). The first question to be asked to explore the roots of volunteer tourism is: Why is this pattern of source countries so closely tied to the evolution of the state of contemporary societies? To pose this question differently: Why are there not many more volunteer tourists from Asia and the Middle East where there are at least parallel and conspicuous pockets of affluence and skills?

A consideration of cultural differences in the values and attitudes of nationality groups appears to lie behind these differences. The same forces which have given rise to European-based or European-derived societies and the pursuit of individual well-being have had two other associated consequences. The first of these is described as alienation between humans and their environment, a Cartesian belief that men and women stand apart from nature and are able to use it for their well-being (Nisbett, 2003; Gore, 2005). Yet paradoxically these same individualistic and exploitative traits also carry the seeds of ethical and moral responsibility – beliefs that individuals are responsible and have the capacity to change and correct mistakes. As Nisbett (2003) reports, this is a different intellectual and cultural tradition, a different way of viewing responsibility and one's place in the world than that which prevails in Muslim, Buddhist and Confucian societies (McGehee, 2002). Viewed in this way, volunteer tourists can be seen as a sociocultural group or movement representing an ethical body of people correcting or at least ameliorating the historical exploitation and environmental mistakes on which their society has been built. This does not mean to suggest that every volunteer tourist is immediately conscious or will report being a part of an environmental or social change group, but at this broad level of explanation which addresses the patterns of volunteer tourism, there is some legitimacy to an overview of the activity as deriving from a collective ethical and remedial effort.

One of the other directly relevant contributions of anthropological analyses to tourism study and volunteer tourism lies in a repeated concern with tourists' quest for otherness (Smith, 1989; Van den Bergh, 1994; Nash, 1996; Harris, 2005). This concern with experiencing other groups of people and other places can be considered as a functionally useful activity for the sending culture. That is, seeking otherness is more than individuals in a society seeking novelty elsewhere; it is culturally sanctioned behaviour of value to the whole society. As Diamond (2005) suggests, societies can collapse due to a number of interconnected forces. Some of these causes for collapse involve failing to interact well with neighbours and outlying trading partners and failing to generate new responses to crises of environmental and social management. In this broad functional view, volunteer tourism enriches the sending society by developing a pool of personnel with international experiences and an embodied awareness of global issues.

One line of argument reinforcing the view that volunteer tourism is culturally sanctioned is the large absence of counter and critical views in the existing literature. While backpackers have had their critics, and tourists from earliest times have been derided for becoming 'more conceited, more unprincipled, more dissipated, and more incapable of any serious application to study or business' than if they stayed at home (Smith, 1775, cited in Hibbert, 1969, p. 224), volunteer tourists have largely escaped such outbursts. Indeed gap years, particularly in the UK, are seen in some circles as an almost obligatory post-secondary school experience and are the source of many younger volunteer tourists.

The macro-sociological level

The roots of volunteer tourism can also be explored with a discussion of the generational differences informing tourism and travel styles. This kind of explanation is based on large-scale, quantitative survey work. Such research typically reports the attitudes and values of different age cohorts and has been conducted in a range of countries with some interesting parallels in the findings. The divisions of interest used in this kind of analysis are broadly referred to as baby boomers (persons born from 1945 to 1964), generation X (those born from 1965 to 1979) and generation Y (the group with birth dates since 1980). The application of this kind of work to tourism markets can be illustrated by reference to the work on young budget travellers and backpackers (Richards and Wilson, 2004; West, 2005). This work is briefly highlighted here because it describes markets and cohorts allied to volunteer tourism. Three stages in backpacker evolution can be detected and these correspond to select travel behaviours appearing in each of the generational cohorts. The phenomenon of hippy drifters as reported by Riley and Cohen describes a subset of baby boomer travel where the influences of a counterculture linked to drugs and experimentation with lifestyles produced what Cohen called nomads from affluence. Such travellers formed small enclaves in preferred destinations and eschewed the comforts of conventional tourism. When generation X started to travel in their post-secondary school years, the labels attached to youth travellers and backpackers were sometimes quite unfavourable, reflecting this earlier association with the hippy drifters of the baby boom era. A range of studies found that the generation X travellers were more affluent than most imagined and were prepared to spend on adventure activities and experiences, if not on luxurious accommodation (Pearce, 1990). The generation X travellers were able to select their experiences from a range of offerings designed by an increasingly attentive tourism sector. More recent accounts of the backpacker market, which increasingly deals with generation Y travellers, has unearthed some further differences with decreasing lengths of time spent travelling, greater use of better quality accommodation, greater involvement in structured experiences and a new dependence on technology for decision making and social support (Noy and Cohen, 2005). In this brief examination it can be seen that the generational analysis seems to matter with the conditions arising from the developmental and social zeitgeist having an influence on travel behaviour.

The application of these generational legacies to volunteer tourism is somewhat more speculative since there is not a rich vein of large-scale survey work.

Nevertheless, the characteristics of the generations appear to fit in different ways with the core ideas of volunteer tourism. While other chapters of this volume outline in more detail the definitional parameters of this form of travel, there is a commonality in most definitions which sees current volunteer tourism activities as being performed as service to others in a novel setting for which an individual pays (Wearing, 2001). Volunteer tourism is a phenomenon which serves all generations but is most marked among generation Y and to a lesser extent generation X travellers. Some of the characteristics of generation Y which support the rise of volunteer tourism include a heightened awareness of global problems, sustainability issues and related travel opportunities fostered by Internet services. Howe and Strauss (2005) report that generation Y individuals are frequent volunteers because they value variety, change, multitasking and believe they can make an impact. Another characteristic of the generation Y cohort is a different decision-making style; there are tendencies for them to make rapid and somewhat emotive decisions with reduced consideration for the long-term or career consequences of their choices. Dougherty *et al.* (2004) describe them as a sheltered and frequently rewarded generation with short time horizons. On this basis, generation Y travellers are more likely to readily decide to volunteer, to go abroad for an activity irrespective of immediate career consequences and to expect to be well looked after and even praised while doing it. There is a related enabling argument here that many generation Y members are effectively supported for longer by their baby boomer parents. Importantly they are considered to get along better with their parents than many previous generations and to value their parents' assistance and input in decisions (Merrill Associates, 2005). Such support gives them an extended adolescence in which to pursue the kinds of causes and experiences which volunteer tourism may yield.

A micro-sociological level

The broad analyses of the forces shaping volunteer tourism provide a perspective on the ultimate causes of the activity. A closer and more detailed approach to the roots of volunteer tourism lies in new conceptualizations of tourism at a micro-sociological level. It is at this level where the proximate causes of alternative and volunteer tourism are most apparent. The kinds of questions about the dynamics of volunteer tourism addressed in this level of analysis are those which ask how tourists manage and respond to the volunteer tourism opportunities. As Franklin (2003) suggests, tourism is as much about a way of seeing the world as it is an industry. He argues, along with de Botton (2002) and Rojek and Urry (1997), that fresh insights for the study of tourism are possible if a new view of the tourist is adopted. He recommends seeing tourists as active, manipulative, selective, embodied and aware individuals whose experiences are linked to, and integrated with, their whole life. As Pearce (2005) states:

> A full understanding of behaviour (and tourist behaviour) requires that the interacting parties be viewed as actively constructing their experiences and their relationships. Tourists, like other social actors, are not passive bodies pushed from place to place and from group to group to group by mechanistic internal

forces and external factors. Rather they are best viewed as organizers of their social world and experiences, acting out roles, communicating their identities and purposefully structuring their time.

(p. 113)

There are perhaps some limits to this view, such as when tour groups are so tightly organized and closely monitored by their guides and tour companies that their immediate freedoms are limited. Here it can be argued that altercasting, the selection of one's roles by others, prevails. Even here, however, such tourists will be interpreting and filtering what they see, and their own experiences and travellers' tales will be unique accounts of the time spent.

The importance of these arguments in understanding volunteer tourism lies in the focus on the travellers' capacities to interpret their experience. In this view, volunteer tourism is not a thing to be consumed but an opportunity to be realized and created. This perspective can now be joined to the previous discussion of the broad commonalities associated with the generations and the implicit cultural approval of volunteer tourism from within the source societies.

The active, embodied and aware tourists we are now conceptualizing are making their choices and creating and maintaining their identities from within predominantly postmodern Western societies. A range of authors have characterized such societies as possessing some distinctive characteristics including being information-saturated and having reduced levels of spirituality (Lash and Urry, 1994; Morley, 2001; Urry, 2002). Additionally, postmodern societies are heavily influenced by the mass media. The physical places people live in change rapidly with consequential losses in earlier forms of community identity and a sense of place (Bauman, 1998). Further, the cultures in which the volunteer tourists are forming their views of the world can be described as service-rich and consumer-oriented.

Some indications of how volunteer tourists actively react to these conditions through their tourism experiences are provided in original data collected by Coghlan (2005). Her detailed study consisted of surveys of over 60 volunteer tourists from six organizations specializing principally in marine conservation. Information from the volunteers was also collected in daily diaries from a smaller number of participants. The key satisfaction findings in Coghlan's study were that the volunteers valued most the opportunity to see things that few others are likely to see. Additionally, they reported very high scores for the statements that the vacation had a special meaning for them and agreed that the volunteering experience had unique and special moments. There was some variability in the satisfaction scores for the different volunteer tourism expeditions. The complexity of the experiences and the different ways in which the activities were realized for individuals are highlighted in some of the following quotations abstracted from the travellers' 10-day self-completion diaries. Mary, a 53-year-old American lawyer, reports:

The trip was fun, educational and an eye opener to scientific research. The crew were great; the research didn't get in the way of the great experiences of seeing the animals.

Jo, a 27-year-old Canadian student, observes:

> The trip was absolutely fabulous. I had a great time doing things I never thought
> I could or would ever do, I learned so much on this trip I feel like my head is
> going to explode.

Simone, a 28-year-old British psychologist, comments:

> My best trip so far made possible by the positive and good temperaments of staff
> and principle investigators... felt we were being treated really well and questions
> and comments, no matter how trivial, were always taken seriously.

Jess, a 24-year-old American social worker, notes:

> There is a part of me that would like to be on this expedition with my head
> here with me, instead of all over the world in many places and times, but
> acknowledging this I am making a conscious decision to continue to drift.

These comments, and many others like them from the diaries, indicate the interconnectedness between the volunteer tourists' world and their on-site experiences. These respondents span the generations but the quest for achievement,
distinctiveness and using the experience to add value and meaning to life is
dominant. What is somewhat less dominant, and remembering that this study
is focused on marine science volunteering, is a strong sense of the usefulness
of the work for conservation and environmental management. The process of
how volunteer tourists work with the opportunities available to them is revealed
in the participants' detailed daily records. Whether the trip is about lifelong
ambitions to work with and see animals, a desire to have time away from problematic relationships or a wish to place oneself in unusual settings with varied
tasks, volunteer tourism is portrayed in these diaries and survey responses as a
managed and created event in the travellers' lives. Coghlan (2005) reports in
integrating the findings from the survey and diary work that four elements are
important in determining a good volunteer experience. These four elements
are skill development and new personal insights, a good social life, experiencing novelty and contributing to a worthwhile project. This micro-sociological
attention to how travellers manage and achieve their goals is richly descriptive
and ideographic. It provides a corrective to etic analyses of volunteer tourism
(and tourist study generally) which imposes standardized scales and researchers'
constructs on the respondents. It suggests that volunteer tourists are certainly
not all alike and that different cohorts will work out their satisfaction with the
activity according to their current personal preoccupations and ambitions.

A psychological level

A further level of analysis pertaining to the dynamics of volunteer tourism seeks to
move beyond the rich descriptions of the volunteers' active participation in mould-
ing their experience. A psychological and social psychological goal for investigating
volunteer tourism lies in attempting to identify models or systems of understanding
which add a predictive component to the consideration of the activity.

One potential candidate for the task of adding such a predictive element to the dynamics of volunteer tourism lies with equity theory. At the heart of equity theory is a model suggesting that a stable state in social relationships and exchanges can only exist if there is a perceived balance between costs and rewards or more specifically between perceived inputs and outputs (Kunkel, 1997). It can be noted immediately that there is an emic component to equity theory as it is the judgement of the participant and not the outside observer which determines the relative worth of what they are giving and getting. This kind of sensitivity to the participants' views of their experiences is congruent with the active, engaged tourist discussed in the section on micro-sociological accounts of the volunteer experience. In the early writing on equity theory, there was a consideration of philanthropist–recipient relationships, that is, relationships analogous to volunteering, and hence there is an a priori case that the further use of equity theory may be of value in the present context (Walster *et al.*, 1978).

The consistent challenge for equity theory is the identification of the inputs and the outputs as perceived and valued by the participant and, in this case, the volunteer tourist. Equity theory proposes that an imbalance between inputs and outputs leads to distress and people in such situations will seek to restore equity. They can do this in one of the two ways: elevate the value of the rewards they are receiving and work harder to get more rewards or decrease their own inputs and hence lower their costs. What they cannot do, according to equity theory, is persist in a deeply inequitable relationship or exchange. The inputs and outputs may not be of the same kind, and often they are not, which is why an intimate examination of the value individuals place on the inputs and outputs is so central to equity analyses. The distress felt by apparently inequitable relationships is illustrated in the following example from a web site forum dedicated to volunteer tourism:

> [W]hy are voluntary organizations such a rip off!!! Why do so called voluntary organizations such as Global Vision International, Coral Cay Conservation, Frontier, etc. charge so much money for their programmes? I mean I've just seen a programme with an organization called Greenforce where they're charging 2,700 pounds sterling for ten (yes ten!) weeks in the Bahamas (flight Not! Included! Flipping rip off!!!).

A notable feature of this example in addition to the emotional energy it reveals is that the individual is not even a participant on this volunteer programme but is angered by the very contemplation of what they see as the inequity involved.

There are several conditions and influences on perceived equity and inequity. There appear to be different individual sensitivities to these distortions in inputs and outputs (Janssen, 2001; Allen and White, 2002). Some individuals may be less troubled than others, possibly due to differences in the strength of their values such as fairness and belief in a just world (Feather, 1999). The methods used to adapt to inequity appear to be linked to the perceived cost of restoring the inequity with most respondents redefining the situation if that is the easier route (Greenberg, 1990; Miles *et al.*, 1994). Another distinction made in the literature is that between intentional inequity and that which is produced as an unforeseen consequence. As an example from the volunteer tourist data collected by Coghlan, one respondent reported her disappointment and frustration at not sighting a species of whale but then provided an apology for this reported annoyance by refusing to blame the captain and crew for the poor weather which prevented her goals from being achieved. By way of contrast, a respondent who believed she had committed her money and time to work with dolphins was more than a little annoyed that the company's plan had obviously been to spend most time on turtle research.

The operationalization of equity theory has followed the path of interviewing respondents and often prompting them by providing a list of inputs and outputs. Of course, care needs to be taken in this approach not to dominate the situation with the researchers' predetermined categories. Mood checklists and rating scales for annoyance have been used to assess respondents' perceived overall level of comfort with the relationship or the exchange. The kinds of inputs which can be identified from the participants' perspectives include money, time, labour, enthusiasm and certain sacrifices in terms of foregoing familiar comforts, while the rewards may be making a difference, access to special locations, new contacts, travel, food and accommodation. There are reports on web sites describing volunteer experiences as well as previous studies which suggest that for some participants the rewards also include having a novel experience, building some skills and acquiring a fund of stories which are socially useful (Wearing, 2001; *Lonely Planet*, 2005). Recognition that the companies have difficulties in funding their expeditions and supporting their personnel is sometimes considered when volunteers assess the money they pay.

It is possible to develop systematically the earlier applications of equity theory to philanthropic recipient relationships developed by Walster *et al.* (1978) to what we now know about volunteer tourism. This is a somewhat more complex task than the usual one-to-one relationships studied in equity theory. For volunteer tourism, there are both individual volunteers to be considered as well as a view of the volunteers on any expedition as a group. The volunteer tour companies themselves consist of those in contact with the volunteers as well as those in head office pursuing administrative roles. When the volunteer tourism includes interacting with communities and their members, there are further webs of complication. Those with a less anthropogenic view of the world would argue that non-human species are also beneficiaries of volunteer tourism and must form some part of the equations of inputs and outputs.

The treatment of volunteer inputs and outputs in Table 11.1 does not extend explicitly to the more difficult cases involving communities and addressing the moral and ethical issues involved in interacting with non-human species. Arguably, the interests of these beneficiaries of the efforts of volunteer tourism could be subsumed in the assessment of the volunteer tourism company's views of the world. The equity approach to assessing the interactions in volunteer tourism as suggested here could form the basis of further study and analysis. The recommendations for actually assessing the ratios of inputs and inputs from the previous literature are varied with perhaps the most promise being offered by holistic treatments of the inputs and outputs rather than fully documenting

Table 11.1. Predictions based on equity theory for volunteer tourism.

One person-volunteer tourism company
(an individual focus)

Outcome 1	Reactions
Volunteer's ratio of inputs to outputs exceeds company's inputs to outputs	Volunteer feels satisfied, marginally guilty; company may not notice but some company individuals in contact with the volunteer who may feel overworked
Outcome 2	Reactions
Volunteer's ratio of inputs to outputs approximately equals company's ratio of inputs to outputs	Volunteer feels satisfied; individuals in company in contact with the volunteer may develop close rapport with the individual
Outcome 3	Reactions
Volunteer's ratio of inputs to outputs is less than company's ratio of inputs to outputs	Volunteer feels angry and annoyed, likely not to travel with the company again and not to recommend volunteer tourism; company individuals may be targeted and criticized

Tour group-volunteer tourism company
(a company focus)

Outcome 1	Reactions
The tour group's ratio of inputs to outputs may be greater than the company's inputs to outputs	The tour company may feel guilty or over benefited but unlikely to act unless group complaints are forthcoming
Outcome 2	Reactions
The tour group's ratio of inputs to outputs may approximately equal the company's ratio of inputs to outputs	Company is satisfied and continues to operate tours
Outcome 3	Reactions
The tour groups' ratio of inputs to outputs is less than the company's ratio of inputs to outputs	The company may reduce services and attempt to raise costs or demand more work from the tour group as a whole

the specifics of what the interacting parties contribute and gain. This means it is preferable to ask and asses the inputs/outputs ratio and the participants' reactions with such questions as: Overall how would you describe the extent of your contributions to this trip? Overall how would you describe your outcomes from this relationship and activity? These items are measured on a rating scale where there is room to locate one's position from extremely positive to extremely negative. For the reactions to this balance of contributions and outcomes the questions include: How content do you feel? How angry do you feel? How guilty do you feel about the experiences you have with this organization or group?

While equity theory offers one pathway to explore the balance between mutual assessments of the interacting parties, a further detailed appraisal of volunteer tourist behaviour resides in the analysis of traveller motivation.

There is a substantial history of motivational studies in tourism with the earliest efforts using metaphors and analogies to describe traveller behaviour. For example, there have been models of forces pushing and pulling tourists, there are one-dimensional bell curve models of a willingness or unwillingness to explore the unfamiliar and there remain approaches built around stable steady states and unstable states of arousal (Plog, 1974; Iso-Ahola, 1982; Beard and Ragheb, 1983). Arguably, the development and consolidation of these earlier approaches have been enhanced through the recognition that a multi-motive view of the forces driving travellers was needed and that a good theory of tourist motivation needed to account for the way individuals and societies change over time (Mansfield, 1992). A continuing attempt to address these difficult requirements in tourist motivation theory, including the further problem of measuring motivation effectively, has been to develop an approach recognizing that tourists have a career in travel and do not just participate in isolated travel events. The career notion has been richly employed for a long time and in slightly different ways in the leisure and recreation literature (Hughes, 1937; Bryan, 1977; Harris, 2005).

One specific approach to tourist motivation constructed with these requirements in mind and which offers the promise of insights into volunteer tourism is the travel career pattern (TCP) approach (Lee and Pearce, 2003; Pearce, 2005; Pearce and Lee, 2005). The TCP view of tourist motivation is an extension and development of an earlier but somewhat more limited travel career ladder approach (Ryan, 1998). Building on detailed traveller motivation survey work with both Western and Asian samples, the TCP identified some recurring patterns in travel motivation dependent on the travellers' previous experience. Fourteen basic factors in traveller motivation were consistently identified from a large pool of travel motivation items employed in multiple previous studies. Less-experienced travellers tend to identify a very large range of the motivation factors as important while more-experienced travellers identify a more restricted range. The travel veterans particularly emphasize involvement with host communities and settings as important to them. Both groups share in common three core travel motives as the most important of all. These three foundation travel motives are the search for novelty, a desire for escape and relaxation, and the opportunity to build relationships. A diagrammatic representation of these patterns is presented in Fig. 11.1.

The potential value of such a travel motivation approach as a level of explanation for volunteer tourism can be outlined. These suggestions may help assist or stimulate future work in this psychological style. The TCP approach could be used to plot the way experienced volunteer tourists remember and recall their set of volunteer experiences with a view that if the model is apposite, then a trajectory of change should conform to the increasingly specific motivational frame driving their behaviour. Additionally, comparisons between less-experienced and more-experienced volunteer tourists could also be considered in cross-sectional approaches to volunteer tourism studies. Here the value of the TCP model lies in providing a structured prediction of which motives should be held in common and which motives should be different between the groups. If this kind of work yields the predicted patterns of motivation, then there are some potentially useful implications for those who design volunteer tourism

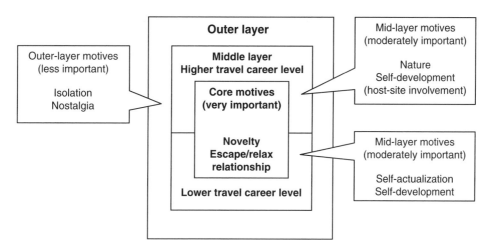

Fig. 11.1. Travel career patterns (TCP). (From Pearce, 2005.)

experiences. It would offer the tour organizers the opportunity of emphasizing and directing their volunteers with different experience levels to different kinds of trips, and, further, they could shape the interactions and activities on those trips to meet the different travel intentions.

Conclusion

In this chapter, the authors have analysed the volunteer tourism sector at a variety of levels in order to capture and reveal some of the complexity and seeming contradictions within the area. By layering the analysis from a macro-scale historical and anthropological level, we are able to pinpoint some of the origins of the sector that guided how it continued to develop. It offers a rationale for the commonly used altruism argument offered by academics and industry alike when discussing the reasons behind volunteering in a tourism context. Yet it also offers insights into some of the apparent contradictions and complexities that a deeper analysis of the sector reveals. Thus, it is shown through the macro- and micro-sociological level that individuals also have their own needs to fulfil through their experience and will approach the volunteer tourism experience with a particular set of expectations and generational imperatives that will influence their actions and interpretation of the volunteering experience. Through this level of analysis, it becomes clear that more emphasis needs to be placed on the individual volunteer tourists as they react to their volunteering setting and interpret their experience depending on their culture, generation and other factors. Finally, this chapter has highlighted some areas for further research, including more in-depth analysis of the generational differences in volunteer tourists' needs and expectations, as well as the role that interpersonal exchange theories may have in explaining the behaviour of volunteer tourists. The kinds of outcomes predicted by equity theory are outlined and how these might impact on both the volunteer tourists and the volunteer tourism are discussed. Clearly, the volunteer tourism sector is a complex phenomenon, which goes far beyond simple altruistic motives. Instead, it is a complex process, where the individual is at the core of understanding the volunteer tourism experience. As research into this sector and the sector itself matures, so will our understanding of the processes that influence the success of a volunteer tourism expedition if researchers address the topic at multiple levels with linked conceptual schemes. As a result, the potential of this sector as a tool for social and environmental good will increase.

References

Allen, R.S. and White, C.S. (2002) Equity sensitivity theory: a test of responses to two under-reward situations. *Journal of Managerial Issues* 14(4), 435–451.

Bauman, Z. (1998) *Globalization: The Human Consequences*. Polity Press, Cambridge.

Beard, J. and Ragheb, M. (1983) Measuring leisure motivation. *Journal of Leisure Research* 15(3), 219–228.

Becher, T. (1989) *Academic Tribes and Territories: Intellectual Enquiry and the Cultures of Discipline*. Open University Press, Milton Keynes, UK.

Bryan, H. (1977) Leisure value system and recreational specialization: the case of trout fishermen. *Journal of Leisure Research* 9, 174–187.

Coghlan, A. (2005) Towards an understanding of the volunteer tourism experience. PhD thesis, James Cook University, Townsville, Australia.

De Botton, A. (2002) *The Art of Travel*. Hamish Hamilton, London.

Diamond, J. (1997) *Guns, Germs and Steel*. Chatto and Windus, London.

Diamond, J. (2005) *Collapse: How Societies Choose to Fail or Survive*. Allen Lane, London.

Dougherty, K., Kirk, H., Harder, R., Hill, M. and Miller, T. (2004) The EchoBoom: what generation Y has in store for the HR community. Available at: http://www.generationsatwork.com/articles/millenials.htm

Feather, N. (1999) *Values Achievement and Justice: Studies in the Psychology of Deservingness*. Kluwer/Plenum Press, New York.

Franklin, A. (2003) *Tourism: An Introduction*. Sage, London.

Galley, G. and Clifton, J. (2004) The motivational and demographic characteristics of research ecotourists: Operation Wallacea volunteers in South East Sulawesi. *Journal of Ecotourism* 3(1), 69–82.

Gore, A. (2005) Dysfunctional society. In: Polman, L.P. (ed.) *Environmental Ethics. Readings in Theory and Application*, 4th edn. Wadsworth Thomson, Belmont, California, pp. 614–623.

Greenberg, J. (1990) Employee theft as a reaction to underpayment inequity: the hidden cost of pay cuts. *Journal of Applied Psychology* 75, 561–568.

Harris, D. (2005) *Key Concepts in Leisure Studies*. Sage, London.

Hibbert, C. (1969) *The Grand Tour*. Weidenfeld & Nicolson, London.

Howe, N. and Strauss, W. (2005) Generation give and give and give. *USA Weekend Magazine*. Available at: http://ww.usaweekend.com/o5-issues/o50424/050424teen-survey.html

Hughes, E.C. (1937) Institutional office and the person. *American Journal of Sociology* 43, 404–413.

Iso-Ahola, S.E. (1982) Toward a social psychological theory of tourism motivation: a rejoinder. *Annals of Tourism Research* 9(2), 256–262.

Janssen, O. (2001) Fairness perceptions as a moderator in the curvilinear relationship between job demands and job performance and job satisfaction. *Academy of Management Journal* 44(5), 1039–1050.

Kunkel, J.H. (1997) The analysis of rule-governed behaviour in social psychology. *The Psychological Record* 47(4), 699–716.

Lash, S. and Urry, J. (1994) *Economies of Signs and Space*. Sage, London.

Lee, U. and Pearce, P. (2003) Travel career patterns: further conceptual adjustment of travel career ladder. In: Busan, J.J. (ed.) *Second Asia Pacific Forum for Graduate Students Research in Tourism*. The Korean Academic Society of Tourism and Leisure, Korea, pp. 65–78.

Lonely Planet (2005) The Thorn Tree Travel Forum. Available at: http://thorntree.lonelyplanet.com/categories.cfm?catid = 30

Mansfield, Y. (1992) From motivation to actual travel. *Annals of Tourism Research* 19, 399–419.

Mayr, E. (1982) *The Growth of Biological Thought*. Belknap Press, Cambridge, Massachusetts.

McGehee, N. (2002) Alternative tourism and social movements. *Annals of Tourism Research* 29(1), 124–143.

Merrill Associates (2005) Call them GenY or millenials: they deserve our attention. Available at: http://www.merrillassociates.net/topic/2005/o5call-them-geny-or-millenials-they-deserve-our-attention

Miles, E.W., Hatfield, J.D. and Huseman, R.C. (1994) Equity sensitivity and outcome importance. *Journal of Organizational Behaviour* 15, 585–596.

Morley, D. (2001) Belongings: place, space and identity in a mediated world. *European Journal of Cultural Studies* 4(4), 425–448.

Nash, D. (1996) *Anthropology of Tourism*. Pergamon, New York.

Nisbett, R.E. (2003) *The Geography of Thought*. Nicholas Brearley, London

Noy, C. and Cohen, E. (eds) (2005) *Israeli Backpackers: From Tourism to Rite of Passage*. State University of New York Press, New York.

Pearce, P.L. (1990) *The Backpacker Phenomenon*. James Cook University, Townsville, Australia.

Pearce, P.L. (2005) *Tourist Behaviour: Themes and Conceptual Schemes*. Channel View, Clevedon, UK.

Pearce, P.L. and Lee, U.-I. (2005) Developing the travel career approach to tourist motivation. *Journal of Travel Research* 43, 226–237.

Peirce, C.S. (1877) The fixation of belief. *Popular Science Monthly*, 12, 1–15. Reprinted in: Moore, E. (ed.) (1972) *Charles S. Peirce: The Essential Writings*. Harper & Row, New York.

Plog, S.C. (1974) Why destinations rise and fall in popularity. *Cornell Hotel and Restaurant Quarterly* 14(4), 55–58.

Richards, G. and Wilson, J. (2004) Widening perspectives in backpacker research. In: Richards, G. and Wilson, J. (eds) *The Global Nomad: Backpacker Travel in Theory and Practice*. Channel View, Clevedon, UK, pp. 253–279.

Rojek, C. and Urry, J. (1997) *Touring Cultures: Transformations of Travel and Theory*. Routledge, London.

Ryan, C. (1998) The travel career ladder an appraisal. *Annals of Tourism Research* 25(4), 936–957.

Smith, V.L. (ed.) (1989) *Hosts and Guests: The Anthropology of Tourism*, 2nd edn. University of Pennsylvania Press, Philadelphia, Pennsylvania.

Urry, J. (2002) *The Tourist gaze*, 2nd edn. Sage, London.

Van den Bergh, P.L. (1994) *The Quest for the Other: EthnicTtourism in San Cristobal, Mexico*. University of Washington Press, Seattle, Washington.

Walster, E., Walster, G.W. and Bersheid, E. (1978) *Equity: Theory and Research*. Allyn & Bacon, Boston, Massachusetts.

Wearing, S. (2001) *Volunteer Tourism: Experiences that Make a Difference*. CAB International, Wallingford, UK.

West, B. (ed.) (2005) *Down the Road: Exploring Backpacker and Independent Travel*. Australian Research Institute, Perth, Australia.

III Journeys at the Edge: Overlaps and Ambiguities

12 All for a Good Cause? The Blurred Boundaries of Volunteering and Tourism

K. LYONS[1] AND S. WEARING[2]

[1]*School of Economics, Politics and Tourism, University of Newcastle, Callaghan, Australia;* [2]*School of Leisure Sport and Tourism, University of Technology Sydney, Lindfield, Australia*

Research has provided a wealth of typological models that help classify tourist behaviours. These taxonomies have been developed based on a broad range of increasingly sophisticated criteria associated with social roles, motivations, activity types, socio-demographics, travel experiences, lifestyles, values and personality (Lyons, 2003). Indeed some of the case studies in this book classify particular forms of volunteer tourism. Proponents of typological research argue that it provides a valuable foundation upon which action can be taken. For example, the principles of market segmentation in tourism are based on the premise that particular types of travellers can be categorized and their needs identified and met through the development of niche products.

Recently, the dominance of typological research has come under criticism. Franklin and Crang (2001) argue that the proliferation of increasingly fine-tuned and elaborate typologies and a general 'craze for classification' (p. 6.) has emerged from viewing tourism as 'a series of discrete, enumerated occurrences of travel, arrival, activity, purchase, departure' (p.13) where tourists are seen as another incarnation of 'Rational Economic Man' (p.13). As a result, there has been an unchallenged belief underlying travel and tourism research that increasingly finer-tuned and elaborate typologies will eventually form a classificatory grid in which definition and regulation can occur (Franklin and Crang, 2001). However, Cohen (1974) argues that it is precisely the fuzziness of tourism categories and the blurred margins it creates that enables conceptual relationships and advancements to be made with other forms of social and cultural activities.

In this chapter we delve into this 'fuzziness' to examine the overlaps and ambiguities of volunteer tourism. This chapter introduces the case studies in this part of the book that provides some critical understandings of volunteer tourism that may be overlooked if a narrower and more rigid view was adopted. In particular, we examine diverse manifestations of the intersections between volunteering and tourism that extend beyond the definition of volunteer tourists as those who 'volunteer in an organized way to undertake holidays that may involve the aiding or alleviating the material poverty of some groups in society, the restoration of certain environments, or research into aspects of society or environment' (Wearing, 2001, p. 240). The following discussion examines three examples of such intersections: service learning, cultural exchange programmes and fund-raising adventure tourism, and considers how each of these challenges conventional views of volunteer tourism.

Service Learners or Coerced Volunteers?

It was once generally agreed that a volunteer was someone who offered service, time and skills to benefit others (Beigbeder, 1991), provided voluntary personal aid while living in developing communities (Clark, 1978) and gained mutual learning, friendship and adventurousness (Gillette, 1968). Volunteers were recognized as those who provided assistance or service for the benefit of the community through formal involvement in an organization, and/or independently as an individual. The concept of volunteering has also been defined as an action perceived as freely chosen, without financial gain, and generally aimed at helping others (Stebbins, 1992).

Many of these early definitions placed altruistic motives at the centre of voluntary behaviour (Lyons, 2003). However, the implied altruism associated with 'helping' has been called into question (see Wearing, 2001). While volunteers almost always help others, the motives for such action are not always primarily altruistic. A number of the cases presented earlier in this book show that contemporary volunteer tourists are motivated by factors such as the opportunity to travel, to develop social connections or to develop skills that will help with one's career (see Chapters 7 and 10, this volume).

The promise of skills development and improved employability underpins a number of international volunteering experiences that are not branded as volunteer tourism but are packaged and marketed, primarily by universities in developed countries such as Australia and the USA, as service learning. Jacoby and Associates (1996) explain that, unlike traditional models of work experience, service learning is unique because it is based upon reciprocity and reflection. Reciprocity refers to what is traditionally the central focus of work experiences where volunteer learners provide their labour and in return, gain skills and knowledge from the experience. The reflection component involves a mirroring process where students examine how an experience relates to how they see themselves and how they would like to be seen (Brown and McCartney, 1999).

The expansion of service learning from domestic experiences to overseas experiences reflects the globalization of higher education (Porter and Monhard, 2001). The advent of specialized areas of study such as international development studies and international business has meant that a growing number of students are being expected to seek out first-hand experiences that will provide a practical foundation to their studies. Likewise, there is growing demand for service-learning experiences in developing countries among service professional education programmes such as teaching, nursing, medicine and social work. The length and nature of these service-learning experiences vary widely from 1-week study tours that incorporate a short volunteering activity, through to semester or year-long study-abroad programmes that feature significant voluntary work commitments (Myers-Lipton, 1996).

The value of international service learning is well recognized in higher education institutions and is increasingly seen as a non-negotiable component of undergraduate education (Roberts, 2003). Increasingly, students who undertake such experiences do so because of the expectation that such experience is essential for one's education and future career. Conceptually, these experiences can be considered a form of what Ellis (1997) describes as mandated or coerced volunteering which also describes work for the dole schemes and court-ordered community service. Ellis (1997) points out that there has been little consideration in the literature given to these volunteer experiences that emerge from contexts where there is little choice.

While the value of these experiences has been analysed and documented (c.f. Myers-Lipton, 1996), warnings have been sounded that reflect similar concerns, raised in this volume, about the impact of volunteer tourism upon host–visitor relationships and understandings. As Grusky (2000) suggests:

> International service-learning programs burst with potential and stumble with the weight of contradictions left unattended. Without thoughtful preparation, orientation, program developments and the encouragement of study, as well as critical analysis and reflection, the programs can easily become small theaters that recreate historic cultural misunderstandings and simplistic stereotypes and replay, on a more intimate scale, the huge disparities in income and opportunity that characterize North–South relations today.
>
> (p. 858)

The implications of this trend in education towards requiring graduates to have undertaken voluntary service abroad raise important questions about efficacy and ethics. It is unknown if the reduction or removal of choice from these volunteer tourists impacts the quality of their voluntary work, the degree to which it creates cultural empathy and understanding and whether it creates more problems for host communities than it solves.

Cultural Ambassadors or More?

Traditionally, volunteers have been seen as those individuals who receive no monetary compensation for their voluntary efforts (Brudney, 2000). However, over the last decade, the blurring of paid and voluntary work has become commonplace (Lyons, 2003). Indeed, it has been the practice of large service agencies such as the US Peace Corps and VISTA to not only include reimbursement to volunteers for out-of-pocket expenses but to also provide cash and in-kind incentives such as college fee payments, thereby blurring the line between 'stipended volunteering and low paying jobs' (Ellis, 1997, p. 29). These blurred boundaries are very evident in new forms of cultural exchange programmes that have proliferated in the last two decades and are major players in providing travel experiences to young people wishing to travel abroad for extended periods (Lyons, 2003).

Cultural exchange programmes have long been associated with promoting tolerance, goodwill and understanding of cultural differences (White, 2002), and have been identified by politicians as a cure-all to a range of deeply ingrained regional conflicts (see Netanyahu, 1998). Proponents of programmes designed to facilitate cultural exchange emphasize their importance in terms of broad macro-level relationships between countries and cultures that help rid nations of 'neo-coloniality' (Altbach and Lewis, 1998, p. 54). However, some critics argue that much of the rhetoric about the value of exchange programmes masks the fact that cultural exchange reinforces capitalism and the values of globalization (Iriye, 1997). These ideological debates about the purpose and role of cultural exchange suggest that these programmes are indeed contexts rife with ambiguities.

Although macro-claims and concerns about cultural exchange programmes are worthwhile considering, it is the direct micro-interactions between participants and host communities that are central to understanding cultural exchange programmes. It is at this micro-level that an overlap between volunteer tourism and cultural exchange becomes more evident. Wearing (2001) has argued that it is the minutia of direct interaction between the volunteer tourist and the host community that promotes long-lasting, socially and environmentally positive impacts. This interactive exchange described by Wearing suggests that volunteer tourism may well be viewed as a subset of cultural exchange. However, it is also at this micro-level of interaction where ambiguities associated with participants' roles in cultural exchange programmes become reality.

Over the last two decades there has been a shift away from primarily education-based cultural exchange programmes that proliferated in the 1960s and 1970s such as teacher and student exchanges, towards more eclectic programmes that incorporate an ever-growing range of occupations and recreational pursuits (Murphy, 1995). Accompanying these newer programmes is a complex relationship between the participant, host organizations, sponsoring agencies and host country legal and political entities. Participants in these contemporary exchange programmes negotiate their way through an array of ambiguous and sometimes conflicting roles. A study of the J-1 Camp Counselor Visitor exchange programme participants demonstrates this (see Lyons, 2003).

The J-1 Cultural exchange programme was designed to promote cultural understanding at summer camps in the USA by enabling young adults from around the globe to work in American camps. However, camp directors, the sponsoring agencies, the US State Department which issues the visas, American camp staff and the participants themselves each had differing views as to what constituted the role of participants in the programme. Ultimately, it was unclear as to whether they were paid employees of a particular camping organization, volunteers or cultural goodwill ambassadors (Lyons, 2003).

The lack of clarity about the role of an individual participating in a cultural exchange programme creates what has been described in the literature as role ambiguity. Role ambiguity describes the degree to which individuals are unclear about the pattern of behaviours that are expected of them (Wolverton et al.,

1999). Role ambiguity has been negatively correlated with job performance and employee satisfaction and is therefore, an undesirable condition from the perspective of any organization. Some researchers differentiate between job task ambiguity and job role ambiguity, with the former referring to the lack of clarity about what specific duties are associated with a role and the latter referring to ambiguity about expected behaviours and relationships that shape and define a role (Tubre and Collins, 2000). In the case of exchange programmes it is the latter definition that is most relevant. The highly convoluted administrative and bureaucratic system that supports many exchange programmes, and indeed many volunteer tourism experiences, creates multiple and contradictory roles for participants (Lyons, 2003). Role ambiguity is a very real and potentially devastating consequence of programmes that suffer from what Oldsen (1983) described as bureaucratic hypotrophy. Multiple levels of organizational, political and governmental controls impinge upon the access to these programmes. In volunteer tourism the multiplicity of agency, operators and host communities encountered by the volunteer tourist creates similar challenges.

Fund-raising Adventurers or Volunteer Tourists?

In the introductory chapter to this book, we argued that NGOs offer and support alternative tourism by engaging in a decommodified process of face-to-face exchange between host communities and volunteers. However, the development of fund-raising adventure tourism, a recent innovation in the way this exchange has been provided by NGOs, raises important questions about whether volunteering and touring components of volunteer tourism need to be in the same temporal and geographical space.

NGOs have had to face the very real issues of economic sustainability that is central to the viability of the community-based projects they provide. In the early 1980s increasing pressure upon NGOs and other non-profit organizations led many executive directors to explore creative alternatives for fund-raising and financial support. While traditional forms of revenue had previously come from grants and philanthropists, the tightening of belts associated with the recession and the economic rationalism of multi-corporates lead to diminishing funds (Dichter, 1999). Increasingly sophisticated approaches to funding NGO projects emerged that moved beyond traditional funding drives such as telethons, or door knock appeals. The notion of value-adding crept into NGOs fund-raising strategies and in the early 1970s, community events such as walkathons, fun runs and other competitive and non-competitive events became important fund-raising products for these organizations (Dichter, 1999). However, the development of fund-raising adventure tours is a departure from these leisure activities, blending the voluntary act of fund-raising with the more traditional hedonic pleasures of a packaged adventure tour, positioning them as an ambiguous form of volunteer tourism.

A recent study of participants in a fund-raising challenge suggests that volunteer tourism might be expanded if we are able to move outside current assumptions about its spatial and temporal boundaries. Lyons (2007) analysed the diaries and web blogs of 25 individuals who participated in fund-raising/cycling adventures with Oxfam Australia–Oxfam Challenge programme. The adventure fund-raising tour conducted by Oxfam Australia is marketed as an adventure experience with a difference. Oxfam Australia recruits participants willing to raise $5000 which in part covers the cost of a 2-week cycling tour through remote villages in China, Vietnam or Cambodia. Fund-raising was done by individuals prior to participating in the tour in a variety of traditional ways such as seeking individual and corporate sponsorship and through organizing fund-raising events such as trivia nights. The bicycle tour itself incorporated scenic and challenging cycling routes that provided opportunities for participants to visit environmental and humanitarian projects where the funds they raised were being used. In some instances, participants had the opportunity to spend a day assisting on a community project as volunteers. While participants were recruited through Oxfam Australia, the adventure tour component of the programme was outsourced to a commercial travel service provider who provided a fully packaged programme including airfares, meals, a bicycle and a guide. This component of the experience is almost identical to any packaged adventure-based tour conducted by a wide range of operators globally.

The findings of this study suggest that while the tourist gaze narrative dominated many of the blogs, a significant component of these narratives emphasized the altruistic experiences associated with volunteering, giving back and helping others through fund-raising (Lyons, 2007). The sense of giving was further enhanced when participants visited communities where the monies they had raised were being used. Moreover, the separation of the act of adventure from the act of giving appeared to have little impact upon the participants' experiences as volunteers. This study argued that participants' motives in this new form of volunteer tourism appear very similar to participants' motives in more traditional forms. However, the strong emphasis upon more hedonic pleasures associated with the physical challenges of cycle-touring suggests that altruism remained in the background while on tour but emerged later upon reflection (Lyons, 2007).

This form of volunteer tourism challenges the necessity for the simultaneity of volunteering and touring in volunteer tourism. It raises questions about the act of volunteering and whether it can be experienced more remotely and independently in space and time from the act of touring.

Conclusion: Meta-ambiguities Ahead

The three examples presented in this chapter challenge current views and approaches to volunteer tourism. They illustrate how a narrow treatment of volunteer tourism does not fully capture the realities of the many who are exposed to a multitude of opportunities and challenges that may at once render them classifiable as volunteer tourists, students, package tourists, exchange participants, employees, fund-raisers, or a number of other designations. Rather than trying to pigeonhole characteristics, interests or behaviours, it is valuable to focus upon how volunteering and tourist behaviours intersect and manifest in a variety of ways.

The remaining chapters extend the ideas presented in this chapter and present case studies that also challenge where we set the boundaries around the phenomenon of volunteer tourism. These chapters consider the overlap between volunteer tourism and other forms of tourism such as cultural and indigenous tourism. They also raise important questions about how we have to date, framed volunteer tourism as a unidirectional phenomenon where volunteers from developed nations serve the needs of developing nations. The final chapter in this volume revisits a central question that underpins this book regarding the commodification of volunteer tourism. In many ways, this debate about the commodification process is a meta-ambiguity that challenges the way volunteer tourism is framed and understood. In closing this chapter we raise a number of questions about the ambiguities of the decommodified/commodified debate that is currently being played out in volunteer tourism.

An ideological proposition put forward in this volume is that volunteer tourism is a sustainable alternative to mass tourism. While each of the case studies confirm this ideological position of volunteer tourism, a number of these contributions reveal that such an ideology can be usurped and diverted by hegemonic forces of late capitalism. A central question that emerges then is whether a philosophy and practice of volunteer tourism that extends beyond market priorities can be sustained in the global tourism marketplace? Areas such as ecotourism have not been able to resist the global commodification in international tourist markets. Can and should volunteer tourism avoid the same fate? Indeed evidence of a move towards the commodification of volunteer tourism is already at-hand with large tour operators competing for a share of this new market. This raises a number of questions that have yet to be answered in the volunteer tourism literature. Does it matter if volunteer tourism becomes commodified as long as it still provides assistance to various projects and communities? Can a commodified experience of tourism satisfy both the need to consume and the desire to assist others? Will the experience become a tranquillizer rather than an awareness-raising experience that prioritizes escape over giving? Will the communities that volunteer tourists visit become 'consumables' that are made palatable under the guise of a 'legitimate' altruistic activity? As the swift rise in number of commercial operators who offer volunteer tourism products continues, answering these questions becomes central in understanding the future of volunteer tourism.

References

Altbach, P.G. and Lewis, L.S. (1998) Internationalism and insularity: American faculty and the world. *Change* 30(1), 54–56.

Beigbeder, Y. (1991) *The Role and Status of International Humanitarian Volunteers and Organizations*. Martinus Nijhoff, London.

Brown, R.B. and McCartney, S. (1999) Multiple mirrors: reflecting on reflections. In: O'Reilly, D., Cunningham, L. and Lester, S. (eds) *Developing the Capable Practitioner: Professional Capability Through Higher Education*. Kogan Page, London, pp. 16–32.

Brudney, J.L. (2000) The effective use of volunteers: best practices for the public sector. *Law and Contemporary Problems* 62(4), 219–255.

Clark, K. (1978) *The Two-Way Street – A Survey of Volunteer Service Abroad*. New Zealand Council for Educational Research, Wellington, New Zealand.

Cohen, E. (1974) Who is a tourist: a conceptual classification. *Sociological Review* 22, 527–555.

Dichter, T.W. (1999) Globalization and its effects on NGOs: efflorescence or a blurring of roles and relevance? *Nonprofit and Voluntary Sector Quarterly* 28(1), 38–58.

Ellis, S.J. (1997) Trends and issues in volunteerism in the USA. *Australian Journal on Volunteering* 2(2), 29–34.

Franklin, A. and Crang, M. (2001) The trouble with tourism and travel theory? *Tourism Studies* 1(1), 5–22.

Gillette, A. (1968) *One Million Volunteers*. Pelican (Penguin), Ringwood, Australia.

Grusky, S. (2000) International service learning: a critical guide from an impassioned advocate. *American Behavioral Scientist* 43(5), 858–867.

Iriye, A. (1997) *Cultural Internationalism and World Order*. John Hopkins University Press, Baltimore, Maryland.

Jacoby, B. and Associates (1996) *Service-Learning in Higher Education: Concepts and Practices*. Jossey Bass, San Francisco, California.

Lyons, K.D. (2003) Ambiguities in volunteer tourism: a case study of Australians participating in a J-1 visitor exchange program. *Tourism Recreation Research* 28(3), 5–13.

Lyons, K.D. (2007) Innovations in volunteer tourism: a case study of fundraising adventure tours. Paper presented at the *BEST Education Network Think Tank VII Conference*, Flagstaff, Arizona.

Murphy, J. (1995) The labour market effects of working holiday makers. *Bureau of Immigration and Population Research*. AGPS, Canberra.

Myers-Lipton, S. (1996) Effect of service-learning on college students' attitudes toward international understanding. *Journal of College Student Development* 37(6), 659–668.

Netanyahu, B. (1998) Prime Minister Benjamin Netanyahu, speech on the requirements of peace, 14 August 1997 (excerpts). *Journal of Palestine Studies* 27(2), 154–157.

Oldsen, W. (1983) The bureaucratization of the academy: the impact on scholarship and culture of professional staff. *Sociologica Internationalis* 21(1–2), 81–91.

Porter, M. and Monard, K. (2001) Building relationships of reciprocity through international service-learning. *Michigan Journal of Community Service Learning* 8(1), 5–17.

Roberts, A. (2003) Proposing a broadened view of citizenship: North American teachers' service in rural Costa Rican schools. *Journal of Studies in International Education* 7(3), 253–276.

Stebbins, R.A. (1992) *Amateurs, Professionals, and Serious Leisure*. McGill-Queen's University Press, Montreal, Canada.

Tubre, T.C. and Collins, J.M. (2000) Jackson and Schuler (1985) revisited: a meta-analysis of the relationships between role ambiguity, role conflict, and job performance. *Journal of Management* 26(1), 155–166.

Wearing, S. (2001) *Volunteer Tourism: Experiences That Make a Difference*. CAB International, Wallingford, UK.

White, C. (2002) Creating a 'world of discovery' by thinking and acting globally in social studies: ideas from New Zealand. *The Social Studies* 93(6), 262–267.

Wolverton, M., Wolverton, M.L. and Gmelch, W. (1999) The impact of role conflict and ambiguity on academic deans. *Journal of Higher Education* 70(1), 80–85.

13 Volunteers as Hosts and Guests in Museums

K. HOLMES[1] AND D. EDWARDS[2]

[1]Lecturer in Tourism, School of Management, University of Surrey, Guildford, UK;
[2]STCRC Senior Research Fellow, School of Leisure Sport and Tourism,
University of Technology Sydney, Lindfield, Australia

Volunteers in Museums

Museums worldwide are very dependent on volunteers. For example, studies have found that nine out of ten museums in the UK involve volunteers (Institute for Volunteering Research, 2002) and it is estimated that they outnumber paid staff two to one (Creigh-Tyte and Thomas, 2001). In Australia it is estimated that volunteers outnumber paid staff by approximately two and a half to one (AusStats, 2004). In Canada, Canadian Heritage estimates that volunteers comprise 65% of the workforce in museums (Canadian Museums Association, 2001). Museum and gallery volunteers even have their own associations, for example the American Association for Museum Volunteers and the Australian Association of Gallery Guides Organization. Additionally, volunteering is common in museums and heritage attractions in countries as diverse as Japan, Mexico, New Zealand, Greece and Taiwan.

Volunteers take on a range of roles including front of house, administration, hospitality, ticket sales, conservation and work to enhance the quality of a person's visit. Many museums are entirely run by volunteers, with a quarter of museums in the UK having no paid staff (Holmes, 1999). Even where museums do have paid staff, when they are registered as charities they will still be governed by volunteer trustees. In studies of museum volunteering, a distinction is made between 'behind the scenes' volunteers, who may help with administration or documenting collections, and 'front of house' volunteers who have direct contact with the visitors. Evidence suggests that front-of-house activities are increasing and becoming by far the biggest area of volunteer involvement (British Association of Friends of Museums, 1998; AusStats, 2004). This increase in front-of-house workers mirrors movements within the museums sector to become more visitor-focused, rather than object-centred (Weil, 1997; Edwards, 2005a). Front-of-house roles have also developed significantly from early days as unpaid security wardens. Indeed in Australia,

Canada and the USA, volunteers often undertake up to a year of training or college-level education before they can act as volunteer teachers, guides or interpreters (Edwards, 2005b).

As museum volunteers have become more visible to visitors, so the literature on volunteering has grown with two conflicting views of volunteering within museums emerging. Volunteers themselves have been regarded as an economic resource (Weisbrod, 1978), while sociologists have argued that volunteering is a leisure activity (Henderson, 1981; Stebbins, 1996). The economic model has dominated in most Western countries and has been implemented through a style of management which views volunteers as unpaid workers. This is called a 'professional' or top-down approach to volunteer management that seeks largely to replicate personnel practices within a volunteer workforce (Cunningham, 1999). A number of both external and internal influences to the museum sector have promoted this professional approach. For example, greater calls for public sector organizations to be more accountable and demonstrate competent management practice have led publicly funded museums to adopt a more professional approach to all areas of management, including volunteers (Kawashima, 1999; Kotler and Kotler, 2001; Kelly et al., 2003; Edwards and Graham, 2006). In addition, concern over the reliability of voluntary workers has led some museums to ask their volunteers to sign contracts or agreements.

In contrast to the economic approach, volunteering as a leisure activity finds its origins in the USA with Henderson's (1981) study of volunteerism. This conceptualization has been further developed by studies of volunteers in various leisure settings (Graham, 2000; Holmes, 2001; Elstad, 2003). Henderson divides all the time available in the day into four categories: paid work; work-related time, such as travel; obligatory time, such as sleeping; and unobligated free time (Henderson, 1981). Since volunteering is not paid work, she argues that it takes place within the last category of unobligated free time, the same category as leisure (Henderson, 1981; Stebbins, 1996). Museum volunteers are predominantly older, retired people, often over the age of 60 (British Association of Friends of Museums, 1998; Edwards and Graham, 2006). This suggests that museum volunteers may fit the leisure model better. Indeed, similar to Stebbins (1996), Edwards (2005a) in a study of volunteers who contribute their time to large Australian museums also found that these volunteers can be considered as serious leisure volunteers: principally they are people who are directed by primary interests, obligations and personal needs which they hope to satisfy while volunteering. Consequently 'people look to volunteer in organizations in which they can pursue their needs and interests...raising the notion of self-interestedness, turning the focus onto the volunteer and what they get out of volunteering rather than the contribution they make to the wider community' (Edwards, 2005a, p. 10). Museum volunteers are participating in leisure consumption that is self-generated, to gain access to the museum social world in order to reap the rewards of serious leisure (Orr, 2006).

This chapter uses the extant research on museum audiences to conceptualize the relationship between museum visiting and volunteering. First, the chapter examines the literature relating to museum visitors; second, it considers research on museum volunteers; and finally these two literatures are compared and a conceptual model of museum visiting and volunteering is presented.

Museum Audiences: the Visitors

A number of audience participation studies have been undertaken on museum visitors. The aim of this research is to understand why people visit museums in order to develop programmes and exhibitions that meet audience expectations and provide satisfying visitor experiences. Audience studies typically focus on the demographic and lifestyle variables of who visits and in compiling lists of reasons to visit. Although the demographics of museum visitors vary depending on the subject matter of the museum (Kirchberg, 1996), visitors are generally highly educated, with professional or intermediate occupations and the people most likely to visit are in the age range of 35–44 years (MORI, 2001; Richards, 2001).

Key reasons for visiting have been identified as opportunities for learning and opportunities for socializing. Thyme (2001) found visitors' reasons for attending museums included educational interest, to be with family, to take their children to see something new, to enjoy a day out and to escape from their daily routine. A study of older visitors (Kelly *et al.*, 2003) established that this visitor segment has a clear knowledge of what their interests are, value museums strongly and see museums as an extension of themselves. In particular, older people visit museums to learn, to take other visitors and grandchildren, to enjoy a social outing with a friend or partner, for entertainment, because they have a strong interest in the topic, to keep up to date and to engage with their special interest. Debenedetti (2003) stated that people's reasons for visiting a museum included sociability, mutual enrichment, recreational outing with family or friends, reassurance through companionship, prestige and to transfer knowledge between parents and children. Museum visitors in Taiwan are predominantly motivated by the opportunity to learn as well as enjoying a low-cost leisure day out (Lin, 2006). The importance of learning as a motivation to visit cultural attractions (including museums) was highlighted in a series of surveys of cultural tourism in Europe, where the most frequently cited reasons for visiting were to experience and to learn new things (Richards, 2001). The social significance of museum visiting has been noted by many researchers (McManus, 1988; Dierking, 1994; Hood, 1994; Goulding, 2000; Debenedetti, 2003). McManus argues that museum visiting is not only a social experience, but that visiting as part of a group makes the visit much more enjoyable, while Hood (1983) and Debenedetti (2003) agree that the social element is particularly important for occasional museum visitors. In addition, evidence suggests that the social interaction between the group members during a museum visit greatly enhances learning (Dierking, 1994; McManus, 1994).

Hood (1983) has developed the theorization of visitors' motives further. She argues that there are six attributes we all look for in an enjoyable leisure activity, which she based on a study of visitors at the Toledo Art Museum in the USA. There is no ranking between these characteristics; they are, according to

Hood, equally important components of an enjoyable leisure experience. If we expect to find these at a museum, we will visit a museum, rather than another type of leisure attraction. These attributes are:

- The challenge of new experiences;
- Doing something worthwhile;
- Feeling comfortable in one's surroundings;
- The opportunity to learn;
- Participating actively; and
- Social interaction.

Although museum visitor motivations are complex, they can be divided into segments depending on their frequency of visit (Merriman, 1991; Hood, 1994; Prentice and Beeho, 1997). Merriman provides the broadest categorization, classifying visitors into frequent, regular, occasional, rare and non-visitors. Frequent visitors will go to a museum three or more times a year, whereas a rare visitor last visited a museum more than 4 years ago. A non-visitor has never visited a museum. Visitors in these different groups also have different lifestyle characteristics (Merriman, 1991; Hood, 1994). Frequent visitors are most likely to have a high level of education, to hold professional occupations and to be regular cultural consumers. Kirchberg (1996, p. 256), in a study of museum visitation in Germany, argues that there is a 'continuum of social and demographic characteristics, from the "high culture" museum visitor through the "popular" museum visitor to the museum non-visitor'. High culture is differentiated as art museums and natural history represents the 'popular' museums. Similar to other researchers, he has observed social and demographic contrasts between non-visitors and visitors of museums. That is, the higher a person's level of education, employment status and affluence, the more likely it is that they will visit a museum and these factors will predict the type of museum they visit. The likelihood of a person expecting to find experiential benefits in a museum is related to demographic factors such as level of education, social class, a general interest in culture and the accumulation of cultural capital (Bourdieu and Darbel, 1991). It is also dependent on how far an individual is introduced to museum visiting as an enjoyable leisure activity in childhood, through the process of socialization.

Museum Audiences: the Volunteers

Volunteers have been described as active visitors (McIvor and Goodlad, 1998) and Smith (2003) found that visiting can lead to volunteering. Recently museum volunteering has been considered as an extension of visiting (McIvor and Goodlad, 1998; Holmes, 2003; Smith, 2003) as museum volunteers have been found to share many of the same characteristics as visitors. They are characteristically highly educated, have professional or clerical occupations and have a general interest in culture. Lifestyle characteristics and frequency of visiting, however, only tell one side of the story. Holmes (2003) identified a link between visiting and volunteering when she found a similarity between Hood's (1983) six characteristics of an enjoyable leisure experience with the benefits reported by respondents to two surveys of volunteers conducted in the UK. Volunteers do tend to be older than visitors, so although both groups are similar, they are at different stages in their life cycle. This suggests that volunteering may be a form of visiting that is more concentrated. The link between visiting and volunteering is also evident within volunteers' motivations. The National Trust for England and Wales is the largest involver of volunteers within the heritage sector in the UK (The National Trust, 1998). In 1997 they surveyed 723 volunteers across their different properties and activities. The respondents reported that the most important benefits they gained from volunteering were:

- I really enjoy it (98% of respondents).
- I meet people and make friends through it (85%).
- It gives me a sense of personal achievement (78%).
- It gives me a chance to do things I am good at (74%).
- It broadens my experience of life (73%).

Only 12% of respondents reported that they hoped it would lead to full-time (paid) employment. These findings are supported by a second survey on training and management of volunteers across the UK heritage sector, conducted by the British Association of Friends of Museums (1998), which found that the most important reason for volunteering was to do something enjoyable. Holmes' own fieldwork with 222 volunteers at museums and heritage attractions in the UK found that the most important benefits gained from volunteering were opportunities for social interaction with paid staff, fellow volunteers and visitors; enjoyment of the activities; and the museum environment and recreation (Holmes, 2003). Similarly, Edwards and Graham (2006) reported that museum volunteers enjoyed satisfying an interest, feeling competent to do the work, being able to use their skills while opportunities for social interaction were benefits gained from volunteering in museums. Volunteering then is not a form of unpaid work experience; rather it is a leisure activity, which involves gaining access to museums and heritage attractions, their staff's expertise and their collections at a level that is often denied the casual visitor.

Motivation of museum volunteers can be said to have eight underlying dimensions: personal needs, relationship network, self-expression, available time, social needs, purposive needs, free time and personal interest (Edwards, 2005a). Of these eight dimensions, personal needs were found to be the strongest dimension and reflected a person's need to broaden their horizons, vary their regular activities and do something that they were interested in, in an organization that they considered to be prestigious (Edwards, 2005b). It is a drive to realize their self-interests that pushes volunteers to seek out organizations that reflect their interests, and in which they perceive they can satisfy their needs (Edwards, 2005b). Volunteering in these institutions helps people to translate their needs into tangible outcomes and they will choose 'to visit a particular place at an in-depth level rather than many more at the relatively superficial level of the average visitor' (Holmes, 2003, p. 352). Many of the reasons for volunteering reported here are identical or similar to those reported within the audience research literature. This discussion is represented in Table 13.1 which reflects the commonalities between volunteers and visitors with respect to their characteristics, motivations and benefits gained.

Table 13.1. Comparison of volunteer and visitor participation in museums.

Visitors	Volunteers
Characteristics	
Educated	High level of education
Professional occupations	Professional or clerical occupations
Motivations and benefits sought	
Interest in culture	Special interest in culture, science, history, art
Challenge of new experiences	Enjoy their experience of volunteering
	Broadens their experience of life
Doing something worthwhile	Doing something they are good at
	Personal achievement
Feeling comfortable in one's surroundings	Immerse themselves in the culture of the museum
Opportunity to learn	Want to use their skills, broaden their skills, learn new skills
Participating actively	Satisfying an interest
Social interaction	Want to meet people and make friends
Take their children for an educational experience/transfer knowledge between parents and children	Continue to educate children about culture, science, history, art
	Early socialization to museums
Prestige	Volunteer for an organization that is prestigious
Values	
Culturally socialized	Culturally socialized
Museum is highly valued	Ensure museums continued to be valued
Passion for history, science, culture, art	Passion for preserving history, science, culture, art

(From Hood, 1983; McManus, 1988; Bourdieu and Darbel, 1991; British Association of Friends of Museums, 1998; MORI, 2001; Richards, 2001; Thyme, 2001; Debenedetti, 2003; Holmes, 2003; Kelly *et al.*, 2003; Edwards, 2005a.)

These findings support Holmes' (2003) argument that there are a number of similarities between museum and cultural heritage centre volunteers and visitors that require further consideration.

Conclusions and Implications

Our conclusion is that volunteering is an extension of visiting and that volunteers and visitors are motivated by similar goals. This line of argument confirms Holmes' (2003) view that volunteers form a distinct group of a museum's audience. As volunteers belong to one organization they could be viewed as the definitive visitors who have ready access to their area of interest and are concerned with supporting and communicating that interest. Drawing together the lines of discussion in this chapter, volunteering could be considered at the extreme end of a continuum of visiting (Fig. 13.1) that includes non-visitors, infrequent visitors, frequent visitors and volunteers (Holmes, 2003).

For a number of reasons, the non-visitor is the market segment least likely to visit museums for leisure. This group may include the unemployed, those with lower levels of education and people who have no interest in museums (Kawashima, 1999). The occasional visitors are perhaps driven by curiosity and a desire for entertainment; they would have knowledge of the museum and may visit high-profile exhibits and special programmes. They could be referred to as the 'cultural window shoppers' (Treinen, 1993). The frequent visitors would have a desire to educate themselves, and in addition to regular visits, may also attend formal lectures or courses. They are most likely to be highly educated, affluent and culturally socialized. The volunteers are both producers and consumers of the museum product using their leisure time to immerse themselves in the museum culture in order to maximize the interests they have in this area and to contribute to sociocultural exchange.

Movement on the continuum can be in both directions as a result of various internal and external factors influencing this progression. An invitation could encourage a non-visitor to visit because of the prospect of sharing the experience with a companion. The warmth and friendliness of a museum may encourage an occasional visitor to visit more frequently and become more immersed in the foci of the museum, while the frequent visitor would consider going one step further and volunteer for personal reasons such as broadening their horizons, varying their social activities with family and friends and wanting to engage more intimately with the culture of the museum that reflects their interests. The volunteer, frequent visitor and occasional visitor can be affected by a range of factors such as changes in health, changed life circumstances, increase in museum entry charges, a change of personal interests and a lack of varied and/or interesting programmes which can result in a decline in visitation and backward movement along the continuum.

The implication is that while museums view volunteers as unpaid staff it is more appropriate to see them as another segment of the museum audience with opportunities for targeting frequent visitors as future volunteers. How can the museum cater to volunteers who wish to have an experience and contribute to the goals of the museum? Although some volunteer programmes provide quality volunteer experiences other museums could do more in the engagement of their volunteers. First, there should be no obstacles to volunteers enjoying the dimensions of their volunteering. These obstacles may include poor management, a lack of resources, not being valued or poor work plans (Edwards

Fig. 13.1. The visitor–volunteer continuum.

and Graham, 2006). Second, the social value of volunteering can be enhanced by offering activities that bring volunteers together and provide opportunities for volunteers to meet each other. Third, museums can assist volunteers to immerse themselves in the culture of the museum through courses and talks with artists, curators and academics to enable a more meaningful relationship between the volunteer and the museum.

Another question is how can museums reach the non-visitor? This may be achieved through museum volunteer programmes that specifically target the disadvantaged which will realize benefits for both the individual and the museum. For example, the Imperial War Museum North in the UK has a much-cited volunteer programme, which recruits small cohorts of 'lone parents; those wishing to return to work; 13–17 year olds at risk of being excluded from school; people from different cultural backgrounds; and people with disabilities' (Imperial War Museum North, 2006, p. 5). All the volunteers are local residents who are unlikely to be typical museum visitors. The museum provides these volunteers with a tailored training programme, work experience in the museum and encourages them into paid employment, further study or socialization into volunteering elsewhere. It is possibly one of the only museum volunteer programmes in the world which can measure its success by the proportion of volunteers who leave because they have realized subsequent opportunities. The participants are usually referred by a third party, for example social services, as their knowledge and experience of museums is so limited they may never have visited a museum for leisure before. Volunteering therefore provides a means of making the museum more relevant to non-visitors, by offering them something tangible, such as formal learning opportunities and valuable work experience. In this context, volunteering is a form of personal development.

The paradoxical role of volunteers acting as hosts to tourists, while being engaged in volunteer tourism themselves, is not well understood, not least by those managers who view their volunteers as an economic resource of unpaid workers, rather than active visitors. According to Orr (2006) the museum has become a leisure space 'where volunteers are active in appropriating their own heritage and contextualising the museum within their own lives' (p. 202). She states that leisure is the process in which the self can be enhanced and expanded, which means that museum volunteers are using the museum to construct and reconstruct their own identities. This means that volunteers need to be managed sensitively and that professional volunteer management practices may not be appropriate for a largely retired group of leisure-motivated volunteers. By viewing volunteers' needs and interests similarly to that of the visitor, museums can offer the volunteer a valuable and enjoyable experience that will be important to the success of the volunteer programme. If museum services are appropriate for volunteers, then they will also be an enjoyable and educational experience for visitors. Additionally, the museum can benefit from engaging the volunteer in programme development and museum advocacy to progress museum goals.

The visitor–volunteer continuum represents an alternative way in which to view both museum visitors and volunteers. The discussion supports the notion that museum volunteering is a committed form of visiting, with the volunteer choosing to visit one museum in depth, rather than making short visits to several museums. Conceptualizing volunteering as a form of visiting also helps us to understand the leisure elements of both activities as captured in the audience and volunteer literature. This theorization raises new ideas for creating more diversity in volunteer programmes and increasing visitor numbers. It is an area rich in research opportunities for further conceptual and empirical development. This chapter has presented a conceptual model that needs to be empirically tested both within museums and other tourism settings. For example, aquaria, zoos, national parks, botanical gardens, festivals and events, and sport organizations are similar in their engagement of volunteers (Caldwell and Andereck, 1994; Cuskelly *et al.*, 1998; Green and Chalip, 1998; Elstad, 2003; Propst *et al.*, 2003) where volunteers act as both host and guest. Application of the continuum to these settings can further enhance our understanding of people who volunteer for tourism-related organizations.

References

AusStats (2004) *Museums, Australia 8560.0.* Australian Bureau of Statistics, Canberra, Australia.

Bourdieu, P. and Darbel, A. (1991) *The Love of Art: European Art Museums and Their Public.* Polity Press, Cambridge.

British Association of Friends of Museums (1998) *Heritage Volunteer Training Project Stage One Report – Draft.* British Association of Friends of Museums, Camberley, UK.

Caldwell, L.L. and Andereck, K.L. (1994) Motives for initiating and continuing membership in a recreation-related voluntary association. *Leisure Sciences* 16, 33–44.

Canadian Museums Association (2001) *The Role and Impact of Voluntarism at Museums.* Canadian Museums Association, Ottawa, Canada.

Creigh-Tyte, A. and Thomas, B. (2001) Employment. In: Selwood, S. (ed.) *The UK Cultural Sector: Profile and Policy Issues.* Policy Studies Institute, London.

Cunningham, I. (1999) Challenges and opportunities in human resource management in the voluntary sector. *Public Money and Management* 19(2), 19–27.

Cuskelly, G., McIntyre, N. and Boag, A. (1998) A longitudinal study of the development of organizational commitment amongst volunteer sport administrators. *Journal of Sport Management* 12, 181–202.

Debenedetti, S. (2003) Investigating the role of companions in the art museum experience. *International Journal of Arts Management* 5, 52–63.

Dierking, L. (1994) Role de l'interaction sociale dans l'experience museale. *Publics et Musee* 5, 19–43.

Edwards, D. and Graham, M. (2006) Museum volunteers: a discussion of challenges facing managers in the cultural and heritage sectors. *Australian Journal of Volunteering* 11, 19–27.

Edwards, D.C. (2005a) It's mostly about me: reasons why volunteers contribute their time to museums and art museums. *Tourism Review International* 9, 1–11.

Edwards, D.C. (2005b) Understanding the organization of volunteers at visitor attractions. *College of Law and Business.* University of Western Sydney, Sydney, Australia.

Elstad, B. (2003) Continuance commitment and reasons to quit: a study of volunteers at a jazz festival. *Event Management* 8, 99–108.

Goulding, C. (2000) The museum environment and the visitor experience. *European Journal of Marketing* 34, 261–278.

Graham, M. (2000) The professionalisation of museum volunteers: an ethical dilemma. In: Mcnamee, M., Jennings, C. and Reeves, M. (eds) *Just Leisure: Policy, Politics and Professionalism*. LSA, Eastbourne, UK.

Green, C.B. and Chalip, L. (1998) Sport volunteers: research agenda and application. *Sport Marketing Quarterly* 7(2), 14–23.

Henderson, K.A. (1981) Motivations and perceptions of volunteerism as a leisure activity. *Journal of Leisure Research* 13, 208–218.

Holmes, K. (1999) Changing times: volunteering in the heritage sector 1984–1998. *Voluntary Action* 1, 21–35.

Holmes, K. (2001) The motivation and retention of front of house volunteers. In: Graham, M. and Foley, M. (eds) *Leisure Volunteering: Marginal or Inclusive?* Leisure Studies Association, Eastbourne, UK.

Holmes, K. (2003) Volunteers in the heritage sector: a neglected audience? *International Journal of Heritage Studies* 9, 341–355.

Hood, M. (1983) Staying away: why people choose not to visit museums. *Museum News* 61, 50–57.

Hood, M. (1994) L'interaction sociale au musée, facteur d'attraction des visiteurs occasionnels. *Publics et Musées* 5, 45–57.

Imperial War Museum North (2006) *Shape Your Future: An Innovative Volunteering Programme*. Imperial War Museum North, Manchester, UK.

Institute for Volunteering Research (2002) *Volunteers in the Cultural Sector*. Resource, London.

Kawashima, N. (1999) Knowing the public. A review of museum marketing literature and research. *Museum Management and Curatorship* 17, 21–39.

Kelly, L., Savage, G., Landman, P. and Tonkin, S. (2003) *Energised, Engaged, Everywhere: Older Australians and Museums*. Australian Museum and The National Museum of Australia, Canberra, Australia.

Kirchberg, V. (1996) Museum visitors and non-visitors in Germany: a representative study. *Poetics* 24, 239–258.

Kotler, N. and Kotler, P. (2001) Can museums be all things to all people?: missions, goals, and marketing's role. *Museum Management and Curatorship* 18, 271–287.

Lin, Y-N. (2006) Leisure – a function of museums? The Taiwan perspective. *Museum Management and Curatorship*, 21, 302–316.

McIvor, S. and Goodlad, S. (1998) *Museum Volunteers: Good Practice in the Management of Volunteers*. Routledge, London.

McManus, P. (1988) Good companions. *Museum Management and Curatorship* 7(1), 37–44.

McManus, P. (1994) Le contexte social, un des déterminants du comportement de l'apprentissage dans les musées. *Publics et Musées* 5, 59–77.

Merriman, N. (1991) *Beyond the Glass Case*. Leicester University Press, Leicester, London.

MORI (2001) *Visitors to Museums and Galleries in the UK*. Resource & MORI, London.

Orr, N. (2006) Museum volunteering: heritage as 'serious leisure'. *International Journal of Heritage Studies* 12, 194–210.

Prentice, R. and Beeho, A. (1997) Seeking generic motivations for visiting and not visiting museums and like cultural attractions. *Museum Management and Curatorship* 16, 45–70.

Propst, D.B., Jackson, D.L. and McDonough, M.H. (2003) Public participation, volunteerism and resource-based recreation management in the US: what do citizens expect? *Leisure and Society* 26, 389–415.

Richards, G. (2001) *Cultural Attractions and European Tourism*. CAB International, Wallingford, UK.

Smith, K.A. (2003) Literary enthusiasts as visitors and volunteers. *International Journal of Tourism Research* 5, 83–95.

Stebbins, R.A. (1996) Volunteering: a serious leisure perspective. *Nonprofit and Voluntary Sector Quarterly* 25, 211–224.

The National Trust (1998) *Volunteering With the National Trust: Summary of the Findings of the 1997 Survey*. The National Trust, Cirencester, UK.

Thyme, M. (2001) The importance of values research for nonprofit organizations: the motivations based values of museum visitors. *International Journal of Nonprofit and Voluntary Sector Marketing* 6, 116–130.

Treinen, H. (1993) What does the visitor want from a museum? Mass media aspects of museology. In: Bicknell, S. and Farmelo, G. (eds) *Museum Visitor Studies in the 90's*. Science Museum, London.

Weil, S.E. (1997) The museum and the public. *Museum Management and Curatorship* 16, 257–271.

Weisbrod, B.A. (1978) *The Voluntary Non-profit Sector*. Lexington Books, Lanham, Maryland.

14 Journeys for Experience: the Experiences of Volunteer Tourists in an Indigenous Community in a Developed Nation – a Case Study of New Zealand

A.J. McINTOSH AND A. ZAHRA

Department of Tourism & Hospitality Management, The University of Waikato, Hamilton, New Zealand

While international volunteering is increasingly recognized as a form of alternative tourism (Stoddart and Rogerson, 2004; Callanan and Thomas, 2005), the nature of the 'alternative' experience gained, and the ensuing narrative between host and volunteer, remains relatively unexplored. Through a case study examination of volunteer tourism in a developed country, New Zealand, this chapter examines the nexus between volunteer tourism and cultural (indigenous) tourism. Previous scholarly attention has concentrated on volunteer tourism involving environmental conservation in developing nations rather than within a cultural context in a developed nation, and thus this chapter poses a new dimension for examining the experiential journey. Specifically, it will explore the nature of the experiences that volunteers gain in their interaction with a Maori host community. The chapter will address: What is the nature of the experience gained? What message does the visitor receive? What perception does the host receive? Is the cultural tourism experience and ensuing dialogue different in the context of volunteer tourism? What are the key problems, impacts or issues arising from this dialogue?

Volunteer Tourist Experiences: a Cultural Context

It is not the intention of this chapter to define volunteer tourism; that can be found elsewhere (see e.g. Wearing, 2001). Importantly for this chapter, volunteer tourism is seen to foster a reciprocal and mutually beneficial relationship between the host and guest. Thus, it is seen as offering the opportunity for sustainable 'alternative' travel that is more rewarding and meaningful than other holidays and focuses on the altruistic and self-developmental experiences that participants can gain and the assistance that can be delivered to communities in terms of community development, scientific research or ecological restoration (Stoddart and Rogerson, 2004; Callanan and Thomas, 2005). The experiential nature, or 'experiences' gained, from volunteer tourism is thus central to the fostering of reciprocity. Wearing and Neil (2000) describe three aspects of the volunteer tourism experience. First, that the volunteer tourism experience is a personal experience that incorporates the perception that it is chosen for its difference and involves intrinsic motivation. Second, that the experience can potentially benefit the participant's life, as well as that of the host community. Third, that meaning is given to the experience through social interaction which may involve a renegotiation of the individual's identity.

While volunteer tourism is inspiring significant discourse in the search for alternative forms of tourism, previous research on volunteer tourism has predominantly profiled volunteer tourists and organizations (Brown and Morrison, 2003; Stoddart and Rogerson, 2004; Callanan and Thomas, 2005) or motivations and the benefits of the volunteer experience on self and society (Broad, 2003; Halpenny and Caissie, 2003; Wearing and Deane, 2003; Simpson, 2004). Although the exact extent to which volunteer tourists make a difference within a community or environment seems to be debated (see Turner *et al.*, 2001), the positive longer-term effects are being noted (see McGehee, 2002; Zahra and McIntosh, 2007). Previous research has also almost exclusively focused on the nature of volunteer tourism within developing countries (Broad, 2003; Simpson, 2004). In addition, these studies have overwhelmingly focused on volunteer tourism as it relates to travel to partake in environmental conservation work, rather than how tourists work interactively with local communities on local projects and whereby the nature of the exchange is mainly cultural or involves interaction with indigenous communities, that is, communities of people who are endemic or native to a destination region (Butler and Hinch, 1996). Cross-cultural experiences can be a rich source of narrative, learning, appreciation, inspiration, cultural respect, solidarity and equality in the search for sustainable models of tourism (Butler and Hinch, 1996).

Within scholarly discourse on cultural tourism, an increasing number of authors have called for 'alternative' cultural tourism experiences that engender authentic, interactive, more meaningful, individualized and sincere experiential offerings through tourism (Richards and Wilson, 2006; Trauer, 2006). The search for these new travel experiences is primarily argued to reflect peoples' increasing recognition and reaction to the homogeneous nature of traditional tourism products as well as their increasing desire for altruism, self-change and to be able to confirm their identities and provide coherence within an uncertain and fragmented postmodern life (Richards and Wilson, 2006).

In New Zealand, there has been a call for the increased development of cultural products based on indigenous Maori culture in an attempt to facilitate economic development for Maori communities. Until recently, much of the consumption of Maori cultural product in New Zealand has been criticized as being centred only on traditional cultural perspectives and leading to predominantly superficial and stereotypical experiences for tourists (McIntosh, 2004). However, in an attempt to meet tourists' demand for more authentic experiences of Maori culture, and in order to preserve Maori cultural identity, Maori communities are now attempting to develop new 'alternative' cultural experiences based on a more engaging, meaningful and sincere interaction with Maori people (Taylor, 2001). One such example forms the topic of this chapter – that of volunteer tourism within an indigenous Maori community.

It has been argued in wider academic discourse that, in the search for alternative models of cultural tourism, many destinations are now using 'creativity' as a development strategy (Prentice and Andersen, 2003; Richards and Wilson, 2006). Whereas traditional cultural tourism often implies the commodification and staging of culture for consumption, creative tourism depends on active involvement and reflexive interaction on the part of tourists and has not been exposed to the critical scrutiny associated with traditional cultural tourism. Creativity-led development implies that creativity becomes an attribute of both the production and the consumption process; thereby recognizing the creative potential of tourists and the subsequent transformation of products into experiences which engage and change the consumer (Pine and Gilmore, 1999). As a process, creativity is seen to create new cultural forms that avoid the 'McGuggenheimisation' of cultural experiences and foster contemporary attractions based on cultural processes that are seen to meet the needs of tourists for more active, meaningful, enduring and worthwhile experiences (Richards, 2001). These experiences may also foster a more sustainable form of cultural tourism through engendering a new type of relationship between host and guest. This chapter proffers that volunteer tourism provides an example of this alternative form of cultural encounter that has been otherwise overlooked in scholarly literature to date.

In short, there has been little previous focus on the nexus between volunteer tourism and cultural tourism, especially in the context of indigenous tourism experiences and the rich narrative that may be created and exchanged between host and volunteer. Key questions thus remain, and pose a context for the present chapter. Key questions include: What is the nature of the experience gained? What message does the visitor receive? Do volunteer tourists gain different meaning from their interactions with indigenous communities than those tourists who participate in traditional cultural tourism? Can the nature of the narrative created proffer an alternative, more sustainable, relationship between host and guest? An ethnographic study conducted with 12 Australian visitors undertaking organized volunteer activities in an indigenous Maori community (*marae*) in the North Island of New Zealand sought to address these questions and to examine the nature of volunteer tourism experiences in a cultural context within a developed country, rather than the more widely reported experiences of volunteer tourists working on environmental projects in developing nations.

The Study

The study involved in-depth interviews, diaries and participant observations to examine the pre-, during and post-trip experiences of 12 Australian visitors undertaking organized volunteer activities in a Maori community while staying on a *marae* (Maori village or traditional meeting place) in the North Island of New

Zealand during January 2005. The respondents represented 80% of the total participants of a volunteer programme organized by an Australian non-governmental organization (NGO) registered with the Australian Agency for International Development (AusAID) that provides community and education development projects in Asia and South America. In addition to community development projects, the NGO organizes projects in which young volunteers from Australia and New Zealand participate in welfare projects around the world. These welfare projects provide 'on the ground' assistance to communities and engage the volunteers and community in a mutual exchange.

This 2-week project in January 2005 involved two locations. The first week was based on a *marae* in the Bay of Plenty in the North Island of New Zealand – a region which has one of the highest proportions of Maori among the local population in New Zealand. The second week of the project was located in Auckland, the largest urban city in the North Island of New Zealand, with the volunteers providing aid to adults with disabilities. The current study focuses on the first week of the project. Typically, participants pay for their own airfare, accommodation and transport in the destination. As the total duration of the trip was relatively short, the participants can be considered 'shallow volunteer tourists' (Callanan and Thomas, 2005). The participants in the present study were all females aged between 16 and 19 years of age.

The organizer, one of the authors, who will also be referred to as the 'participant observer' has been involved in volunteer tourism and with this particular NGO for 18 years, as participant, organizer of projects and as a director of the organization. The participant observer had worked with one of the local NGOs called Rural Education Action Programme (REAP) and the *Kaumatua* (Maori elders) of the *marae* in a previous project in 2003. The objectives of the project were to engage the volunteers in physical work and community activities. The programme in the Bay of Plenty included a welcome on to the *marae* where the group was staying, a session with the *Kaumatua* explaining the history of the *marae* and the local Maori people, and cleaning, water blasting and painting on the *marae*. The community work entailed organizing and running a 5-day holiday programme for children from the Awatapu community, a suburb of Whakatane that has a low socio-economic ratio and that received severe flood damage in July 2004. The population of Awatapu is approximately 50% Maori, with 80% of the children being Maori. Awatapu is a separate suburb of Whakatane from the *marae* where the volunteers were living. The holiday programme also involved art, crafts, drama, music and sports activities. The activities were orientated to performances, props and exhibitions that took place on the last day as a fun day for the whole community, especially for the parents and extended family, to participate in a sense of community and celebration.

Study Method

To explore the deep, personal and experiential aspects of the volunteering experience, each volunteer was interviewed individually before and during their stay on the *marae* by the participant observer, as well as collectively during a focus group session led by the other researcher at the end of their stay in the

Bay of Plenty. Each in-depth interview lasted between 45 and 90 min. Each of the 12 volunteers was also asked to keep a research diary throughout the duration of the stay in which they were asked to write down, at the end of each day, their key observations, memories and feelings, as well as things they had learned about Maori culture. The participant observer also kept a diary. The aim of the research was to record the experiences of respondents (i.e. of both volunteers and hosts) as accurately as possible before, during and immediately after their stay, and to examine the volunteer experience from the volunteer's own perspective (Broad, 2003). These research methods were selected in preference to others, for example a survey, due to the small sample size of volunteers participating in this case study project and the need to record in-depth personal experiences (McIntosh, 1998).

The in-depth interviews and focus group session followed a semi-structured format, which allowed for variation in the order of questions; however, the main topics covered remained unchanged. Key questions asked during the individual and group interviews with volunteers included their reasons for deciding to take the trip, what they expected to gain from the trip, the most memorable experiences, the least memorable experiences, their knowledge about Maori culture, their views and experiences relating to staying on the *marae* and what they felt they had gained from their trip. Consistent with previous studies of the tourist experience, the in-depth interviews and focus group session employed the principles of the 'Laddering Technique' used in marketing to further probe the responses of participants in order to elicit the deeper personal values gained from their experiences (see Reynolds and Gutman, 1988). Nine in-depth interviews with the Maori hosts, including six *Kaumatua* (elders), and two non-Maori social workers involved in the project were also undertaken before, during and after the visit to establish the attitudes, motivations and experiences of hosts. It is important that host communities have their voices heard in any examination of tourism experience (Wearing, 2004), and that cultural acceptance and control is paramount for sustainable tourism encounters (Butler and Hinch, 1996; McIntosh *et al.*, 2004).

Each host and volunteer interview and the focus group was tape-recorded and later transcribed to ensure the accuracy of data. Each author, separately, used content analysis, summation of the transcripts and research diaries to identify categories that integrate and generalize major themes. The authors then came together for comparison and to confirm the common themes emerging from the data. An inductive approach to the data analysis was used, whereby a set of categories grounded in the data were established so that key themes that emerged were described by respondents using their own words (Strauss and Corbin, 1990; McIntosh, 1998). This approach was chosen to mitigate any potential participant observer bias as a consequence of one of the author's past volunteer tourism experiences and her role as the organizer of the group. The volunteer participants were also given the opportunity, through a follow-up focus group, to review and comment on the study's findings to further enhance validity and reliability of the interpretative themes and conclusions drawn.

The Volunteer Tourist Experience in an Indigenous Community in a Developed Nation

Key themes emerging from the data showed the nature of the interaction and cultural experiences gained by the 12 volunteer tourists volunteering at the Maori *marae* to be different from that reported in previous studies of cultural tourism more generally. The nature of the experience gained by the volunteer tourists involved a different narrative and constituted an 'alternative' Maori cultural product – one that was rich in authentic cultural content and personal interactions, genuine and reflective of modern Maori life in New Zealand society. These findings are elaborated below in relation to volunteers' motivations and experiences of the trip, and are demonstrated with quotes taken from the personal journals and interviews conducted. Potentially, these reported alternative experiences may facilitate a more sustainable form of tourism compared to traditional cultural tourism consumption.

Motivation for undertaking volunteer tourism on a *marae* in New Zealand

Findings of the study showed that the main motivation for undertaking the volunteer project was not primarily related to sightseeing but volunteering, to 'work; not just being tourists', 'to give' and 'to experience a service project'. The service project was also seen to allow participants to experience 'real' New Zealand people through a cultural encounter; 'to see how they live and to make connections'. One respondent explained: 'My main motivation was to give; because I know in giving you are happy. I saw and spoke to others who had done this type of project and I could see it was so rewarding I wanted to do something like this.' Other volunteers explained: 'I really wanted to do volunteer work. It was really attractive and I thought it was important that I do something like this'; 'I wanted to do a service project [volunteer project]. This came up so I said why not. New Zealand was not the real attraction. I would have done any project that had the combination of overseas and volunteer work; and mum and dad said yes'; 'It was not about New Zealand, tourism or Maori, but it was expectations about volunteering'; 'I was looking for new experiences, ones that challenged me, seeing other countries, but not as a traditional tourist; I actually like helping people'.

Most of the participants had made contact with others who had participated in volunteer work and they explained that 'you could see they had got so much out of it'; 'when they talked about their experiences their face glowed'; 'they were so happy because they gave'; 'you could see it was a special experience and I wanted it too'; 'when I heard what they did and saw the photos of the kids and the impact they made I made up my mind "yes" I am going to do a service project'. That volunteer tourists exhibit greater altruistic motives for travel than other cultural tourists potentially confirms previous conclusions drawn elsewhere (see e.g. Wearing, 2002; Uriely *et al.*, 2003).

The 'alternative' nature of volunteer tourists' experiences of Maori culture

The experiences gained by the volunteers on the *marae* and working in the Awatapu Holiday Programme could be conceptualized as three layers of experience: their experiences of Maori culture; their experiences relating to self; and their experiences of their interaction and relationship with their Maori hosts. The integration of these three layers makes the nature of the experiences gained by the volunteer tourists different, or 'alternative', to those gained by cultural tourists experiencing traditional cultural products, as reported in previous literature. Instead, they pose a different narrative between host and guest – one that is potentially more sustainable (Wearing, 2001). The three layers of experience are elaborated below.

Experience of Maori culture

Consistent with previous studies of indigenous tourism (see McIntosh, 2004), most of the volunteers held very little previous knowledge about Maori culture and held very traditional stereotypical impressions about Maori people prior to their visit. Respondents commented that they 'didn't know anything about Maori culture; all I knew was the haka [Maori war challenge]'; 'I only knew about rugby and the haka; the visible things'; and 'I had watched the movie "Whale Rider" but I didn't really know anything'. One respondent described their expectation of a traditional encounter with Maori people:

> I don't really know much about the *marae*. I thought we might be living in little huts that would house three of us in one hut, so when I saw it with all our mattresses lined up next to each other, it was completely different to what I had expected. The welcome was different to what I had expected as well. I had this little vision that they'd all be in their national costumes and that we'd be welcomed over a bridge on a lake with a waterfall in the background; it's all very different to that; I think I maybe expected too much of traditional Maori.

While volunteers expected to receive a traditional view of Maori culture, their experience on the *marae* and dealing with the children and their families in Awatapu related predominantly to the contemporary lifestyle of Maori, including, for example, experiences of contemporary Maori family values, association with tribal gangs and drugs, cultural 'rules' and the sense of community spirit. This is in contrast to the majority of tourists' experiences or gazing of traditional cultural tourism reported elsewhere (see McKercher and Du Cros, 2002; Ryan and Huyton, 2002). Respondents described how 'the kids have let us see what life is *really* like for them'; 'it's more hands-on; learning about everyday'; 'we even got involved in the subculture'; 'this is a modern and "real" experience; we were treated like we were from here'. As one volunteer commented to the organizer after the briefing session with the host community organizer: 'I did not realise we could get involved with gangs; that is stuff out of the movies.' The participant observer similarly noted in her diary:

> The volunteers are commenting a lot and very fascinated about the gangs and culture associated with gangs. This is an aspect of the culture they did not expect to encounter. The volunteers discuss how the kids talk about how their parents are in the gangs and how they will join the gangs when they get older. The kids are recruited for the gangs at a young age.

The nature of Maori family values was also a feature of what the volunteers learned about Maori culture from their trip. They described Maori culture as 'having such a strong feeling of family'; 'the kids all look out for each other'; and 'they put themselves last'.

As volunteers, the respondents learned a lot about contemporary Maori lifestyle by visiting Maori in their own homes. One participant recounted:

> I went to one of the kid's family home; Jess came with me. The home was small, simple and tidy; everything was normal. But when we went to another little boy's house, you could see the attitude of lack of care; junk in the garage and backyard, kitchen a mess, kids toys everywhere and clothes. We asked his sister, who was very shy, where their mother was and she said in the bedroom stoned with her boyfriend. Us two girls felt very uncomfortable and scared. We had never been near anyone so close who was stoned before; it was the stuff of movies and hip hop songs.

The participant observer noted:

> The conversation at dinner tonight was very interesting; everyone was passing on their experiences but the focal point was the three families and why they are so different. They all live in the same community, all Maori, but why has there been such different impacts on the kids, on the family and their outlook on life. The volunteers asked lots of questions about the history of Maori culture, why some were marginalised and the Christianisation of Maori. Are the complexities in Maori culture just a mirror of the complexities in wider western society? Why is western society like this? What is the connection between economic development, family stability, cultural integrity and identity? The experience is really making them think about things they have never thought about before.

While previous studies have concluded that cultural tourists demand more authentic experiences of indigenous culture by interacting with their indigenous hosts in the host's own community (Ryan and Huyton, 2002; McIntosh, 2004; McIntosh and Johnson, 2004), it is unlikely that other cultural tourists will gain the same depth of interaction and experience as a volunteer tourist. Indeed, it has been argued that 'institutionalised mass tourists' and tourists who engage in a cultural encounter based on 'economic exchange' have less opportunity for direct, genuine and meaningful encounters with their hosts (Uriely and Reichel, 2000; McKercher and Du Cros, 2002). However, this conclusion requires further empirical validation.

The volunteers also compared their experiences of staying on the *marae* and working in the community with a day visit to a commercial Maori cultural attraction centred on a traditional Maori cultural performance in Rotorua. Their perception was that the nature of the experience they had gained on the *marae* was more genuine and 'real'. The participant observer noted that the volunteers had to make adjustments and accommodate both dimensions of the same culture: the commodified version in Rotorua and the cultural experience in the Maori community. The following quote from a volunteer illustrates this:

> To think this is all the tourists see; I think we are going to leave New Zealand so much more enriched having seen the real Maori; how they live in the modern world yet they still have their identity.

While the volunteers' experiences predominantly related to experiences of contemporary Maori lifestyle, aspects of the traditional values and customs of Maori culture were also experienced by the group, although the traditional values were arguably experienced within a contemporary context. This can be illustrated from the following quotes:

> The actual *powhiri* (welcome) was quite laid back and informal. I learned that there were many rules; how we had to be welcomed on the *marae,* how you couldn't wear shoes, the rules about the women and a division of gender and gender roles.

> I thought [during the *powhiri*] they would translate what they said in Maori into English. They did speak a little in English but you could feel it was not everything they said in Maori. I asked one of the ladies later what was said and she explained it to me. She said, 'We are welcoming you into our home, our community, our ancestors will look over you'. It was nice; if I did not ask I would not have known. I asked her why it was not explained by the man in the welcoming ceremony. She said the welcoming ceremony is, 'Not only for you but it is part of our ritual and culture; it is for us'.

As such, the experiences gained by the volunteer tourists in their interaction with Maori people were potentially more informal, interactive and authentic than that experienced by visitors to traditional Maori tourist attractions (Taylor, 2001; McIntosh, 2004).

Experience of self

Although the experience gained by the volunteers centred on an appreciation of Maori culture, it additionally involved an experience related to self. Self-reflection and personal development are characteristic of the volunteer tourism experience generally (Broad, 2003; Wearing and Deane, 2003). While appreciation of one's current life has been a feature of tourists' reactions at some cultural attractions (see Phelps, 2001), arguably, a deeper experience that develops the potential of the individual, or an experience that is considered cathartic (Zahra and McIntosh, 2007), is not widely associated with traditional cultural tourism consumption.

The participant observer noted the volunteers' reflections of self in her diary:

> Another thing that is happening to the volunteers is that they are reflecting on and evaluating their own lives, their families and the choices they have made and the attitudes they are forming. One commented about how coming here, seeing the kids, hearing about family backgrounds made her appreciate everything she has.

This was echoed in the reflection of one volunteer on her own family life:

> Seeing these kids with their blended families and living with aunts and grandmothers made me think about my own family. I did not realise how much mum and dad have done for me and for my brothers and sisters. They must have sacrificed a lot. Mum and dad have nothing for themselves, everything is for us.

Other volunteers described how 'by reflecting on my own culture, I've had spiritual growth' and 'our western society is so defined by materialism and I can see how I have been caught up in it'. The participant observer noted that 'the issue of suffering came up in the conversation at the dinner table; why some people suffer and others don't; why some are lucky – you don't choose the family you are born into'. One of the volunteers expressed the following:

> I knew it would be a life changing experience, and that you learnt about other cultures and a different way of life from other people, and it is life changing because you don't know what you have and now you know you're better off than other people; the education I've got and to be able to help other people. I think from now on, I'll be more involved in other forms of projects like donating more to World Vision; helping more in the community, listening more at home, helping mum more often.

Thus, reflection of self was evident in the nature of the volunteer experience, as noted in the above quotes from participants. However, this experience remains distinct from most traditional cultural tourism encounters.

Meaningful interpersonal experience

In addition to situating their own lives within the context of the experience, the experience involved interpersonal narratives and relationships – a creative cultural exchange. The volunteers described how their experiences had been influenced by the relationships they had developed with the Maori children, and from generally mixing with people from another culture. The essence of the experience they defined as a 'personally meaningful relationship'; 'the more you give of yourself in the relationship, the more you enjoy yourself and the more you get back'; 'it feels like you've just gone away for a bit and come back. We felt really cool; everyone treats you like you're from here'. Similarly, Brown and Morrison (2003) argue that volunteer tourists make genuine friendships in the process of interaction. However, the extent to which traditional cultural tourists, in contrast to volunteer tourists, experience a meaningful and lasting relationship with the indigenous hosts with whom they interact remains an issue for further investigation. Previous literature has argued that the short time frame and generalist nature of most cultural tourism experiences render the experience shallow and less authentic (Ryan *et al.*, 2000; McKercher and Du Cros, 2002).

The nature of the volunteers' experiences and the relationships they developed with their hosts can be illustrated in the following quotes:

> We learned a lot from the experience but the biggest things we got out of it were the personally meaningful relationships. We got to know them so well; it was like we'd known them our whole life. The smallest things could bring a smile to their face and if you remembered their name, it meant so much. They smiled all the time and it made you feel so good; we touched those kids.

> I felt more like a New Zealander than an Australian because I feel so welcomed and it was really good to say when people asked me that I was staying on the *marae*. This girl gave me a photo and it was the only photo she had and she gave it to me because she wanted me to remember her. One girl also gave me a greenstone pendant that had been given to her by her grandmother and it was the first time it had been outside of her family. That was a really powerful moment.

In considering the interactions between volunteers and their hosts, the nature of the volunteer tourism experience appeared to engender deep host–volunteer connections and meaningful relationships.

The Host Community's Response

What remains to be addressed is to examine how open and responsive was the host community initially, and throughout the volunteering project, and what impact did the volunteers leave on the community. The following narratives portray the perspectives reported by *Kaumatua* from the *marae*, the non-Maori social worker who organized the holiday programme in Awatapu and members of the Awatapu community who helped with the holiday programme and its activities and interacted with the volunteers.

Hosts' attitudes towards the volunteer tourism project

The *Kaumatua* reported favourable attitudes towards the volunteer project on the *marae*; primarily, this attitude was based on the precedent set by a previous group of volunteers who had visited the *marae* 3 years earlier and the trust that had been established with the organizer. He explained:

> I took a risk last time [in 2003] in inviting a group of young volunteers onto the *marae*. I was concerned about late night parties, drinking, the bad boys of Whakatane hanging around the *marae*. I was concerned about the impact all this would have on the Maori families living around the *marae*. But I took the proposal to the Board. One advantage of this group was that the women did not have to cook and take care of the group. They were going to cook and clean for themselves, but not only that, they were going to help us with activities for our very young and clean around the *marae*. They were coming to give, not to take. Anyway the first project went well.

The senior social worker expressed his apprehensions about the volunteer tourism project but these, he reported, were alleviated relatively quickly:

> I wasn't quite sure what the group was going to be like, the make up, the actual backgrounds, what their expectations were going to be and their experiences prior to this project. I thought they were a really good group. When I met them I laid down some ground rules, I talked about Maori and some of the gang influences. I think I went over the top but it kept them in line and they did not take risks and they were very positive. I was really happy with the group; with the way they rose to the occasion and got involved.

Thus, both the *Kaumatua* and one social worker had initial reservations about the volunteer group, especially regarding their young age. However, the performance and interaction of the volunteers with the host community removed any concern and prior apprehensions.

Hosts' perceptions of the volunteers

The host respondents were generally positive in their perceptions of the volunteers and their conduct during volunteering activities. For instance, both the *Kaumatua* and the adults accompanying the volunteers during the welcome on to the *marae* reported that they were very impressed with the effort the volunteers made to prepare a Maori *waiata* (song) for the *powhiri* (welcome) and how well they sang it. As one elder commented, their *waiata* showed they 'came with an openness and wanting to make an effort to appreciate our culture'. The social worker further explained:

> The two groups [the children and the volunteers] just met and it was on, there was no animosity, there was an openness, open friendliness that caused them to react straight away, both groups came together, they supported each other, had fun, they enjoyed that closeness, they did share their own stories, especially the boys that want to be little gang members; they were open. They felt quite big talking about their experiences and their families and the fact that someone from the outside was genuinely interested was cool for them and probably important at their stage of development. There were no ruptures or conflicts; it was a two-way thing.

A member of the Awatapu community further confirmed the positive perception held of the volunteers:

> The volunteers came in with no 'airs'; 'hey we are better than you', 'you can learn from us', etc. The message they gave out to those kids was 'we want to be with you'. We want to know you and we want to have fun with you. You saw that in the first hour. They were interested in the kids. They gave the kids their undivided attention. They were not interested in their own things or wanting to rush off at lunch time or later. They were there as long as the kids wanted them to be there.

What has been highlighted here is that the volunteers embraced the host community and their culture.

Hosts' perceptions of the impact of the volunteers on the community

Generally, the hosts believed that the volunteers had had a positive impact on the community. For the *Kaumatua*, the example set by the volunteers was reported to be the biggest impact on the community. One elder explained:

> The positive thing was seeing young people, *Pakeha* (non-Maori), coming to do all this community volunteer work. They give up their time, they pay for everything. Sometimes the elders complain about the negative influences of Western society on our young. They get all these negative images that lead our young to only be interested in self, ignoring the *whanau* (extended family/smaller tribal unit) and the community. Our young sometimes do not take on board Maori cultural values such as giving back to the community because of all these negative influences. It helped the elders to see young *Pakeha* serving them and wanting to help them. It helped the young people and brought them closer their own Maori community. No, the group contributed a lot to our community.

For one Maori member of the Awatapu community, an ex-gang member, the benefit came from the cultural exchange:

> This holiday programme with the volunteers from Australia helped the kids identify with their culture. These volunteers were interested in them and in

their culture and it made them proud to be Maori. They were important to strangers, to outsiders. These people engaged with them personally. The kids had something to share, their life, themselves, their culture. Since the programme more kids are part of the *kapahaka* (Maori song and dance) at school. The boys want to get into the music. There is more interest in the local legends and local identity, devoid of gang culture which has dominated too many of our lives for too long. The volunteers contributed to this but we still have a long way to go.

The volunteers were also felt to be positive 'role models' for the Maori children and this was translated through the interaction and positive conversations between the children and the volunteers. One community member explained:

In their conversations and through their friendships they were a wonderful role model for the kids. I heard some of the conversations. There was one of the volunteers with two 10–11 year old girls and they were painting one of the props for the drama. They were talking about children. One of the young girls asked the volunteer does she want to have a baby. She said she wanted a husband first, who can be the father of the baby, and then I want a baby. They said to her so you do not want a baby to your boyfriend. She replied I do not know yet if my boyfriend is going to stay with me to see our baby grow up. I want my baby to have their mother and father with them if possible. The volunteer just explained what she wanted, she did not ask the girls personal questions. They asked her straight, she answered them straight. There was no moralizing, but a positive message was delivered.

There is previous scepticism among scholars that the process of volunteer tourism can have a negative impact on host communities and only deliver superficial benefits to the volunteers. This study appears to suggest that this is not always the case. Indeed, it provides evidence of the beneficial impacts of volunteer tourism within an indigenous community in a developed nation.

Conclusion

This chapter examined the nature of the volunteer tourism experience in the search for alternative experiences through cultural tourism. Qualitative research undertaken with community hosts and 12 Australian volunteers working on a *marae* in the Bay of Plenty region of New Zealand found the nature of the volunteer tourism experience to be mutually beneficial to both host and volunteer. The case study presented here represents volunteer tourism in a cultural context within a developed country and showed that the nature of the experiences gained by the volunteers were seemingly different from those gained by tourists experiencing traditional cultural products; specifically, it was more authentic, genuine, reflexive, of contemporary cultural content and a meaningful interpersonal experience. This extends the conceptualization of the cultural tourism experience more commonly reported in the academic literature to date; it thus adds to our understanding about less traditional forms of cultural tourism. Indeed, volunteering is arguably central to a model of alternative cultural tourism as the experience gained was found to evoke intrinsic motivation, is beneficial to both host and volunteer and is based on meaningful interaction (Wearing and Neil, 2000).

This case study has highlighted that with volunteer tourism more intense rather than superficial social interaction can occur; a new narrative between host and guest is created; a narrative that is engaging, genuine, creative and mutually beneficial. The narrative and traditional interaction between host and tourist is thus potentially rewritten as the tourist experience is actively constructed by the host as well as the tourist. In this way, volunteer tourism has the potential to foster creative, alternative *and* more sustainable forms of tourism activity. This case study has demonstrated the positive social benefits of volunteer tourism at a micro-level. Critics, however, may argue against the ethics of volunteer tourism as a 'best practice' form of tourism (Wearing, 2004), for example, viewing it as contributing to the curtailment of self-sufficiency in communities. Thus, future research should more closely examine the cross-cultural nature of the interaction between volunteer tourists and indigenous hosts, as well as the longer-term sustainable benefits attributing to both in order to move beyond the precursory evidence provided here.

In particular, this study involved volunteers of a similar (younger) age, gender and culture, and highlighted their role of interacting volunteer not only making a positive contribution to the indigenous community but also discovering who they were and returning home with an experience impacting on self. Further research is needed to examine how cultural experiences may be experienced by volunteers of differing profiles, and how cross-cultural experiences may differ among participants (hosts and guests) of relative greater cultural diversity. Furthermore, quantitative research is needed so that potential differences between volunteers and traditional cultural tourists can be validated. Comparison to different cultural contexts is also required. For example, this study provides insights into volunteer tourism in a cultural context in a developed nation; how this compares to a range of other cultural contexts in other developed nations, or how this contrasts with the experiences gained in developing nations, also requires investigation. Moreover, this study only considered one volunteer tourism organization. There is thus further scope to draw a comparison between differing volunteer organizations. Of particular note, the volunteers in this study were primarily motivated by volunteering; travel was a secondary motivation. This may not be the case for all volunteer organizations and, thus, the resulting interaction between host and volunteer may also be different.

Although rich insight into the experiential nature of the volunteer tourism experience in a cultural context was gained in this study, further qualitative research is required to more deeply examine the narratives between hosts and volunteers in other case study contexts. The precursory findings presented here provide some evidence to suggest that the host–volunteer encounter has the potential to be authentic, mutually beneficial and more sustainable than traditional cultural tourism consumption. Thus, the study provides further evidence in addition to anecdotal conclusions elsewhere (McIntosh, 2004) that indigenous tourism products based on more genuine and meaningful encounters are potentially the most sustainable option for indigenous communities in sharing their culture with tourists. For this reason, we argue that the nexus of volunteer tourism and cultural tourism requires more pressing research attention in the search for alternative cultural experiences through tourism.

References

Broad, S. (2003) Living the Thai life – a case study of volunteer tourism at the Gibbon Rehabilitation Project Thailand. *Tourism Recreation Research* 28(3), 63–72.

Brown, S. and Morrison, A.M. (2003) Expanding volunteer vacation participation: an exploratory study on the mini-mission concept. *Tourism Recreation Research* 28(3), 73–82.

Butler, R. and Hinch, T. (eds) (1996) *Tourism and Indigenous Peoples*. International Thomson Business Press, London.

Callanan, M. and Thomas, S. (2005) Volunteer tourism: deconstructing volunteer activities within a dynamic environment. In: Novelli, M. (ed.) *Niche Tourism. Contemporary Issues, Trends and Cases*. Butterworth-Heinemann, Oxford, UK, pp. 183–200.

Halpenny, E.A. and Caissie, L.T. (2003) Volunteering on nature conservation projects: volunteer experience, attitudes and values. *Tourism Recreation Research* 28(3), 25–33.

McGehee, N.G. (2002) Alternative tourism and social movements. *Annals of Tourism Research* 29(1), 124–143.

McIntosh, A.J. (1998) Mixing methods: putting the tourist at the forefront of tourism research. *Tourism Analysis* 3(2), 121–127.

McIntosh, A.J. (2004) Tourists' appreciation of Maori culture in New Zealand. *Tourism Management* 25, 1–15.

McIntosh, A.J. and Johnson, H. (2004) Exploring the nature of the Maori experience in New Zealand: views from hosts and tourists. *Tourism: An International Interdisciplinary Journal* 52(2), 117–129.

McIntosh, A.J., Zygadlo, F. and Matunga, H. (2004) Rethinking Maori tourism. *Asia Pacific Journal of Tourism Research* 9(4), 331–351.

McKercher, B. and Du Cros, H. (2002) *Cultural Tourism: The Partnership Between Tourism and Cultural Heritage Management*. The Haworth Press, New York.

Phelps, A. (2001) Visiting places with 'added value': learning from pilgrimage to enhance the visitor's experience at heritage attractions. In: Horne, J. (ed.) *Leisure Cultures, Consumption and Commodification*. Leisure Studies Association, Eastbourne, UK, pp. 131–144.

Pine, B.J. and Gilmore, J.H. (1999) *The Experience Economy*. Harvard University Press, Boston, Massachusetts.

Prentice, R.C. and Andersen, V. (2003) Festival as creative destination. *Annals of Tourism Research* 30(1), 7–30.

Reynolds, T. and Gutman, J. (1988) Laddering theory, method, analysis and interpretation. *Journal of Advertising Research* February/March, 11–29.

Richards, G. (ed.) (2001) *Cultural Attractions and European Tourism*. CAB International, Wallingford, UK.

Richards, G. and Wilson, J. (2006) Developing creativity in tourist experiences: a solution to the serial reproduction of culture? *Tourism Management* 27(6), 1209–1223.

Ryan, C. and Huyton, J. (2002) Tourists and aboriginal people. *Annals of Tourism Research* 29(3), 631–647.

Ryan, C., Hughes, K. and Chirgwin, S. (2000) The gaze, spectacle and ecotourism. *Annals of Tourism Research* 27(1), 148–163.

Simpson, K. (2004) 'Doing development': the gap year, volunteer-tourists and a popular practice of development. *Journal of International Development* 16(5), 681–692.

Stoddart, H. and Rogerson, C.M. (2004) Volunteer tourism: the case of Habitat for Humanity South Africa. *GeoJournal* 60, 311–318.

Strauss, A. and Corbin, J. (1990) *Basics of Qualitative Research: Grounded Theory Procedures and Techniques*. Sage, Newbury Park, California.

Taylor, J.P. (2001) Authenticity and sincerity in tourism. *Annals of Tourism Research* 28(1), 7–26.

Trauer, B. (2006) Conceptualizing special interest tourism: frameworks for analysis. *Tourism Management* 27(2), 183–200.

Turner, R., Miller, G. and Gilbert, D. (2001) The role of UK charities and the tourism industry. *Tourism Management* 22, 463–472.

Uriely, N. and Reichel, A. (2000) Working tourists and the attitudes to hosts. *Annals of Tourism Research* 27(2), 267–283.

Uriely, N., Reichel, A. and Ron, A. (2003) Volunteering in tourism: additional thinking. *Tourism Recreation Research* 28(3), 57–62.

Wearing, S. (2001) *Volunteer Tourism: Experiences That Make a Difference*. CAB International, Wallingford, UK.

Wearing, S. (2002) Re-centring the self in volunteer tourism. In: Dann, G.M.S. (ed.) *The Tourist as a Metaphor of the Social World*. CAB International, Wallingford, UK, pp. 237–262.

Wearing, S. (2004) Examining best practice in volunteer tourism. In: Stebbins, R.A. and Graham, M. (eds) *Volunteering as Leisure, Leisure As Volunteering: An International Assessment*. CAB International, Wallingford, UK, pp. 209–224.

Wearing, S. and Deane, B. (2003) Seeking self: leisure and tourism on common ground. *World Leisure* 1, 6–13.

Wearing, S. and Neil, J. (2000) Refiguring self and identity through volunteer tourism. *Society and Leisure* 23(2), 389–419.

Zahra, A. and McIntosh, A. (2007) Volunteer tourism: evidence of cathartic tourist experiences. *Tourism Recreation Research* 32(1), 115–119.

15 Absences in the Volunteer Tourism Phenomenon: the Right to Travel, Solidarity Tours and Transformation Beyond the One-way

F. HIGGINS-DESBIOLLES[1] AND G. RUSSELL-MUNDINE[2]

[1]School of Management, University of South Australia, Adelaide, Australia;
[2]Southern Cross University, Lismore, Australia

Volunteer tourism is one of the most prominent niches of the alternative tourism movement and it is witnessing a rapid rate of growth. Wearing defines volunteer tourism as applying to those tourists 'who, for various reasons, volunteer in an organized way to undertake holidays that may involve the aiding or alleviating the material poverty of some groups in society, the restoration of certain environments, or research into aspects of society or environment' (2002a, p. 240). Volunteer tourism attempts to bring the humanistic and ecological values and impacts of tourism into focus and thus it may serve as a challenge to the dominant neoliberal paradigm that currently holds sway. However, to date the literature has overwhelmingly focused on the impacts upon the volunteer tourists rather than their hosts or those that are excluded from the volunteer tourism opportunity. This chapter attempts to fill a gap in the volunteer tourism literature by exploring the exclusions/inclusions of volunteer tourism and by examining the little-studied phenomenon of solidarity and reality tours.

This discussion begins with the new interest among tourism academics in the inclusions and exclusions of tourism (Botterill and Klemm, 2005) and investigates the foundations of the universal right to tourism and travel and the social tourism movement which has attempted to make such a right a reality. This analysis suggests that the right to tourism and travel is least developed among the poor and the marginalized of the developing world despite the fact that many of the world's nations have endorsed a universal right to tourism and travel and have committed to social tourism in the 1999 Global Code of Ethics for Tourism (United Nations World Tourism Organization, 1999). In such circumstances, the transformative and cross-cultural capacities of volunteer tourism become restricted to the privileged volunteer tourist having an interaction with the often underprivileged developing world 'host'. Because the volunteer tourism research to date has not sufficiently focused upon the experience and attitudes of the developing country hosts, it is difficult to ascertain the full impacts of such a one-way interaction through volunteer tourism, but it is logical to assume the restricted nature of its transformative capacities as a result. This chapter explores the understudied phenomenon of solidarity exchanges in which people from developing countries are enabled to travel and interact with people in developed communities through church-based, activists and developmental networks. This tourism phenomenon enticingly reveals the potentials of an implemented universal right to travel and tourism and offers volunteer tourism a missing piece of the puzzle of developing a tourism paradigm which could contribute to transformations that would fully 'make a difference'. The study of these solidarity exchanges reveals a tourism phenomenon that actually undermines the commodification of tourism and advocates profound shifts in social and environmental paradigms and which challenges the current status quo in a way that contemporary volunteer tourism arguably does not.

Inclusions and Exclusions of Tourism and the Human Right to Travel and Tourism

Frequently, tourism has been characterized either as a trivial phenomenon with its focus on the hedonistic pursuit of fun (Weaver and Lawton, 2002) or as an industry of considerable economic worth (Higgins-Desbiolles, 2006b). More rarely, attention turns to the serious social implications of tourism and its potential to fulfil a variety of human needs including self-realization, cross-cultural understanding, community development and cultural maintenance (Reid, 2003; Higgins-Desbiolles, 2006b). However, since the market ideology of neoliberalism has held sway, tourism analysts have tended to focus upon such issues as satisfying tourists' demand, marketing destinations and experiences and managing tourism to obtain greater growth rates and profits. Wearing *et al.* (2005) have recently championed a decommodified tourism research agenda. They argue that tourism analysts should turn to the alternative perspectives offered by feminism, ecocentrism, post-structuralism and community development in order to foster a tourism geared to true sustainability and community empowerment. Similarly motivated by equity concerns, Botterill and Klemm (2005) have edited a special volume of *Tourism Culture and Communication* dedicated to tourism's social inclusions and exclusions. Here they propose an alternative tourism research agenda to the traditional focus on the tourists and the 'positives of tourism', one that problematizes tourism and provides an 'account of tourism that foregrounds absences and negativities and asks what and who is absent from tourism and why' (Botterill and Klemm, 2005, p. 4). Their vision of inclusion arises from the social sciences concept of 'a process whereby all citizens can enjoy full participation in society' and in this examination, they look at access or lack of access to tourism opportunities (Botterill and Klemm, 2005, p. 1). However, this volume only focuses upon the case of the UK and those Britons who are marginalized due to such factors as race, gender, sexual orientation, age, disability or poverty. This is a very narrow focus that could be widened by examining the universal right to travel and tourism and the social tourism initiatives developed to realize them.

The right to travel and tourism has been incorporated in key international documents including the Universal Declaration of Human Rights of 1948, the International Covenant on Economic, Social and Cultural Rights of 1966, the World Tourism Organization's (UNWTO) Tourism Bill of Rights and Tourist Code of 1985 and the Global Code of Ethics for Tourism of 1999. The Universal Declaration of Human Rights has two passages that underpin the right to travel: articles 13(2) and 24. Article 13(2) states that 'everyone has the right to leave any country, including his own, and to return to his country' (UN, 1948), which O'Byrne (2001) describes as underpinning the human right to travel. Combined with article 24, which states that 'everyone has the right to rest and leisure, including reasonable limitation of working hours and periodic holidays with pay' (UN, 1948), this fundamental document underpinning international law is credited with situating travel and tourism as a human right. The justification for asserting such new rights can be gleaned from the words of the UNWTO's Manila Declaration on World Tourism, which declares:

> Tourism is an activity essential to the life of nations because of its direct effects on the social, cultural, educational and economic sectors of national societies and their international relations. Its development is linked to the social and economic development of nations and can only be possible if man [sic] has access to creative rest and holidays and enjoys freedom to travel within the framework of free time and leisure whose profoundly human character it underlines. Its very existence and development depend entirely on the existence of a state of lasting peace, to which tourism is required to contribute.
>
> (UNWTO, 1980)

The more recent code promulgated is the Global Code of Ethics for Tourism (UNWTO, 1999), which reiterates the human right to travel and tourism and also advocates government support of initiatives such as 'social tourism' to promote access to tourism for potential disadvantaged groups in their societies including the disabled, youth, seniors and families.

The basic principle of social tourism is 'access to travel and leisure opportunities for all' (International Bureau of Social Tourism, 2002). In particular, social tourism advocates the provision of tourism opportunities for the 'economically weak or otherwise disadvantaged elements of society' (Hunzinger, cited in Murphy, 1985, p. 23). The precepts of modern social tourism were being laid early in the 20th century when the principle of paid leave for workers became adopted. For example, France has a long tradition of social tourism through the trade union movement (Ouvry-Vial et al., cited in Richards, 1996, p. 157). Switzerland created the Swiss Travel Saving Fund (REKA) in 1939 to assist low-income workers with funding for holidays (Teuscher, 1983). A distinctive form of social tourism was developed in the socialist countries of Eastern Europe and the Soviet Union to serve several needs. These ranged from provision of rest and relaxation for the workers of socialist production in order to improve their future output, to fostering communist solidarity by touring fellow communist countries and to the use of tourism as a method of fostering 'socialist education' for youth (Allcock and Przeclawski, 1990, p. 4). But social tourism initiatives are found around the world with examples discernible in most countries.

This global distribution is supported by an international body, the International Bureau of Social Tourism (BITS). BITS is an umbrella organization for national social tourism organizations to cooperate on the development and promotion of social tourism. It was founded in 1963 in Brussels and now represents members from around the world and includes 12 governmental authorities. BITS has formulated a strong argument for the right of all to tourism, travel and leisure, and exhorts governments in particular to move beyond 'recognition of the right' to tourism to actual pragmatic programmes to enable all to enjoy the exercise of their right (BITS, 2002). In their Montreal Declaration (1996), BITS outlines the context which makes the promotion of social tourism so vital. This states that in today's world:

- Growth in the wealthiest countries is spasmodic, and whole sections of the population suffer increasing deprivation, resulting in serious social unrest.
- Large economic alliances are formed, operating according to their own free-market logic.
- Some countries experience rapid growth, opening up to the possibility of domestic tourism.
- Other countries, and even whole continents, are trapped in appalling poverty.
- The right to a search for meaning is claimed everywhere.
- In this world, tourism is growing rapidly (BITS, 1996).

In sharp contrast to the economistic perspective of tourism, this declaration asserts that the 'subjugation' of tourism to the service of human needs is imperative in such a context (BITS, 1996). First Secretary General of BITS Arthur Haulot described social tourism as 'a type of tourism that concentrates essentially on Man and his destiny [sic], and not on the profits to be made from his status as a consumer' (1985, p. 220).

However, despite the social tourism phenomenon and its supporting body of BITS, it is obvious that the human right to travel and tourism is not universally enjoyed. In particular, there is a clear divide between the developed and developing worlds in this respect, with the former providing the vast bulk of international tourists and the latter increasingly serving as their hosts. In this era of the ascendancy of the market, it has largely been forgotten that important international tourism declarations acknowledge the need to bridge the divide between the developed and developing world's ability to fulfil the human right to travel and tourism (UNWTO, 1980, 1999). It is within such a context that volunteer tourism operates.

Volunteer Tourism: Transformative Force or Penitence for the Privileged?

Stephen Wearing was the first to comprehensively analyse the phenomenon of volunteer tourism which he labelled 'a new form of alternative tourism' (2002a, p. 257). He defines volunteer tourism as applying to those tourists 'who, for various reasons, volunteer in an organized way to undertake holidays that may involve aiding or alleviating the material poverty of some groups in society, the restoration of certain environments, or research into aspects of society or environment' (2002a, p. 240). Volunteer tourism has been examined from a multitude of perspectives, but one relevant lens to this analysis is to see it as a catalyst to necessary social and ecological change. Uriely *et al.* suggest:

> [V]olunteering in tourism should be seen as an expression of what is recognized in tourism literature as the 'other' dimension of postmodern tourism, which emphasizes the growing appeal of concepts such as 'alternative', 'real', 'ecological', and 'responsible' forms of tourism. These developments in the context of tourism are congruent with anti-globalization and environmental awareness in contemporary Western cultures.
>
> (2003, p. 61)

McGehee (2002), McGehee and Norman (2002) and McGehee and Santos (2005) have begun the important work of researching how participation in volunteer tourism experiences leads individuals to heightened consciousness of political and social issues and as a result to join new social movements and support activism. Clearly elements of volunteer tourism possess a potential to transform the nature of contemporary social and human–environmental relations. Wearing's (2001, 2002a) analysis suggests that volunteer tourism challenges the very foundations of contemporary tourism and capitalist globalization. It challenges the former by undermining the 'othering' of tourism and 'the dialogue that volunteers have with other cultures' views of the world through their often elongated and more intense travel experiences provides a different perspective . . . it de-centres an excessive focus on the self that has hitherto been at the core of tourism analysis' (Wearing, 2002a, p. 249). Additionally, the volunteer tourism experience can lead tourists to question the ethos of their own society. Illustrative of this is this quote from one of the volunteer tourists Wearing interviewed:

> It [the volunteer tourism experience] made me a lot more critical of a consumer's society. I think there are a lot of things here that are all very nice and convenient and are good for status. But there are a lot of things we just don't need. If something is broken, we go down to the shop and buy another one, or buy a dishwasher instead of doing it yourself. I have become more critical of my environment, because each time I buy something, I have to really justify to myself, do I need this or is it just something to do with money I'm spending my life earning.
>
> (2002a, p. 250)

Volunteer tourism clearly delivers significant transformations in tourism and the tourists, including the fostering of an ethos of 'self-other care' (Wearing, 2002a, pp. 254–255), promoting sustainable community development through which the host community is empowered (see Wearing, 1993), fostering involvement in new social movements and activism (McGehee, 2002; McGehee and Norman, 2002; McGehee and Santos, 2005) and demonstrating a powerful example of how tourism can be redirected away from a narrow economic focus to human welfare and ecocentrism (Wearing, 2002a; Wearing *et al.*, 2005; Wearing and Ponting, 2006). Despite these laudable outcomes, a critical analysis of volunteer tourism reveals at least one significant absence in both the phenomenon and its analysis.

Currently volunteer tourism is predominantly a story of western privilege as it is the rich who visit the poor and marginalized communities of the world who are in need of their financial and non-financial assistance. Research and analysis by Wearing (2001, 2002a) and others (e.g. Broad, 2003; Lyons, 2003; McGehee and Santos, 2005) have largely focused on transformations in the privileged volunteers. Seldom are the voices of the members of the host community heard in these musings on volunteer tourism and even rarer is a consideration of how the underprivileged can receive the extraordinary benefits of a volunteer tourism experience. Wearing has recognized the limitations that volunteer tourism suffers as a 'consumer' activity of the privileged when he suggests that perhaps volunteer tourism 'provides another source of consumption which will only endanger the very communities and environments that the volunteer tourists seeks to protect' (2001, p. 15). In fact, volunteer tourism is being co-opted as a lucrative niche market as travel agencies jostle to attract the privileged volunteer tourists. Thus, we see organizations such as Travellers Worldwide turn the mediating of volunteer tourists with work projects abroad into a business and sell their experiences to potential volunteer tourists as curriculum vitae building opportunities (Travellers Worldwide, 2006). If volunteer tourism is truly anticipated to 'make a difference' and change things, it cannot remain limited in this way. One way of overcoming such limitations is to expand the conceptualization of volunteer tourism to include the solidarity tours of justice tourism.

Justice Tourism and Solidarity Tours

Although justice tourism is new to the tourism lexicon, the critical evaluation of tourism in terms of its impacts on human rights and justice has been long enduring (Scheyvens, 2002, p. 102). Holden's description of alternative tourism makes justice a key: it is 'a process which promotes a just form of travel between members of different communities. It seeks to achieve mutual understanding, solidarity and equality amongst participants' (cited in Pearce, 1992, p. 18).

One type of tourism that fits these criteria has recently received attention, 'reality tourism'. Reality tours attempt to move tourists to engage with the lived reality of the locals and to establish interactions based on equity and respect. Perhaps the most exemplary case is the reality tour programme of Global Exchange which aims to:

- Provide individuals with the opportunity to understand issues beyond what is communicated by the mass media and gain a new vantage point from which to view and affect US foreign policy;
- Link travelers [sic] with activists and organizations from around the globe who are working towards positive change;
- Prompt participants to examine related issues in their own communities (Global Exchange, 2007).

A related type of alternative tourism is the solidarity tours that began in the 1960s. At that time the counterculture, student and civil rights movements marked a supportive wave in the developed world for decolonization, civil rights and justice in solidarity with people around the world seeking self-determination and human rights. Solidarity tours, also known as solidarity exchanges and immersions, describe organized visits to communities in need of understanding and external support in the face of negative circumstances such as occupation, poverty, colonization, trade sanctions and conflict. Examples include the visits to Cuba organized by Cuba solidarity groups around the world to study the impacts of Fidel Castro's socialism and express solidarity against the US-imposed sanctions in effect since the 1960s. Another example is Olive Travel and Tours' solidarity visits to Palestine which provide opportunities to:

- See at first-hand the current situation in Israel/Palestine;
- Show solidarity with Israelis and Palestinians working for peace and justice;
- Learn from experienced guides;
- Visit key political and religious sites;
- Meet and stay a night with Palestinian and/or Israeli families;
- Travel, laugh and exchange experiences with your fellow travellers; and
- Return informed and motivated to work effectively for a just and lasting peace (Olive Co-operative, 2007b).

One specific tour that Olive organizes annually is a solidarity tour bringing visitors to assist Palestinians in the olive harvest which has been made difficult under Israeli occupation. These visitors not only assist as workers but may also deter Israeli Occupation Force intimidation of these Palestinian farmers by serving as external witnesses during the harvest. Interestingly, the Olive Co-operative offers travel bursaries to assist unemployed and low-income British activists to participate in the solidarity tours (Olive Co-operative, 2007a) – an example of social tourism.

There are solidarity tours and exchanges which address the need to foster social and environmental transformations by arranging exchanges across the divide between the developing and developed worlds. For example, the reciprocal youth exchanges of the International Palestinian Youth Exchange and YMCA Sweden focus on raising awareness about youth concerns and problems in both countries (International Palestinian Youth League, 2004). In the UK, Voluntary Service Overseas (VSO) has been running a programme for 6 years called Global Xchange with the British Council and Community Service Volunteers. Global Xchange teams up nine young people from the developing world with nine young people from the UK. They spend 3 months working together in the UK and 3 months in the developing country on community-initiated, community development projects. Over 50 teams have been through the programme so far. Former volunteer Bethan McDonald states: 'I believe that when young people from different socio-economic and cultural backgrounds work together and understand each other, we may begin to have a more peaceful and tolerant society' (Global Xchange, 2005). Similar visits are organized around the world by non-governmental organizations (NGOs), church groups and activists' networks aimed at fostering social and environmental change. This chapter will now review a case study of one such project.

A Case Study in Creating Transformations Through Tourism: the Ladakh Project

The Ladakh Project of the International Society for Ecology and Culture (ISEC) contains a solidarity/reality tourism component that deserves further analysis. Ladakh is located in the Indian Himalayas. It has a strong, vibrant Buddhist culture similar to Tibet, hence its appellation of 'Little Tibet'. ISEC was founded by Helena Norberg-Hodge, a Swedish linguist who visited Ladakh in 1975 (Norberg-Hodge, 1992). This was just at the time that India imposed a programme of planned development for the region which included tourism, industrialized agriculture and other aspects of the modernization programme that development analysts advocated as the model to move such developing areas to western-style development status (ISEC, 2005b). After spending time in Ladakh and learning the language, Norberg-Hodge grew concerned that the cultural impacts of external development were changing the autonomous and proud traditions of Ladakh and imposing a 'psychological pressure to modernise' as 'idealised images of western consumer culture' undermined the economy and damaged Ladakhi cultural confidence (ISEC, 2005a). Anecdotal evidence of this can be seen in the transition in perspective evident in these statements by a Ladakhi youth, Tsewang Paljor, recounted by Norberg-Hodge:

> I remember being shown around the remote village of Hemis Shupachan by a young Ladakhi called Tsewang. It seemed to me that all the houses I saw were especially large and beautiful, and I asked Tsewang to show me the houses where the poor people lived. He looked perplexed for a moment, then replied: 'We don't have any poor people here'. Eight years later, I overheard Tsewang talking to some tourists. 'If you could only help us Ladakhis', he was saying, 'we're so poor'.
> (Norberg-Hodge, cited in Graydon, 2003)

In addition to this, Norberg-Hodge witnessed numerous negative consequences of the development process in Ladakh over many years, including undermining of the local economy, community and family breakdown, unemployment, rapid urbanization and pollution (ISEC, 2005a). But Norberg-Hodge also recognized that witnessing changes in Ladakh as the western development model was imposed provided important lessons for the developed countries that had also suffered such negative impacts from the modernization process but had forgotten the sources of these problems as their transition phase from more locally based lifestyles had occurred so much earlier (Norberg-Hodge, 1991, 1992). After much thought, Norberg-Hodge came to the conclusion that the problem lay with a monolithic and monocultural development model that globally reduces cultural diversity, undermines local economies and damages human–ecological relationships (Norberg-Hodge, 1992). This led Norberg-Hodge and her husband to establish the ISEC and the Ladakhi Project in order to 'promote locally-based alternatives to the global consumer culture' (Graydon, 2003) in a vision that Norberg-Hodge has entitled 'counter-development' (Norberg-Hodge, 1991).

The Ladakhi Project has two 'tourism' programmes which support this vision: the Tourism for Change Programme and the Education and Cultural Exchange Programme. The Tourism for Change Programme is meant to address the impacts that the imposition of mainstream tourism has had on Ladakh since the 1970s by opening up a realistic encounter between interested tourists and Ladakhi people. ISEC claims that misunderstandings between tourists and Ladakhis

> are born of a lack of complete information and real communication between tourists and Ladakhis. We have found that greater knowledge about what is happening around the world, not isolationism, is the surest way for Ladakhis to take control over their own future. Recognizing that tourism is a powerful agent of change, we make great efforts to reach out to visitors to invite them to participate in solutions at every level: from cultural awareness, to ecologically sensitive behaviour, to supporting alternatives in Ladakh and in their own home communities.
>
> (ISEC, 2005a)

To accomplish this, ISEC offers a daily workshop to tourists in the capital, Leh, which features a showing of ISEC's film *Ancient Futures: Learning from Ladakh* (1993) that portrays Norberg-Hodge's concept of learning from Ladakh. Since this project has begun, over 3000 tourists have participated annually (ISEC, 2005a). Another measure ISEC has taken to educate the tourists so that their impact is more benign if not beneficial is to develop an extensive set of guidelines for visitors advising how they can support the local economy, display cultural sensitivity and avoid damage to the environment (see ISEC, 2005a). ISEC additionally offers intensive reality/volunteer tours where tourists can stay with a Ladakhi family and work with them to experience lives lived on a more 'human scale' as Norberg-Hodge describes it (Paradise with side effects, 2003).

The Educational and Cultural Exchange Programme targets the lack of information that Ladakhis have about life in the developed countries. ISEC seeks to counter the idealized images of western culture that tourists, expatriates and media often portray so that Ladakhis can decide their own future fully informed (ISEC, 2005a). One facet of this is to conduct 'reality tours' for Ladakhis which take them to developed countries so they can experience what life is really like. Some 50 Ladakhis have experienced these reality tours over the years. ISEC has created a film entitled *Paradise with Side Effects* (2003) depicting the reality tour experiences of two Ladakhi leaders of the Women's Alliance, Dolma Tsering and Tsewang Lden, touring London with Norberg-Hodge. Anticipating her experience, Tsering says: 'I'm really looking forward to this trip. Some people say it's not very nice in the West and others say it is wonderful. On television you only see the positive things. I can't wait to see everything with my own eyes' (*Paradise with Side Effects*, 2003). As part of the effort to provide insights into the lived experiences of Londoners, Norberg-Hodge hosts Tsering and Lden in her family home and takes them to see places where the contrasting dynamics of western life are in sharp relief to Ladakh, including an aged-care facility indicative of a breakdown in family and community values and a massive rubbish dump demonstrating the impacts of a wasteful society. (However, Norberg-Hodge also takes Dolma Tsering and Tsewang Lden to see evidence of transitions in British society to more humanistic and ecologically sustainable living such as seen in the organic cotton garments in high demand in speciality shops.) On returning to Ladakh, Tsering concludes that 'people there don't have any time. We always think people in the West are the ones who are rich but in many ways we are better off' (*Paradise with Side Effects*, 2003). Another Ladakhi reality tourist, Stanzin Tonyot, stated:

> Spending time in the West showed me a side of Westerners I never imagined. I found that they have lots of money but they don't have time for each other. Many of them are looking for community and a life closer to nature – a Ladakhi lifestyle!
> (ISEC, 2005a)

Insights that have moved the Ladakhis include the loneliness and isolation of the elderly, the waste of western society, the breakdown into nuclear families where young and old rarely mix, and how hard people in the west must work to earn a living, which makes the reality tourists reflect more favourably on the Ladakhi traditional lifestyle where work and leisure are still entwined and time for people is more ample (*Paradise with Side Effects*, 2003). Norberg-Hodge states that such messages can 'help to establish a balance so that they realize there is something to be lost' in the move to western-style development (*Paradise with Side Effects*, 2003).

Reflecting on the success of these reality tours to the west, Norberg-Hodge claims that almost one-half of the Ladakhis who have undertaken such experiences have changed their attitudes and subsequent activities; many getting involved in NGOs (H. Norberg-Hodge, Devon, UK, 2006, personal communication). Norberg-Hodge did note that some Ladakhi reality tourists are awed by their experiences of the west and some have proceeded to fully integrate into the modernizing lifestyles occurring in urban areas such as Leh. However, Norberg-Hodge acknowledges that the Ladakh Project is not 'unproblematic' (Norberg-Hodge, 1991, p. 178). Certainly some might criticize Norberg-Hodge for imposing her values on Ladakh, but this can be countered by highlighting that the Ladakh Project is focused on enabling Ladakhi informed decision making and is committed to working with Ladakhi NGOs.

Despite such potential ambivalence, the Ladakh Project presents one model of holistic social and environmental transformations through tourism from which volunteer tourism proponents could learn. It includes an educational programme for tourists visiting Ladakh similar to initiatives in other places focused on sensitizing tourists to their impacts and harnessing their visits for better outcomes for Ladakhis. Similar to volunteer tourism projects in other places, it also includes a specialized volunteer/reality tourism experience dedicated to providing opportunities for tourists to live and work with Ladakhi families. However, uniquely the Ladakh Project organizes reality tours for Ladakhis to visit the west in order to ensure that the opportunity to expand consciousness goes beyond the privileged of the developed world. Fully gauging the impacts of the reality tours remains a task for future research which should survey the Ladakhi reality tourists, conduct longitudinal studies of their lifeways and conduct participant observation of their tours. None the less, this example invites us to expand the horizons of volunteer tourism operations and analysis to be more inclusive and innovative. The social and ecological transformations required demand nothing less.

For the number of solidarity and reality tour initiatives to increase, funding is vital. Currently numerous activities which could be placed under this umbrella are organized around the globe by international NGOs (INGOs), NGOs, churches, trade unions and other entities. This facet of tourism is worthy of further research. However, this analysis suggests that more considerable funding of solidarity tourism is justified from the public purse because of the commitments made through the international declarations on the human right to travel referred to above. This could form a new facet of social tourism, international social tourism, and be justified by the need to foster global citizenship. Wealthier countries could incorporate this in their governmental welfare spending and poorer countries could access funds from international aid. Of course, this is unlikely under the current neoliberal paradigm. However, the international obligations assumed by the nations of the international community through such documents as the Universal Declaration of Human Rights and the International Covenant on Economic, Social and Cultural Rights provide grounds for challenging the current paradigm (see Higgins-Desbiolles, 2006a).

Conclusion

Volunteer tourism analyst Stephen Wearing sets a challenging vision for volunteer tourism when he enquires: 'To what extent does volunteering in tourism contribute to global peace, understanding and solidarity?' (Wearing, 2002b, p. 3). The ability of volunteer tourism to contribute to such vital goals would be vastly improved if the universal right to travel and tourism were fully applied to the volunteer tourism sector resulting in exchanges across the divide between the developing and developed world. This chapter has only provided a preliminary analysis and singular case study to expose this research opportunity.

In fact, there is a well-recognized need for further research in order to fully gauge the impacts that volunteer tourism is having on localities, peoples and the global order (Halpenny and Cassie, 2003; Lyons, 2003; Wearing, 2004). This chapter has provided only a brief exploration of the need to expand the inclusions of volunteer tourism beyond the provinces of the privileged. This analysis indicates a need for further research into the scale, scope and impact of such reality and solidarity tours across the divide that now separates the people of the developing and developed worlds. There is a particular need to search out projects which are locally initiated in contrast to the Ladakh Project studied here.

This analysis suggests that change must occur not only in the privileged but also in the thoughtful tourists who seek to learn through meaningful volunteering opportunities in tourism. The direness of the difficulties that human societies confront and the universal right to travel and tourism necessitate that all individuals in all societies must be enabled to experience the consciousness-raising opportunities innate to volunteer tourism. For volunteer tourism to truly 'make a difference' (Wearing, 2001), volunteer tourism and its analysis must move beyond the one-way nature of its contemporary form and embrace inclusivity fully.

References

Allcock, J.B. and Przeclawski, K. (1990) Introduction. *Annals of Tourism Research* 17, 1–6.

Ancient futures: Learning from Ladakh (1993) Videorecording. International Society for Ecology and Culture, Devon, UK.

Botterrill, D. and Klemm, M. (2005) Introduction: tourism and social inclusion. *Tourism, Culture and Communication* 6(1), 1–6.

Broad, S. (2003) Living the Thai life – a case study of volunteer tourism at the Gibbon Rehabilitation Project, Thailand. *Tourism Recreation Research* 28(3), 63–72.

Global Exchange (2007) Global Exchange Reality Tours. Available at: http://www.globalex change.org/tours/index.html

Global Xchange (2005) Global Xchange. Homepage. Available at: http://www.vso.org. uk/globalxchange

Graydon, N. (2003) Seeds of Hope. *The Ecologist (online)*. Available at: http://www.theecolo gist.org/archive_detail.asp?content_id=386

Halpenny, E.A. and Cassie, L.T. (2003) Volunteering on nature conservation projects: volunteer experience, attitudes and values. *Tourism Recreation Research* 28(3), 25–33.

Haulot, A. (1985) The environment and the social value of tourism. *International Journal of Environmental Studies* 25, 219–223.

Higgins-Desbiolles, F. (2006a) Another world is possible: tourism, globalisation and the respon-sible alternative. PhD thesis, Flinders University of South Australia, Adelaide, Australia.

Higgins-Desbiolles, F. (2006b) More than an industry: tourism as a social force. *Tourism Management* 27(6), 1192–1208.

International Bureau of Social Tourism (1996) Montreal Declaration. Available at: http://www. bits-int.org/declaration.asp?lang=en 3

International Bureau of Social Tourism (2002) The Right of All to Leisure, Holidays and Tourism. Available at: http://www.bits-int.org/quest_ce_que.asp

International Palestinian Youth League (2004) Exchange Programmes. Available at: http://www. ipyl.org/ste.html

International Society for Ecology and Culture (2005a) The Ladakh Project. Available at: http:// www.isec.org.uk/ladakh.html

International Society for Ecology and Culture (2005b) Tourism For Change: Some Guidelines for Visitors to Ladakh. Available at: http://www.isec.org.uk/ladakh.html

Lyons, K.D. (2003) Ambiguities in volunteer tourism: a case study of Australians participating in a J-1 Visitor Exchange Program. *Tourism Recreation Research* 28(3), 5–13.

McGehee, N. (2002) Alternative tourism and social movement. *Annals of Tourism Research* 29, 124–143.

McGehee, N.G. and Norman, W.C. (2002) Alternative tourism and consciousness-raising. *Tourism Analysis* 6, 239–251.

McGehee, N.G. and Santos, C.A. (2005) Social change, discourse and volunteer tourism. *Annals of Tourism Research* 32(3), 760–779.

Murphy, P.E. (1985) *Tourism: A Community Approach*. Methuen, New York.

Norberg-Hodge, H. (1991) *Ancient Futures: Learning from Ladakh*. Sierra Books, San Francisco, California.

Norberg-Hodge, H. (1992) Rethinking Development, Interview by David Barsamian. Available at: http://www.lol/shareworld.com/zmag/articles/barhodge.htm

O'Byrne, D. (2001) On passports and border controls. *Annals of Tourism Research* 28(2), 399–416.

Olive Co-operative (2007a) Bursary Fund. Available at: http://www.olivecoop.com/bursary.html

Olive Co-operative (2007b) Olive Travel and Tours. Available at: http://www.olivecoop.com/ tours.html

Paradise with Side Effects (2003) Videorecording. International Society for Ecology and Culture, Devon, UK.

Pearce, D.G. (1992) Alternative tourism: concepts, classifications and questions. In: Smith, V.L. and Eadington, W.R. (eds) *Tourism Alternatives*. Wiley, Chichester, UK, pp. 15–30.

Reid, D.G. (2003) *Tourism, Globalization and Development*. Pluto, London.

Richards, G. (1996) *Cultural Tourism in Europe*. CAB International, Wallingford, UK.

Scheyvens, R. (2002) *Tourism for Development: Empowering Communities*. Prentice-Hall, Harlow, UK.

Teuscher, H. (1983) Social tourism for all – the Swiss Travel Saving Fund. *Tourism Management* 4(3), 216–219.

Travellers Worldwide (2006) Voluntary Work Placements Overseas. Available at: http://www.travellersworldwide.com

United Nations. (1948) Universal Declaration of Human Rights. Available at: http://www.fourmilab.ch/etexts/www/un/udhr.html

United Nations World Tourism Organization (1980) Manila Declaration on World Tourism. Available at: http://www.world-tourism.org/sustainable/concepts

United Nations World Tourism Organization (1999) Global Code of Ethics for Tourism. Available at: http://www.world-tourism.org/pressrel/CODEOFE.htm

Uriely, N., Reichel, A. and Ron, A. (2003) Volunteering in tourism: additional thinking. *Tourism Recreation Research* 28(3), 57–62.

Wearing, S. (1993) Ecotourism: the Santa Elena rainforest project. *The Environmentalist* 13(2), 125–135.

Wearing, S. (2001) *Volunteer Tourism: Experiences that Make a Difference*. CAB International, Wallingford, UK.

Wearing, S. (2002a) Re-centering the self in volunteer tourism. In: Dann, G.S. (ed.) *The Tourist as a Metaphor of the Social World*. CAB International, Wallingford, UK, pp. 237–262.

Wearing, S. (2002b) Volunteer tourism editorial. *Tourism Recreation Research* 28(3), 3–4.

Wearing, S. (2004) Examining best practice in volunteer tourism. In: Stebbins, R.A. and Graham, M. (eds) *Volunteering as Serious Leisure, Leisure as Volunteering: An International Assessment*. CAB International, Wallingford, UK, pp. 209–224.

Wearing, S. and Ponting, J. (2006) Reply to Jim Butcher's response (Vol. 14, No. 3) to 'Building a decommodified research paradigm in tourism: the contribution of NGOs' (Vol. 13, No. 5). *Journal of Sustainable Tourism* 14(5), 512–515.

Wearing, S., McDonald, M. and Ponting, J. (2005) Building a decommodified research paradigm in tourism: the contribution of NGOs. *Journal of Sustainable Tourism* 13(5), 424–439.

Weaver, D. and Lawton, L. (2002) *Tourism Management*, 2nd edn. Wiley, Milton, Queensland, Australia.

16 Mediating Volunteer Tourism Alternatives: Guidebook Representations of Travel Experiences in Aboriginal Australia

T. YOUNG

School of Economics Politics and Tourism, University of Newcastle, Callaghan, Australia

> [T]he 'voluntourism' phenomenon is rocking the travel world.... By staying in one place and interacting with the local people, you will learn far more about the local culture and form genuine friendships.
>
> (Lorimer, 2006, p. 200)

The notion of alternative tourism as an experience that can provide opportunities for cultural learning and cultural interaction is not new. Indeed, such an ideal is central to the construction of the alternative tourism experience within travel media such as guidebooks. Since early critiques of tourism, particular forms of travel, such as those that fall under the umbrella of 'alternative tourism', have been exalted above mass tourism which is most often associated with mere escape and hedonism. The distinctions between mass tourism and alternative tourism present an interesting conundrum. In this chapter, I examine the role that guidebooks can play in commodifying alternative experiences. I suggest that the contemporary alternative travel experience has, in many ways, become a commodified activity that is shaped and framed by a number of travel texts, specifically guidebooks. As a result, the distinction between mass and alternative tourism is enhanced and undermined. The volunteer travel experience as alternative thus becomes, in the words of Lonely Planet, a 'voluntourism phenomenon'.

A textual analysis of three guidebooks to Australia reveals that the alternative travel experience is constructed in opposition to mass tourism by focusing on authenticity, cultural learning and cultural interaction. The alternative traveller is constructed by guidebooks as one who should actively seek out particular types of experiences, in particular, those that are authentic, responsible and culturally appropriate, particularly those that can provide benefits to indigenous communities. Drawing on interviews with independent travellers in Australia, the chapter explores how the discourses of alternative travel can influence the traveller, the types of experiences they wish to have (or, indeed, believe that they can have) and also the type of traveller-self that they consider themselves to be.

Tourism Alternatives: Travel 'off the Beaten Track'

> I've been travelling for a bit and I want to get off the beaten track and see more of the things that I haven't seen. I want to see different people, different cultures. That's how you take advantage of your travels. I see it as a way for me to learn as much as possible.... You have to see outside your own backyard. That's why I'm travelling. To get to know and to get to learn. To develop as a person, you know.... When I've seen it I get the knowledge, and I know things because I've been there.... My feeling about travelling is that I want to take part in the local culture. I just don't want to be one of the crowd, you know, it's easy to sort of hang round the tourist areas but that's not my wish.
>
> (Stefan, 22, from Sweden)

Travel as an educational pursuit is related to personal development and often self-improvement – there is significant cultural capital to be gained from long-haul, long-term travel (Desforges, 1998). In the above quote, Stefan discusses learning as the fundamental reason for travelling. He believes that experience is the best way to gain knowledge and speaks of his desire to experience 'different' people and cultures, and of the opportunities that travel can provide for fulfilling this desire. He acknowledges that learning about different cultures through travel would contribute to his education and personal development. He also emphasizes his desire for cultural interaction and says he wants to 'take part in the local culture'. He also alludes to the traveller–tourist oppositional relationship by stating that he does not want to be 'one of the crowd' or 'hang round the tourist areas'. He wants to separate himself from 'tourism' and thinks that 'getting off the beaten track' would lead to the most authentic learning opportunities. This quote illustrates a desire for a particular type of alternative travel experience that goes beyond the activities associated with mass tourism.

The traveller versus tourist debate represents an axis around which many critiques of tourism have been discussed (Butcher, 2003), and raises questions relating to identity (Dann, 1999). Wearing (2002, p. 245) notes:

> To date, sociologies of tourism have developed two major themes concerning the self of the traveller. First, there has been an emphasis on tourism as a means of escape from everyday life, even if such escape is temporary. Secondly, travel has been constructed as a means of self-development, a way to broaden the mind, experience the new and different and return in some way enriched.

According to Wang (2000, p. 178), the 'discourse of the traveller versus that of the tourist is one of the most typical tourism discourses on taste in the West'. The distinction between traveller and tourist raises questions about the identity of the tourist, the nature of the tourist's quest and of relationships with people at the destination – 'the presumed object of the quest' (Dann, 1999, p. 159). Cohen

(1989, p. 31) noted that the most common way to distinguish between travellers and tourists is by 'their quest for authenticity [which for travellers] is on the whole more serious and demanding than that of the ordinary mass tourist'. The context in which the traveller–tourist debate has developed is explored below.

The growth of modern mass tourism and the subsequent development of the tourism industry as a major economic enterprise are emblematic of the various economic, technological, social and political changes that occurred in the latter half of the 20th century. The growth of tourism in the west has been dramatic, and corresponds with major social changes including increases in leisure time and higher disposable incomes. The rapid growth of the tourism industry, and an increased recognition of its sociocultural and environmental impacts, ensures that tourism has faced much controversy and debate. The development of, and interest in, alternative forms of tourism aims to ameliorate many of the negative aspects of mass tourism.

According to Butcher (2000, p. 45), alternative tourism is 'counter-posed to a conception of mass tourism as problematic, destructive of the environment and insensitive to cultural differences'. As a result, people who are averse to conventional mass tourism are now seeking a plethora of 'alternative' and 'new' travel experiences. These changes have resulted in the increasing fragmentation of the tourism industry and the development of niche and specialized markets, in particular small-scale ventures that contrast with the mass, large-scale enterprises of established tourism. Some examples of the terms assigned to these alternative or new forms of tourism include: adventure, cultural, ethnic, nature, wildlife, sustainable, responsible and volunteer.

The emergence of these specialized markets in tourism is described by Munt (1994, p. 119) as a consumer reaction against being part of a mass – a 'craving for social and spatial distinction from the golden hordes'. Furthermore, Mowforth and Munt (1998, p. 103) state that new forms of tourism reflect the desires of the 'new middle classes' for exclusivity in their holidays. These authors go on to highlight a number of key characteristics of postmodernism and its relevance to (specifically developing world) tourism including:

> The emergence of specialist agents and tour operators (and its adjunct, more individually centred and flexible holidays); the de-differentiation of tourism as it becomes associated with other activities; and the growth of interest in *other* cultures, environments and their association with the emergence of new social movements.
>
> (Mowforth and Munt, 1998, p. 126, original emphasis)

Even Krippendorf, writing in the 1980s, stated that for the tourist seeking an alternative tourism experience the guiding principle is 'to put as much distance as possible between themselves and mass tourism. They try to avoid the beaten track, they want to go places where nobody has set foot before them' (Krippendorf, 1987, p. 37). Alternative tourists are said to be in pursuit of the primitive and the remote; they are searching for 'authentic and unspoilt areas beyond the boundaries of the established touristic circuits' (Cohen, 1989, p. 31), and thus the quest for the 'authentic' experience is central to much alternative tourism.

According to Wearing and Neil (1999, p. 3), a key feature of alternative tourism is cultural sustainability and that many alternative tourism pursuits are underpinned by a respect for 'the cultural realities experienced by the tourists through education and organized encounters'. Thus, in the alternative tourists' search for authentic experiences there is an increased interest in seeking cultural contact and educational experiences. While 'new' and 'alternative' tourists are seemingly more aware of their capacity as tourists to impact upon indigenous cultures, according to Butcher (2000, p. 46) they are certainly 'not satisfied with staged aspects of the host's culture' and seek to go 'beyond that, potentially into the backstage world of the host society'. He argues that the 'new tourist' is:

> a tourist who seeks selfhood through experiencing other cultures.... The new tourist is often seen as intent on gaining an understanding of the host society's culture, and through this, discovering something about themselves.
>
> (Butcher, 2000, p. 45)

Theoretically, the search for alternative and more authentic experiences is central to the motivation of those tourists who consider themselves travellers, particularly in terms of their ideological positioning relative to mass tourists. The supposedly commodified and mundane world of the modern western tourist is eschewed and frequently 'meaningful' experiences of indigenous cultures are sought. As alternative tourists search for experiences of, and contact with (what they consider to be), an authentic other, there is growing interest in, and appreciation of, indigenous cultures and traditions, with travel providing opportunities for learning experiences. Munt (1994, p. 104) argues that an increasing respect for the natural environment and for indigenous cultures as a 'critique of mainstream culture' means that a dominant characteristic of contemporary alternative travel is the involvement of otherness.

Mowforth and Munt (1998) have suggested that the publication of guidebooks is motivated by the traveller's desire for real and authentic experiences. Guidebooks supposedly allow travellers to move away from the mass tourism industry – to get 'off the beaten track' – to find more real, natural and authentic experiences. Using a guidebook is also a marker of one's independence as a traveller and of one's status as not being part of the mass tourism phenomenon. Until recently, users of most 'alternative guidebooks' were almost exclusively backpackers and independent travellers (Sørensen, 2003, p. 859); however, in the latter half of the 20th century there was a significant increase in the range of users, titles and publications. Guidebooks can play an influential role as mediator between the traveller, the travel experience and the travelled destination.

Shaping Experiences: Guidebooks as Mediators

Travellers come to know about the places, peoples and cultures of travel destinations in various ways. The relationship between the traveller and the travelled destination is a mediated one; indeed, as Chambers (1997, p. 4) has noted, 'tourism is a mediated activity'. Guidebooks, for example, play a very influential role as mediator between the traveller and their experiences of destinations. These texts provide a socially and culturally constructed lens through which travellers come to see and know their travelled and untravelled world. Particular guidebooks have apparently 'managed to escape the stigma travellers associate with most tourist-oriented texts, clearly belonging to the "good" traveller world, rather than the "bad" tourist world' (McGregor, 2000, p. 35).

The research discussed in this chapter is drawn from a broader qualitative study that examines the relationships between traveller texts (guidebooks), travellers (backpackers) and travelled cultures (Aboriginal Australia) (Young, 2005). The empirical data discussed in this chapter are drawn from the textual analysis of three popular guidebooks to Australia (published by Lonely Planet, Rough Guide and Let's Go) and in-depth interviews conducted during a period of fieldwork in the Northern [...] August to December 2000 with a s[...]lia. The three guidebooks [...] the backpackers I interviewed [...]nely Planet dominated as the [...]ew-ees carrying *Lonely Pl[...]* [...]der (O'Byrne *et al.*, 2000). [...]4% carrying *Australia: The[...]* 11% carrying *Let's Go: Aust[...]* [...]vees indicated that they wer[...] only two of the interviewees [...]

Each of the guidebo[...] They are large books of arou[...]e and territory of Australia, a[...]rovide factual and contextual [...]stream publications and readi[...] Despite the ostensibly bohemi[...]ree, the publishers of Lonely Planet claim that they are [...] dependent travel publisher' and that they 'cover every corner of the planet' (www.lonely planet.com). For the travellers interviewed in my study, Lonely Planet was the most popular choice of guidebook which seems to confirm Laderman's (2002, p. 95) claim that the 'Lonely Planet guidebook message reaches more people than those of other guidebooks'. In the following section, a textual analysis of the Introductory and Northern Territory chapters is presented to examine the ways in which these three guidebooks draw upon and reproduce aspects of the discourse of alternative travel.

Framing Interpretations: Constructing the Traveller and the Travelled

The guidebooks to Australia published by Lonely Planet, Let's Go and Rough Guide have fundamentally the same objectives in relation to their target audience. They are all aimed primarily at travellers seeking experiences alternative to that of the mass tourist. The various audiences of travellers are identified as 'adventurous travellers' (Lonely Planet, p. 16), 'budget-minded travellers' (Let's Go, p. v) and 'independent-minded travellers of all ages on all budgets' (Rough

Guide, p. iv). In each case, the guidebook reader is positioned as different to the mass tourist. For instance, this distinction is promoted on the cover text of Let's Go with the reader advised to 'be a traveller, not a tourist...avoid tourist traps, discover local secrets, and create your own adventure'.

The alternative travel experience is thus constructed in opposition to the mass tourist experience from the outset. The reader is encouraged to '*be a traveller*', not simply to partake in travel. The implication is that the traveller is a fundamentally different kind of *being* than the tourist, and in many ways is defined as its antithesis. These implicit criticisms of tourism draw on popular conceptions of travel as being desirable, positive and to be pursued, with mass tourism suggested as negative, undesirable and to be avoided. The traveller ethos is presented as being achievable through the use of guidebooks – they provide a means through which tourism can be avoided, and the status and experience that comes from travel pursued.

Lonely Planet says its 'main aim is to help *make it possible* for adventurous travellers to get out there – to explore and better understand the world' (p. 16, my emphasis). The publishers of Lonely Planet promote what they refer to as 'responsible travel practices' (p. 16). Thus, they position their guidebooks and travel advice within the 'morally superior' (Butcher, 2003, p. 1) alternative tourism framework by focusing on responsible and sustainable travel, as illustrated in the guidebook's foreword:

> At Lonely Planet we believe travellers can make a positive contribution to the countries they visit – if they respect their host communities and spend their money wisely. Since 1986 a percentage of the income from each book has been donated to aid projects and human rights campaigns.
>
> (Lonely Planet, p. 16)

This aim is further reinforced on the Lonely Planet web site:

> Lonely Planet is passionate about bringing people together, about understanding our world, and about people sharing experiences that enrich everyone's lives. We aim to inspire people to explore, have fun, and travel often....Travel can be a powerful force for tolerance and understanding. As part of a worldwide community of travellers, we want to enable everyone to travel with awareness, respect and care.
>
> (www.lonelyplanet.com)

This clearly defined aim positions the traveller as responsible and aware, and travel as a catalyst for peace and understanding. Indeed, simply by selecting and purchasing the guidebook, the reader has apparently already made a contribution to improving developing world living conditions and ensuring human rights via Lonely Planet's donation of a percentage of their profit from the sale. By association, Lonely Planet has positioned itself as a 'force for tolerance and understanding', as 'respectful of host communities', and as making a 'positive contribution'. The reader is invited to become part of a worldwide community of like-minded individuals who share these values of 'awareness, respect and care', and this invitation is facilitated or 'enabled' by the reader's close attention to the information and advice contained within the Lonely Planet publication. From the above passage it can be seen that in constructing the traveller

Lonely Planet mobilizes discourses of the adventurous, responsible and culturally interested traveller. Moreover, it endorses travel as a way to 'bring people together' and respect for other cultures is promoted. Lonely Planet, therefore, is actively defining and reinforcing the meanings associated with being an alternative tourist:

> *Let's Go* also aims to appeal to the adventurous traveller; however, it targets the more budget-conscious traveller. The publishers of *Let's Go* contend that:
>
> We don't think of budget travel as the last recourse of the destitute. We believe that it's the only way to travel. Our books will ease your anxieties and answer your questions about the basics so you can get off the beaten track and explore.
>
> (www.letsgo.com)

Promoting the traveller ideal of getting 'off beaten track travel' is central to the Let's Go aim and mission, and can be interpreted as a reference to the supposedly 'authentic' experiences that exist beyond the well-worn circuits of popular tourism destinations. The publishers of Let's Go advise their readers that they assist them in making travel happen as their guidebooks can be relied upon for 'inside information' on these 'undiscovered' sites and sights. Likewise, the 'travelling on the cheap' aspect of the Let's Go message could almost be seen as a kind of insurance against the highly commodified and highly lucrative mass tourism industry. By promoting budget travel, Let's Go is ostensibly both encouraging and making it possible for their readers to immerse and interact with local cultures – to have an authentic travel experience.

Rough Guide, while less overt in its self-positioning as a traveller text, and lacking explicit reference to elements of the narratives of adventure, responsible travel and authentic experience, still identifies its target market as 'independent travellers of all ages, on all budgets' (Rough Guide, p. iv). The emphasis on the 'independent' traveller highlights the differentiation from the mass tourist common to all three guidebooks. 'Independent' potentially refers to both travelling individually (as opposed to mass tourists) and without a structured itinerary imposed by a tour organization. Rough Guide claims to have been developed to fill a niche apparently ignored by other travel guidebooks concerning aspects of 'contemporary life – its politics, its culture, its people, and how they lived' (Rough Guide, p. iv). The experience of culture, therefore, is a central dimension of the Rough Guide's message alongside 'accounts of every sight, both famous and obscure'. The confluence of these themes can be seen to outline a familiar set of principles – the alternative traveller should be interested in the 'obscure' as much as the well known, and their travels should focus upon experiencing the living culture alongside visiting destinations more commonly associated with mass tourism.

In order to appeal to travellers with the desire for alternative experiences, the guidebooks select and present information that promotes and defines the 'authentic' experience in relation to people, cultures and landscapes. As guidebooks are often 'the only fixed structure with the ability to hold and transfer information and culture from one cohort to the next' (Sørensen, 2003, p. 859), the nature of these texts is to offer advice to readers through the process of interpretation. As Bhattacharyya (1997, p. 381) states, 'a guidebook shapes the image of a destination through both selection of sights and providing information about them, [but] it is the process of interpretation that is perhaps the most crucial in this regard'. Places of interest are selected, identified and described through a process of evaluation grounded in the supposed ideals of the traveller. Descriptions of sites are interwoven with prescriptive information offering advice to readers about how they should behave, for example, through the provision of information on culturally appropriate behaviour. The following passage is illustrative:

> As in any country, politeness goes a long way when taking photographs; ask before taking pictures of people. Note that many Aboriginal people don't like having their photo taken, even from a distance.
>
> (Lonely Planet, p. 88)

Information about culturally appropriate behaviour can be drawn upon by the reader to guide their interactions at their destinations. These 'appropriate' behaviours are grounded also in the central values of the alternative traveller as constructed and portrayed by the guidebooks. In so doing, the guidebooks contribute to the mobilization of a particular form of 'sight' – a 'second gaze' (MacCannell, 2001) or 'traveller gaze' (cf. 'tourist gaze' in Urry, 1990). The above quote illustrates aspects of this gaze – a level of respect for the travelled culture, and a concern for both the cultural values and emotional well-being of any potential indigenous subjects of traveller photography. The traveller is constructed as a subject who is not only interested in other cultures, but is also culturally aware and responsible when interacting with them.

Notions of responsibility also are evident in the presentation of Aboriginal-owned and Aboriginal-operated tours as the best option for gaining access to Aboriginal Land. Importantly, Aboriginal cultural tours are presented as an excellent way through which to learn about, and gain first-hand knowledge of, Aboriginal cultures. Lonely Planet provides comprehensive information in relation to Aboriginal tours, which is not surprising considering this guidebook positions itself most explicitly within discourses of 'responsible travel', as evidenced by references to responsible travel practices in its mission statement. Lonely Planet's presentation of information regarding Aboriginal-owned and Aboriginal-operated cultural tours precedes any discussion of other recommended organized tours; thus, at every opportunity, Lonely Planet recommends Aboriginal cultural tours.

Lonely Planet advises that taking tours is the best way to visit Aboriginal communities and, therefore, such tours provide the greatest opportunity for 'authentic' experiences, even allowing some access to Arnhem Land 'and other places that are normally off limits' (p. 364). According to Lonely Planet, Aboriginal-owned and Aboriginal-operated cultural tours offer travellers the opportunity to 'delve into' Aboriginal culture (p. 376; p. 437). Aboriginal cultural tours are promoted as providing important opportunities for learning about culture through the leadership of an Aboriginal guide, as it is considered more appropriate and no doubt more authentic to be guided by Aboriginal interpreters rather than non-Aboriginal people.

Moreover, Lonely Planet presents its readers with reasons why taking an Aboriginal-owned cultural tour is beneficial, not only in terms of education and providing access for the traveller, but also readers are informed that they can contribute to Aboriginal communities in two ways: '[T]he more obvious is the financial gain; the other is that introducing Aboriginal culture and customs to non-Aboriginal people helps alleviate the problems caused by the ignorance and misunderstanding of the past' (p. 363). By emphasizing this aspect of traveller discourse – an apparent concern for the well-being of toured cultures – Lonely Planet is defining a certain type of experience as worthwhile and culturally appropriate. Although no volunteer experiences are specifically referred to in this guidebook, the narrative of 'giving something back' that is central to responsible travel discourses can be seen to underpin the recommendation to participate on Aboriginal cultural tours.

The above discussion has sought to demonstrate that by drawing upon and reproducing particular ideals associated with responsible tourism experiences, guidebooks play a role in helping to shape alternative tourism discourse. In this sense, they are 'tools of discourse' (Moore, 2002, p. 58) that influence the way that their readers can behave, assisting in the interpretation and, often, the creation of new and unexpected cultural situations. The traveller is constructed through a conceptually oppositional discourse as having the desire for experiences that are marked as authentic. In guidebook representations of Australia, narratives of authenticity are mobilized in representations of Aboriginal people and their cultures. Each of the selected guidebooks presents the view that experiencing aspects of Aboriginal Australia is an important and integral part of the authentic travel experience. I now turn to an analysis of the Northern Territory chapter of each of the guidebooks to examine how and why readers are directed to the Northern Territory, and consider the places and experiences that are recommended as authentic.

Be a Traveller, Not a Tourist: Constructing the Authentic Indigenous Experience

The guidebooks suggest that the Outback of the Northern Territory is where Aboriginal people have 'best been able to preserve their ancient culture and traditions' (Lonely Planet, p. 19) and where they have 'managed to maintain a traditional way of life' (Rough Guide, p. xi) and a 'persistent spirituality with the land even today' (Let's Go, p. 3). The guidebooks present three reasons why this is the case. First, that a higher proportion of the population of the Northern Territory comprises Aboriginal people. According to Lonely Planet 'around 38,000 of the Territory's 190,000 people are Aboriginal' (p. 360), for Let's Go 'nearly 30% of the Territory's population is indigenous' (p. 242) and for Rough Guide 'nearly a quarter of the Territory's inhabitants are Aborigines' (p. 518). Irrespective of the statistics, what each is promising is that the traveller is more likely to experience Aboriginal culture in the Northern Territory than anywhere else in Australia. Underpinning this 'promise' is an assumption that readers want opportunities to experience 'authentic' Aboriginal culture.

Second, the Northern Territory is described as having the most recent history of colonization. The subtext here is that it is the least spoilt by modernity and thus the least affected by the encroachment of western culture. This information conjures images of the Northern Territory as a locale for potential adventure, and a site of possible authentic cultural interaction. For example, Rough Guide states that 'within the Territory's boundaries there's evidence of the most recent colonial presence set among the oldest-occupied sites in Australia' (Rough Guide, p. 516). The third reason pointed out by the guidebooks is that the Northern Territory has the greatest proportion of Aboriginal land ownership compared to other Australian states, with Aboriginal people owning 'around 50% of the Northern Territory' (Lonely Planet, p. 362) and 'over one-third of the Territory is Aboriginal Land' (Rough Guide, p. 518). The reader is told that as a result of the Northern Territory land rights, and the 'handing back' of land to traditional owners, Aboriginal people 'began to leave the settlements and return to a more traditional, nomadic lifestyle on their own land' (Lonely Planet, p. 363).

Paradoxically, however, readers are also informed that travel on Aboriginal land is 'generally restricted' (Lonely Planet, p. 363), and 'out of bounds to casual visitors' (Rough Guide, p. 516), because visiting Aboriginal communities and travelling through Aboriginal land without a permit or invitation is not an option. Despite the higher proportion of Aboriginal people and Aboriginal-owned land in the Northern Territory, readers of all three guidebooks are warned that their experiences with Aboriginal people and culture may be, to some extent, difficult. Within historical discussion about colonialism and associated issues of cultural ignorance, readers are told that 'there are still yawning gulfs between cultures' (Lonely Planet, p. 363), that 'separatism [between cultures] is rampant' (Let's Go, p. 242), and that 'the chasm between the two vastly different cultures is actually far greater than most visitors realize' (Rough Guide, p. 518). Thus, for the traveller seeking experiences with Aboriginal people and cultures, 'meaningful contact' is 'hard' or 'unlikely' (Lonely Planet, p. 363; Rough Guide, p. 518) and Aboriginal people 'often prefer to be left to themselves' (Lonely Planet, p. 363) in 'self-imposed isolation' (Rough Guide, p. 518). As a result, 'most exchanges' between Aboriginal people and the 'short-term visitor' (Lonely Planet, p. 363; Rough Guide, p. 518) can be 'awkward and superficial' (Rough Guide, p. 518).

As this warning is directed at 'short-term' visitors, the implication is that travellers who spend an extended period of time in the Northern Territory may have more opportunities to have meaningful and, thus, authentic experiences and interactions with Aboriginal Australia. While the long-term visitor is positioned as having advantages in this regard, these statements could also be read as revealing the limitations of all types of recreational travel. By acknowledging the limited possibilities for travellers to achieve this ideal, the guidebooks, arguably, are contributing to a more realistic and self-reflexive perspective as part of the traveller gaze. At the same time, the guidebooks are suggesting that if the reader moves beyond experiences of both travel and tourism, they may indeed be able to have a more authentic experience. The implications of such differentiation between the types of experiences that can be had by short-term and long-term visitors are further explored below with reference to backpacker expectations of their travels and themselves.

Be a Volunteer, Not a Traveller: Ambiguities in Lived Experience

Many of the backpackers I spoke to identified a desire for both cultural learning and cultural interaction in their travels. These backpackers believed that the best, and perhaps the only way, to learn about culture is to actually meet and talk to Aboriginal people. In this sense, they often expressed a desire to access the 'backstage' (MacCannell, 1989) to experience authentic interaction with Aboriginal culture. For instance:

> I was really interested... to find out more and to learn about Aboriginal culture.... I was interested in meeting Aboriginal people and talking to them. That was one of the things I really wanted to do.
>
> (Isobel, 24, from Ireland)

Many of the backpackers suggested, however, that 'true' cultural interaction cannot easily occur saying that the 'backstage' is somewhat difficult to access and that travellers in Aboriginal Australia are most often only able to experience the 'frontstage':

> I am really interested in Aboriginal culture, and I just want to know, to learn, more about it.... [But] it is hard to access [culture] on a non-tourism level, on a more one to one basis. I would get more out of interactions than going to a [cultural] centre.... I would prefer to do it on a personal level, sit down and have a chat to somebody, but I believe this is difficult.
>
> (Andre, 22, from the Netherlands)

There was a belief that the most 'authentic' cultural experiences could only be achieved through long-term interaction, such as 'living with' or 'working with' Aboriginal people. Indeed, as discussed above, the guidebooks that were used by the backpackers advise them that it is potentially difficult for 'short-term visitors' to have 'meaningful' experiences (Lonely Planet, p. 363; Rough Guide, p. 518). Authenticity of experience, therefore, was sometimes deemed to be an immersion into local culture and this belief has resonance with the view of travelling that is epitomized, for example, by the original backpacker travellers such as 'explorers' and 'drifters' (Cohen, 1972, 1973). In this light, some backpackers believed that cultural immersion was beyond the scope of a travel experience and that one needs to be more than a traveller to really learn about and experience Aboriginal culture:

> I think if you want to experience Aboriginal life, to learn about Aboriginal culture, if you are interested in something like that then you'd have to go and live with them for months. You can't just expect to turn up for a week and have the Aboriginal experience.
>
> (James, 21, from England)

> I'm quite interested in the whole Aboriginal culture thing. I am actually keen to do something, maybe do something to get involved, like I volunteered in Nepal. That's the best way to learn about [a culture], to get involved.
>
> (Cathryn, 24, from England)

> I've been looking at various Aboriginal cultural tours.... But I think what I'd prefer to do is to find a job somewhere... and get the experience through meeting people and getting to know them.
>
> (Melissa, 27, from England)

The above statements indicate that the transitory nature of travel itself works against the goal of cultural immersion and associated authentic cultural interaction. While backpackers are considered, in the main, to be relatively long-term travellers, the large number of destinations of interest in a country the size of Australia means that they are constantly on the move and rarely in one place long enough to develop the necessary social contacts that would facilitate greater levels of involvement with Aboriginal people. Those backpackers I interviewed who had spent extended periods of time in particular destinations overwhelmingly chose to stay in the major cities of Sydney (New South Wales) and Melbourne (Victoria). In those destinations, the desire for cultural interaction with Aboriginal Australia was secondary to the dimensions of play and hedonism, perhaps because the guidebooks do not mobilize discourses of authentic indigenous cultural experiences in relation to these places (Young, 2007).

The possible experiences described by backpackers as having the potential for cultural immersion all consist of overcoming the transitory nature of travel. In this sense, proposed means for cultural immersion involved not simply getting beyond tourism but, indeed, getting beyond travel, for example by volunteering (as mentioned by Cathryn, above). These narratives draw upon other discourses of alternative tourism, such as volunteer tourism and the working holiday. The belief that cultural learning is hard to achieve outside long-term interactions means that backpackers often consider those experiences that can occur as somewhat superficial and often limited to those experiences that are prescribed by the guidebooks. Although the guidebooks do not state outright that travellers will not find these experiences, they provide a set of cultural understandings that can be seen as actively producing limits on these kinds of opportunities.

The ideals and values of cultural learning and cultural interaction are represented by the guidebooks in association with particular destinations (notably the Northern Territory). Due to the backpacker's tendency towards situational engagement with guidebooks, these desires potentially increase and decrease in prominence according to the place the backpacker is in (Young, 2007). For example, the guidebooks describe the potential for cultural interaction as being most likely to be achievable in the Northern Territory and, as discussed above, learning about Aboriginal culture became a prominent desire for backpackers when they were in the Northern Territory. However, the ideal of cultural interaction was perceived as desirable only in relation to the authenticity of experiences. And 'true' or 'authentic' cultural interaction was understood as the ultimate means of cultural learning and, simultaneously, recognized as being somewhat unattainable. Thus, these perceptions reflect to an extent the representation in the guidebooks of the traveller ideals and the extent to which they may be fulfilled in relation to various destinations and specific experiences.

Conclusion: Implications for Volunteer Tourism

This chapter, through an analysis of guidebook representations of the travel experience in Aboriginal Australia, reveals that the selected guidebooks shape and frame particular travel pursuits as offering the traveller an alternative experience of the destination and of indigenous people and their cultures. Central to these representations is a quest for authentic cultural engagement – an experience that is supposedly achievable for the long-term traveller. The analysis also reveals that such information can be interpreted by the readers of guidebooks as only being achievable if the traveller is to move beyond the boundaries of travel and tourism. According to the backpackers interviewed, perhaps the best way to fully immerse oneself and to learn about Aboriginal cultures is to pursue alternative experiences, in particular volunteering.

The empirical research has demonstrated that there is certainly a desire for authentic experiences with indigenous cultures. This desire is reflexive of broader trends in society which have not been elaborated on in this chapter; however, what is of interest is the role that popular travel guidebooks play in shaping this desire. Guidebooks construct their readers (who tend to be backpackers and other independent travellers) as alternative tourists and offer ways to avoid mass tourism through certain experiences. At the same time as promoting alternative experiences in opposition to mass tourism, it has to be noted that guidebooks are mass-produced and used *en masse*. Thus, guidebooks can be considered as an exemplar of the commodification of alternative tourism. Guidebooks direct their readers to many of the same types of mediated activities and experiences at destinations inscribed in well-worn tourism circuits. Thus, the distinction between the alternative travel experience and the mass tourism experience is increasingly blurred. This dialectic has various implications for contemporary volunteer tourism.

Volunteer tourism is certainly an expanding sector of the tourism industry in many countries in both the developed and developing world. Lonely Planet and other popular guidebook publishers are increasingly promoting responsible alternatives to travel and tourism, and Lonely Planet's recent publications, *Code Green: Experiences of a Lifetime* (Lorimer, 2006) and *Volunteer: a Traveller's Guide* (Lonely Planet, 2007), are examples of this trend. The publication of these books demonstrates that the alternative travel experience is increasingly becoming a marketable commodity. The rhetoric used to sell such experiences is premised on the idea that by volunteering the traveller will be able to have a more authentic experience. This point is clearly stated on the cover of the recent Lonely Planet publication: 'Code Green is about discovering a more authentic travel experience. One that will challenge, change and inspire you.' Arguably, alternative travel and volunteer tourism have become packaged versions of the authentic experience. At the same time, however, the travel experience is increasingly constructed as being an avenue through which to 'give something back' and this trend offers positive benefits to host communities and cultures. In this light, alternative travel, although being increasingly mediated and commodified, can serve to provide positive outcomes for both the traveller-self and the travelled culture.

References

Bhattacharyya, D. (1997) Mediating India: an analysis of a guidebook. *Annals of Tourism Research* 24(2), 371–389.

Butcher, J. (2000) The 'new tourist' as anthropologist. In: Robinson, M., Long, P., Evans, N., Sharpley, R. and Swarbrooke, J. (eds) *Reflections on International Tourism: Motivations, Behaviour and Tourist Types*. Centre for Travel and Tourism in Association with Business Education Publishers, Sunderland, UK, pp. 45–54.

Butcher, J. (2003) *The Moralisation of Tourism: Sun, Sand…and Saving the World?* Routledge, London.

Chambers, E. (1997) Introduction: tourism's mediators. In: Chamber, E. (ed.) *Tourism and Culture: An Applied Perspective*. State University of New York Press, Albany, New York, pp. 1–11.

Cohen, E. (1972) Toward a sociology of international tourism. *Social Research* 39(1), 164–182.

Cohen, E. (1973) Nomads from affluence: notes on the phenomenon of drifter tourism. *International Journal of Comparative Sociology* XIV(1–2), 89–103.

Cohen, E. (1989) 'Primitive and remote': hill tribe trekking in Thailand. *Annals of Tourism Research* 16(1), 30–61.

Dann, G. (1999) Writing out the tourist in space and time. *Annals of Tourism Research* 26(1), 159–187.

Daly, M., Dehne, A., Leffman, D. and Scott, C. (1999) *Australia: The Rough Guide*. Rough Guides, London.

Desforges, L. (1998) Checking out the planet: global representations, local identities and youth travel. In: Skelton, T. and Valentine, G. (eds) *Cool Places: Geographies of Youth Cultures*. Routledge, London, pp. 175–192.

Krippendorf, J. (1987) *The Holiday Makers: Understanding the Impact of Leisure and Travel*. Heinemann, Oxford, UK.

Laderman, S. (2002) Shaping memory of the past: discourse in travel guidebooks for Vietnam. *Mass Communication and Society* 5(1), 87–110.

Lonely Planet (2007) *Volunteer: A Traveller's Guide*. Lonely Planet, Footscray, Australia.

Lorimer, K. (2006) *Code Green: Experiences of a Lifetime*. Lonely Planet, Footscray, Australia.

MacCannell, D. (1989) *The Tourist: A New Theory of the Leisure Class*. Schocken Books, New York.

MacCannell, D. (2001) Tourist agency. *Tourist Studies* 1(1), 23–37.

McGregor, A. (2000) Dynamic texts and tourist gaze: death, bones and buffalo. *Annals of Tourism Research* 27(1), 27–50.

Moore, K. (2002) The discursive tourist. In: Dann, G. (ed.) *The Tourist as a Metaphor of the Social World*. CAB International, Wallingford, UK, pp. 41–60.

Mowforth, M. and Munt, I. (1998) *Tourism and Sustainability: New Tourism in the Third World*. Routledge, London.

Munt, I. (1994) The 'other' postmodern tourism: culture, travel and the new middle classes. *Theory, Culture and Society* 11, 101–123.

O'Byrne, D., Bindloss, J., Draffen, A., Finlay, H., Harding, P., Horton, P., McGaurr, L., Mundell, M., Murray, J., Ross, H. and Saxton, P. (2000) *Australia: Up Front, Outback, Down Under*. Lonely Planet, Hawthorn, Australia.

Sheppard, B., Levy, E. and Bacon, L. (eds) (2000) *Let's Go: Australia 2000*. Let's Go, Cambridge, UK.

Sørensen, A. (2003) Backpacker ethnography. *Annals of Tourism Research* 30(4), 847–867.

Urry, J. (1990) *The Tourist Gaze: Leisure and Travel in Contemporary Societies*. Sage, London.

Wang, N. (2000) *Tourism and Modernity: A Sociological Analysis*. Elsevier, Oxford, UK.

Wearing, S. (2002) Re-centring the self in volunteer tourism. In: Dann, G. (ed.) *The Tourist as a Metaphor of the Social World*. CAB International, Wallingford, UK, pp. 237–262.

Wearing, S. and Neil, J. (1999) *Ecotourism: Impacts, Potentials and Possibilities*. Butterworth-Heinemann, Oxford, UK.

Young, T. (2005) Going by the book: backpacker travellers in Aboriginal Australia and the negotiation of text and experience. PhD thesis, The University of Newcastle, Australia.

Young, T. (2007) Framing experiences of Aboriginal Australia: guidebooks in backpacker travel. *Tourism Analysis* Special edition: Tourism and the Media (in press).

Index